Happy Birthday, Joe!

OUR SERVICE
OUR STORIES

Indiana Veterans Recall Their World War II Experiences

VOLUME 2

Ronald P. May

RONALD P. MAY

Jim Bonner

Enjoy~
Love you,
Rosanne

ISBN: 978-1-948638-95-1

On the cover: Watercolor by combat artist Dwight Shepler, 1944; National Archives. Depicts the *USS Emmons* (DD-457) bombarding enemy positions at Omaha Beach, Normandy, on D-Day, June 6, 1944. After escorting minesweepers prior to H-Hour and firing on assigned turrets as the landing commenced, the *Emmons* dueled with enemy shore batteries and fired at targets of opportunity from about three quarters of a mile off shore. During this action, she expended 914 rounds of 5-inch 138 ammunition and 1,014 rounds of 40mm.

PRINTED IN THE UNITED STATES OF AMERICA

TABLE OF CONTENTS

Foreword..*vii*

Introduction...*ix*

EUROPEAN THEATER

WILLIAM BIRD
Rings of Promise and Protection 1

ENNIS GRAY
Slogging Across Southern Europe 7

GENE GROVES
Pushing into Germany 23

HOWARD KWITNY
Beating the Odds... 29

EILEEN JONES McCLARNON
Memphis Belle Leaves Home for War 41

JAMES LOUIS POWERS
Basketballs and Bombs.. 51

JOHN REDMOND
Across Europe on a Motorcycle 65

FRANCIS "FRAN" SCHIFFHAUER
Letters From the War Front... 71

RODNEY "ROD" SIECK
Duty From the Belly of a Bomber... 83

SCOTT THOMPSON
A Forgotten Christmas & Uncertain Future 93

JACK WELSH
Landing Troops All Around Europe 105

CHINA-BURMA-INDIA

RALPH "DUANE" COLLINGS
Traversing the Dangerous 'Hump' 129

WILLIAM "BILL" McCOLGIN
Here, There and Everywhere 147

PACIFIC THEATER

ROBERT ANDERSON
Combat in the Pacific with the Marines 165

ROY BLACKWOOD
Finding His Way Through the Pacific 175

CARROLL BOTTOM
Signaling on the High Seas 189

WILLIAM "BILL" GABONAY
Surviving Combat in the Philippines 197

ROBERT KEARNS
Adventures on a Troop Carrier 213

RAY McDONALD
Occupation Duty in Japan 223

DONALD SPEES
Gunner on the High Seas 235

ED WHITE
Experiment in the South Pacific 243

ON THE HOME FRONT

HILDA BROWNING
    Duty Over Fear 253

MARILYN FOWLER
    On a Farm at the Homefront.. 259

KAY GRAY
    Duty with the SPARS... 269

FERN METCALF
    From the Farm to the Big Apple 275

BETTY ROBLING
    A Rosie the Riveter 285

Acknowledgments... 289

About the Author 293

PHOTO BY KARLIE ANN MAY

Foreword

World War II (1939–1945) is the largest and most destructive event in the history of mankind. The Second World War was a total war, covering the entire globe. The war touched every continent on earth. The totality and complexity of World War II are almost impossible to convey. Novelist John Steinbeck's description of the war, "As dirty a business as the world has ever seen…" seems a fair caption. At least 60 million people died as a direct result of World War II.

For most of us, World War II is just a string of long-ago muzzle flashes in old black-and-white newsreels. World War II seems like a historical fairy tale of massive armies arrayed against an unambiguous evil. Normandy, Guadalcanal, the Battle of the Bulge, and Okinawa are famous battles and campaigns during World War II. As a boy, these battles with bizarre sounding names were just a blur on a map that seemed impossibly exotic and far away, until two of my uncles and my grandfather, all veterans of World War II, made the war real to me. Now, these names serve as a kind of brutal shorthand for scenes of mass carnage and unbelievable courage.

Ron's book *Our Service, Our Stories Vol. 2*, a collection of World War II veteran service stories, does the same thing for a reader.

The Greatest Generation is disappearing. Of the 16 million Americans who served during World War II, only about a half-million are still alive. The numbers of veterans who fought in the war are rapidly dwindling. Most of those who fought in World War II are dead or in their nineties, with close to 400 veterans passing away each day. There are only a small number of Americans who have grandparents or other relations who still remember World War II all too well as children. The conflict will soon be a distant history and not within graspable, living memory.

Ron May is trying to change that. Ron is a writer and historian-turned-chronicler. In *Our Service, Our Stories Vol. 2*, he does something special. He collects the first-hand recollections of the veterans and allows us to see the war that shaped the Greatest Generation. Ron's storytelling helps to frame their heroic tales for a wide audience. This is important because there was never a collective effort to capture, record, and catalog the experiences of World War II veterans until almost a half-century after the war.

The stories in *Our Service, Our Stories Vol. 2* touch on many different aspects of the war. There are naval battles, stories of combat, and other tales of young, lonely soldiers far from home facing the prospect of death. Ron's tales remind us of another America after the Great Depression where idealism met realism, and brave young Americans fought against the evil of fascism. For those who survived the war, it would be the most vivid and intense experience of their lives. Most of those who fought in the war were in their late teens or early twenties- a time when most people are just starting their lives.

As a veteran of the wars in Iraq and Afghanistan, I know how important it is to make sure the sacrifice of your fallen comrades is never forgotten. As a retired Navy Chaplain, Ron knows first-hand the cost of war. Ron's book has fulfilled a long overdue obligation to our World War II veterans. *Our Service, Our Stories Vol. 2* isn't merely eye-opening history. Ron's book offers Americans a chance to ponder the sacrifices of past wars like Vietnam and the current veterans of Iraq and Afghanistan.

For Ron, capturing the stories of the Greatest Generation is an obsession. He's a man on a mission. Ron wants all Americans to know about the noble sacrifice of our soldiers in World War II. His writing makes that history come alive and helps us to understand not just the past, but the choices we make today.

Our Service, Our Stories Vol. 2 lets us see, know and, feel what that awful battleground of World War II was like and what actually happened there. Ron's book captures the service of the disappearing Greatest Generation, a generation that survived the poverty of the Great Depression, won a global war and rebuilt America. That group of intrepid Americans gave us a world far better than they inherited. *Our Service, Our Stories Vol. 2* is a permanent monument to their sacrifice and an important contribution to the literature of World War II.

Lieutenant Colonel Dominic Oto
USAR, Retired

INTRODUCTION

When I published *Our Service, Our Stories* in 2015 there was never a doubt in my mind that I would write another volume. The experience of interviewing veterans and preserving their stories continues to enrich my life and compels me to publish them for posterity. And I hope to continue doing so with future volumes.

This 2nd volume includes 26 World War II veteran stories. While that is 10 stories fewer than in my first book, this volume is actually quite a bit longer. The stories in this volume are more in-depth, and they include more photographs.

Some of the stories are quite a bit longer than others. The length and depth of each story are determined by the memory and willingness of each veteran to share his or her experiences. In several cases, the added length of stories comes from veterans sharing with me their personal unpublished memoirs of their time of service. In these cases, I try to include most of their reflections with some minor editing. I think you will agree that the memoirs not only extend these veterans' stories, they enhance them.

Regardless of the length of each story, in my opinion all of them are wonderful and worth reading; not because I wrote them, but because the veterans lived them and shared them with us.

As with my first book, I make every effort to augment each veteran's story with some background information on his or her specific job as well as his units' history and contribution to the war effort.

In this second volume, I am pleased to include some service stories of women. Their contributions to the war effort cannot be overestimated; but they have sadly been overshadowed by the stories of men in uniform, and they have often been overlooked by the public.

Women served at home as "Rosie the Riveters" who helped to build and send the equipment needed for the war front. Women served in the service auxiliaries of the Army, Navy, Marines, Air Force and Coast Guard. Some even served overseas. Women also served as Red Cross volunteers and in many other capacities.

And many more women served at home as devoted wives and mothers of service members and as good citizens; doing their part by writing letters, growing victory gardens and feeding their families in spite of the rationing of food and resources.

As with my previous book, I have organized the stories under theaters of war sections which include Europe, China-Burma-India, and the Pacific. I have included a new section with this volume called the "Home Front" for the stories of women (and men) who contributed to the war effort at home. It required the efforts of our entire nation to support and win World War II. And that goes for England as well. One of the stories in this section is about a British woman, Hilda Browning, who served in the Women's Land Army.

In my first volume, the majority of the veterans I interviewed were from Morgan County, Indiana. This was due to my writing and submitting these stories as a freelance writer for the *Martinsville Reporter Times* newspaper, and the *Mooresville-Decatur Times*; both of which are Morgan County newspapers.

This second volume only has 4 stories of veterans from Morgan County. Although I still write for the *Martinsville Reporter Times*, my move to the north side of Indianapolis has precluded me from getting down to Morgan County as often as I once did. Most of my more recent articles for that newspaper have been focused on World War II battle sites and memorials, as well as places in Indiana that commemorate the war and honor those who fought in it. I intend at some point to collate those stories and publish them as a book.

Over half of the stories in this second volume are from veterans who live at Hoosier Village Retirement Center in Zionsville, Indiana. Since I serve as the full-time chaplain there I have the privilege of personally getting to know these veterans and have easy access to them for doing the interviews.

I have made every attempt to make sure that the photos used in this book do not infringe upon any copyright. The photos have either been personal photos shared with me by the veterans or photos identified as being in the public domain that I uploaded from the internet (usually Wikimedia Commons). If I have mistakenly used a copyrighted photograph in this book, I sincerely apologize. When the error is brought to my attention I will make every effort to exclude the copyrighted photo or give proper credit to the copyright holder in future printings.

Two things have enhanced my writing for this second volume. The first was my trip to Europe in 2016 to visit World War II battle sights and memorials in France, Belgium, Luxembourg and Germany. I had an amazing 11-day tour with a travel company called "Beyond Band of Brothers". It was a phenomenal experience! I gained insight from seeing where so many of our veterans lived and fought. I encourage any World War II enthusiast to make such a pilgrimage if possible.

The other source of enrichment was my reading of Ernie Pyle. As most of you know, he was one of the press correspondents who covered much of World War II. He traveled extensively and wrote about those who served in North Africa, Italy, England, France and the Pacific theater. He became the most popular and well-loved of all the correspondents of that era.

While his writing was superb, he was best known for telling the stories of the common soldier, sailor, airman or Marine and sharing with the American citizens back home the experiences of these young men as they endured combat and deprivation. He did that by getting close to them and living among them for a time. That meant he was also close to combat. Too close! He cheated death several times over the years. But his luck ran out on April 18th, 1945 when he was killed by a Japanese sniper on the island of Ie Shima (near Okinawa).

As I visited his museum in Dana, Indiana (he is a native Hoosier) and read more of his stories, I found myself experiencing a special bond with Ernie Pyle. This is not because I think I write like him. I'm not even close to displaying his craftsmanship with words. Rather, the bond is because I have been privileged to do what he did 70-plus years ago.

He wrote stories of 18, 19 and 20-year old young men who were in the thick of combat; some of whom died. I write stories of 90, 91, and 92+ year old men (and women) who look back at their time of service over 70 years ago and are willing to share their experiences and recollections with me. Hearing their stories has been for me a special privilege as well as a sacred responsibility for me to share them. And, I like to think that Ernie Pyle would be delighted to know that the military service stories of these aged veterans are still being preserved today, and that there continues to be interest in reading them.

There isn't much time left for capturing these eyewitness accounts of the men who fought in World War II and the women who supported the war effort in so many ways. According to the VA Administration there are only 558,000 of the 16 million veterans who fought in World War II alive today. They are dying at a rate of 362 per day. But there is still a brief opportunity to capture the stories of those who are still with us.

I encourage every reader of this book to consider interviewing some veterans. Just ask them to share their recollections of serving and use a recorder to capture what they say. Even if you don't consider yourself to be much of a writer, you can type out what the veteran said in the recording and then give the veteran the typed transcript to share with his family. Keep a copy of the transcript yourself and offer it to someone who might like to write a story about the veteran; perhaps a reporter from your local newspaper.

I know that I'll continue doing this work as long as I can and as long as there are veterans who are alive and willing to share. In fact, I've already started work on my third volume of World War II stories. And I hope I will be able to complete a fourth volume as well.

As I stated in the introduction of my first volume, I made a deliberate decision when I started interviewing veterans to accept each veteran's memory of the events connected with his time of service without trying to verify the accuracy of the details. Memory is imprecise for each of us. The combination of advanced age and the passing of time for events that took place over 70 years ago are bound to produce some inaccuracies. I accept that, and I hope you the reader will as well. This is a book about *their* stories, which, for me, means that **their** memories of the events are more important than the precise details of what may have actually happened.

That being said, if I noticed in their interview a glaring historical error of chronology or a mistake pertaining to their unit history, their ship or some other detail that I had clear knowledge of, I went ahead and made that correction. In all cases, and there weren't many, doing so had almost no effect on their story.

Because my primary interest is preserving as much of the "voice" of each veteran, I have intentionally used frequent and long quotes in these stories. Most of my contribution to each story is in summarizing parts of their life story, assigning a title and theme to each story, and providing some historical background on unit history, battle details, and descriptions of planes, ships, weapons and other equipment used. I am not an expert in any of those areas, but I have done my best through research to speak briefly to them for the readers' benefit.

I hope you get as much from reading these stories as I have from preserving them. Our world is a better place because these veterans and citizens rose up to the challenge, defeated their aggressor enemies, and preserved freedom for countries across the globe at a critical time in history. There is hardly a more significant blessing or a better story than that!

~ Ronald P. May

EUROPEAN THEATER

Rings of Promise and Protection

Soldier survives combat and capture
to return home to his sweetheart

William James Bird wore a special ring during his combat in World War 2. It was an engagement ring of sorts — a Mizpah ring — part of a set that his parents had loaned to him and his fiancé when he went off to war.

Bill's parents had each worn one band of the Mizpah ring set while his father was off fighting in the Great War (World War 1) in Europe. For both father and son, the rings symbolized not only commitment to their sweethearts but also faith in God to protect each person while they were absent from one another.

> *"It was also called Mizpah because he said, 'May the LORD keep watch between you and me when we are away from each other.'"* (Genesis 31:49)

The rings and their symbolic reminder of God's protection proved to be prophetic in Bill's survival as a POW.

Born in Kansas City, Kansas on January 19th, 1925, Bill was the oldest of three sons. Following his graduation from Wyandotte High School in Kansas City, he was drafted into the U.S. Army.

He reported to Camp Gruber in Muskogee, Oklahoma in September of 1943. Trained as an infantryman, he eventually became squad leader for two 81 mm mortar teams. "The Lieutenant would give the order and then I would decide where to set up the two guns," Bill explained of his role.

Mortar Team in Leyte.

He and the men he trained with were assigned to the 2nd Battalion, 242nd Regiment, 42nd Infantry Division. It was part of the "Rainbow Division"; so named because it consisted of men from each of the 48 states. Once the division arrived in Europe, it came under the 7th Army.

In mid-November of 1944, the 42nd Division left Camp Gruber and traveled by train to Camp Kilmer, New Jersey. A week later, the men boarded a troop transport and crossed the Atlantic Ocean, arriving at Marseille, France on December 8th.

"After leaving the ship we went up a hill and set up camp," remembered Bill. "It was colder than blue blazes!" They stayed there getting organized for a few days and then began moving forward in a motor convoy. For two weeks they traversed France without resistance. "The towns we went through had been blown to bits," recalled Bill of the destruction left behind by both German and Allied bombers.

Late December, the division reached Strasbourg, on the far eastern part of France, near the Maginot line — a snake tail of fortifications built after World War 1 to protect France from an aggressive attack from her eastern German neighbors.

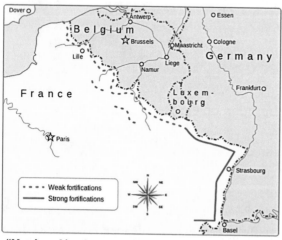

"Maginot Line In-en svg" by Goran tek-en. Licensed under CC BY-SA 3.0 via Wikimedia Commons

"We could hear gunfire out in the distance," Bill recalled. It was along this line that Bill's division met heavy resistance as the Germans attempted their last major offensive actions of the war in an operation they called, "Nordwind."

After turning the Germans back, Bill's battalion was assigned to the 12th Armored Division to support an attack on the enemy along the Rhine River bridgehead at Herrlisheim, France. During the violent fighting between January 8—17, 1945, the German defenders repulsed the Allied attack and overwhelmed the units. The division suffered 1,700 casualties. Among them were Bill and some other men, who had been captured by the Germans.

Bill recalled, "A lot of firing was going on, and very little from us, as we had run out of ammo. We set out to get more. Suddenly there was a rifle pointing at me from inside some bushes 4 feet away. The man didn't shoot. Why didn't

StaLag_IVB POW Camp Entrance (Eingang StaLag IVB by LutzBruno - Own work. Licensed under CC BY-SA 3.0 via Wikimedia Commons)

it go off? I'll never know. I owe many thanks to the man on the other side of it."

It was nothing short of a Mizpah miracle for Bill. "God's influence was surely there," he concluded.

"I've thought about it a gazillion times. I was that close to being in the national cemetery."

After helping to calm the other dozen or so men from his unit who were around him, Bill surrendered himself and his squad to the Germans. "The Germans gathered us up and took us to their officers for interrogation," Bill said. His future was now uncertain. Would he ever see his fiancé again? Would the Mizpah rings hold true to the promise of God's protection?

The captured soldiers were then placed on a train and transported across Germany to "Stalag IV-B" — a Prisoner of War camp near Muhlberg, in the eastern part of Germany. One of the largest prisoner camps in Germany, Stalag IV-B was expansive, covering about 74 acres and housing over 30,000 prisoners.

"It was cold," said Bill. "We slept in bunks that were raised just off the dirt floor." Each day, Bill and other prisoners went out along the countryside to gather firewood for their barrack's stove. And then, the men waited. That's all they could do. Wait, pray and hope to be liberated.

That liberation came in April when the Soviet Army, pushing into Germany from the east, reached Muhlberg. Bill remembered the Russians entering the camp on horseback as the German soldiers fled.

Street in StaLag IVB

Bill was among the 30,000 prisoners when the Russians arrived. Initially detained, the Americans were soon released on their own cognizance. Bill and other Americans walked out of imprisonment and headed west, eventually linking back up with Allied Forces.

Betty Cunningham as a young woman.

On June 9th, Bill and other former POW's departed from France on board a ship. Having suffered from dysentery in the POW camp, Bill received medical attention during the transit. He returned to the U.S. on June 18th.

Bill didn't waste any time getting back to the person that mattered most and was waiting for him back in Kansas City — Betty Cunningham.

Bill and Betty had been born in the same hospital a week apart. They attended school together and had started dating in Junior High. It was the classic love story. Betty was a cheerleader, while Bill played on the basketball team. A friend introduced them. "I said I'm going to marry that boy," said Betty. "And I did!" "We fell in love pretty quickly," added Bill.

The couple married on July 29, 1945 at an outdoor wedding near Betty's home. Their union brought to fulfillment the hope of the Mizpah rings that they had worn. They were safely back together again. "We returned the rings to my parents," said Bill, noting the exchange of the Mizpah rings for their wedding bands.

Bill and Betty.

Bill completed two more years of Army service before receiving his honorable discharge in January of 1947.

The couple moved back to Kansas City after his discharge. Bill worked in automotive repair for a few years, served as a milkman, and even owned a gas station.

Meanwhile, Betty gave birth to two children: Connie (1949) and William, Jr. (1951).

In the early 1950's, Bill started working in Quality Control at General Motors of Kansas City. He visually inspected new parts and checked them against the blue prints. A few years later, he was transferred to GM in Indianapolis, beginning work there on May 1, 1955.

The family settled briefly in Speedway, Indiana before moving out to Decatur Township in October of 1956. The Bird's built a home and remained there until 1987, when Bill retired from GM after 31 years of service.

In retirement Bill and Betty moved to northern Minnesota, where they had vacationed for many years. They purchased several acres of land along Big Elbow Lake and erected a manufactured home. They loved everything about their life there — the fishing, the people, and the beauty.

In 2002, they moved to Zanesville, Ohio and spent a decade living near their son. They returned to the Indianapolis area in 2012 to live closer to their daughter.

Seven decades later, Bill still struggled with the "guilt" of surrendering in Germany. "I don't know if I did the right thing or not," he said, choking up over the memory.

William and Betty Bird and their 69th Wedding Anniversary celebration.

But the blessings of his decision beg for a different interpretation. His wife of 70 years sits beside him. A loving daughter lives in town and looks after them. Shelves are filled with photos of their two children and their grandchildren, great-grandchildren and their wonderful life.

Sometimes the bravest thing to do is to survive — even by means of surrender — and achieve something greater than a battle win or a heroic death — a family. The Mizpah rings would agree, I think.

William Bird died on April 19, 2015. He was 90 years old. His wife, Betty died on January 23, 2017. She was 92.

Slogging Across Southern Europe

Veteran Reflects on Horror of War in Italy, France and Germany

Ennis Gray fought in Europe during World War II. Two years later, he came out of that war on the winning side. But what he remembers most about his time of service was not the victory but the horror and cost of combat.

Born on April 6th, 1923 in Manhattan, New York, Gray's family moved to Queens in his infancy. He attended New Town High School in Queens for two years before gaining a track scholarship to La Salle Military Academy on Long Island, a prep boarding school. Following his graduation in 1942, he accepted a track athletic scholarship at Fordham University, a Jesuit school, in New York. "Running was a big thing in my life, right up to the service," Gray said.

He decided to enlist in the service while he was a freshman at Fordham University. Gray recalled, "I went to the Marines first. They didn't want me because I wore glasses. That annoyed me, so I went down to the Army office, and they were delighted to get me."

He was sent to basic infantry training at Camp Wheeler in Georgia. "They were really getting ready to go to war over there in Europe," he recalled of the time.

With his training completed, Gray and the other soldiers waited for word on when they would depart for war. "One day they called us to fall out in front of the barracks," remembered Gray. "The Sergeant comes out who was our training Sergeant, and he had a smile on his face. And I looked at the guy next to me and

Empress of Scotland Troop Ship

said, 'This is not good news.' The message he had for us was, 'Go back and pack your stuff. You are all going to Newport News, Virginia and then on to Europe."

When Gray and the other soldiers reported to Virginia they had to undergo a physical and psychological interview before being released for deployment. Gray remembered, "We are standing in a gym somewhere with hundreds and hundreds of soldiers. We had to get a psychiatric interview before we went overseas. And there was a hallway with three or four doors in it with people who were going to psychoanalyze you or something. They were psychiatrists. And so you wait and wait and wait. Finally, I get up in the front. So an office opens up and I walk in the door and a young officer behind the desk asks me, 'How do you feel about going overseas?' And I look at him and said, 'Does it matter what I feel?' And he calls out, 'Next!' That was the whole interview. I was standing there all day just for that."

CROSSING THE OCEAN

Gray and 8,000 other soldiers with him soon boarded a troop transport in New York City and headed across the Atlantic Ocean on the *Empress of Scotland*, a Canadian luxury liner converted into a troop carrier during World War 2.

The trip was an unpleasant experience for Gray and the others. He recalled, "I'm telling you, if you want to see one of the most disgusting things in the world, see a troop ship. You start to feel the ocean and some people just can't take it. It's a terrible thing! People start getting sick. And I couldn't stand the people getting sick. It was so much slime sliding around on the deck. I went to the latrine, and there were men there, sliding around in their own vomit. I grabbed my stuff (blanket and personal belongings) and headed up toward the deck of the ship. And once I got up there I stayed up there until we reached port."

ORAN, ALGERIA

Their first stop was Casablanca in North Africa. After getting off the ship a boxcar train took the men to Oran, a port city located on the northwestern Mediterranean coast of Algeria.

Gray recalled of his time in Oran, "We are at a pretty big camp in Oran, and it has a lot of British soldiers. And in the morning we happen to be on the dividing line in tents. Guys on one side of the aisle were British and guys on the other side were American. We both fell out at the same time in the morning. We heard bells and shouts and everyone fell out. The American Army was fully dressed and ready to go when falling out. Not the British! They just came out any goddamn way that they wanted to. They were in their shorts and whatever, barely awake. But the difference between the two was that on the American side an officer would walk by to give an inspection. He just kind of walked through the ranks and that was it. But on the British side, the officer stopped at every man and looked at his rifle. And I thought that was significant! He would take each rifle and look at it thoroughly, and there the men were standing in their PJs. They (British Officers) chose to put the importance on how the rifle looked and not how the man looked at the moment."

From Oran the American troops boarded another ship that would take them to Italy. Recalled Gray, "As we are going up to the pier we saw people on the ship throwing all of these mattresses over the ship. Hundreds and hundreds of

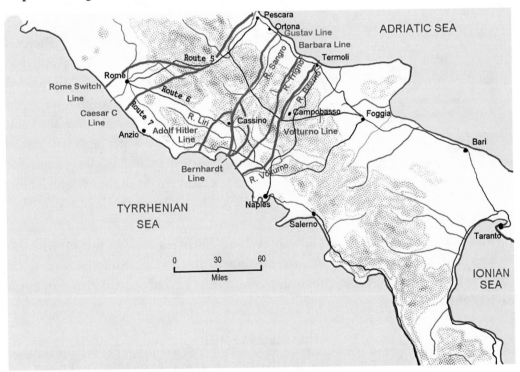

Italy defense lines south of Rome, 1943. (Stephen Kirrage)

mattresses! They were all full of bugs! Then we were on the ship, and we didn't have a mattress. We lay on metal springs without a mattress."

The ship headed for Anzio, Italy for an Allied amphibious landing and offensive code-named, *Operation Shingle*. The men on Gray's ship were arriving as replacement troops for the ongoing invasion of Italy. And they were about to experience their first taste of combat.

INVASION OF ANZIO, ITALY

Anzio landing.

In the middle of the night on January 22, 1944, Gray and the others climbed down cargo nets on the side of their ship and dropped into Higgins Boats that were waiting for them on the surface of the water. The smaller crafts were rising up and down on the swells of the sea.

Gray recalled the scene once everyone was in a landing craft, "The Higgins boats form a circle. Other boats join the circle — there are many boats circling. Then on a signal, they all formed a line parallel to the shore; the engines roar … We headed in. The boat scrapes bottom, the ramp drops down and we all run out of the boat, waist deep, in the water and get to the shore. We move inland. We have landed at a place called Anzio, Italy. What is about to develop is a major battle of World War II with the objective of entering Rome."

After their landing at Anzio, Gray and about 300 other soldiers met up with the Army's 3rd Division, to which they were assigned. The 3rd Division, nicknamed the "Marne Division," had the distinction of engaging in combat with Axis forces on each of the major European fronts.

THE COLUMN OF MEN

Gray observed the men of the 3rd Division. He said, "If you want to see war, see a column of men walking up to the front; to the line as they say. The atmosphere is different than anything I have ever encountered. It is a long column of young men who have been with the Division for a while. They are veterans of the line, and they know what they are headed for. It is a completely different atmosphere than when they were new to the Division and making their first trip to the line, because now they know what lies ahead for them. In most cases, it is pure horror! And they know it. They walk along solemnly, deep in thought with no talking or kidding. These are men that are truly men. They are doing their duty to the highest possible degree and they all should be recognized for their deeds. There should be a tribute to their dedication and spirit."

THE SIZE OF THE DIVISION

He was also impressed by the sheer size of the division. "We were in awe seeing the Division for the first time — its sheer size! We were just coming from the states now and you look out and see this company, that company, a tank company, artillery company all along the road, it went on and on and on. It's a big unit. I'm thinking wow. You know, now you are starting to realize you are in a war. Here it comes!"

"All these guys are waving at you saying, 'You'll be sorry. You'll be sorry.' It's huge. It's devastating. And the power that comes out of the Division when it is coordinated in action. People are getting killed left and right. The highest number of people getting killed were probably only age 19 or so."

"That's the thing — the death & carnage — I think that is overlooked. They only talk about the victory like it was a romp. It was not a romp!"

3rd Division soldiers in formation.

Gray recalled his rendezvous with the division: "We were in tents sleeping. During the night the Army pulled in with two-ton trucks. We got on them and took off. We didn't know where we were going or why. They very seldom told you. And it turns out we were going to the 3rd Division line. Dawn broke and we were standing up in these two and a half ton trucks going by some of the veterans of the division there along the road. And you start to realize how big the division is that just came off the line. (They had previously been in Africa and Sicily.) And there is just an aura going by it all."

"Then the next thing that happened brought you really closer to the war. People were assigned to units. They dumped us off in the field. There must have been about 300 soldiers. We are all replacements troops. I was assigned to the command post for the security regiment. Now the war is coming closer."

MONTHS OF COMBAT AT ANZIO

From late January until early June, the 3rd Division engaged their German enemy in the Battle of Anzio. Gray recalled, "Initially, the enemy offered little or no resistance. But they quickly adjusted to provide a major force opposing the Division. Plus, they were holding the high ground. The Division held low, muddy, flat farmland. The enemy had the advantage and knew how to use it. The Division was forced into a defensive position for the first time. This resulted in a violent standoff that raged for four months. The Division was facing a very persistent enemy."

Lucca Italy, 1944.

The enemy was also attacking at night from the sky. Gray recalled, "At night the German planes would come over toward the shore to bomb the ships. And all the ships had guns on them. And when the German planes came over all the ship's guns would go off at once — they were coordinated in some way — and it made the most fantastic display, like a huge light fountain, because each huge shell from the anti-aircraft fire had tracers (one tracer for every 4 bombs). They fill the sky with bullets. It is unbelievable. But it was beautiful. Like a huge fountain."

In the weeks ahead, the Germans made several intensive attacks against the Division. Gray remembered, "During this period, the enemy launched two massive attacks with the objective of driving the Division back into the sea. Both efforts failed because of the tenacity of our men on the line plus the devastating accuracy of the Division artillery. (Note: It is times like these that men learn about war. But the men of the line, the true infantrymen, the 'dog-faced soldiers,' learn about the HORROR of the war. They will have my everlasting, highest respect.")

The horror of war became especially horrible on February 29th of 1944 as the 3rd Infantry Division repelled an attack by three different German divisions at Anzio. While the division was successful in fighting off the Germans, the battle resulted in over 900 casualties for the 3rd Division. That was the most casualties for a single American division on one day of battle during World War II.

Gray served with a security group of 10 guys in his regiment's command post. He recalled of his combat duty, "I was with an officer. He was getting the lay of the land. I went up to cover him if anything happened. I did a lot of that (covering fire)."

Living conditions were rough throughout that time, especially for the men in the line companies. Gray remembered, "There were irrigation ditches for the farms. We were in this ditch. I saw this is how guys were living. They were dug into

U.S. soldiers moving through Italy.

the side of the ditch. And water had come up and was going right through where they had dug. They were in half water and mud. You can't imagine anything more miserable!"

BREAK-THROUGH TO ROME

The 3rd Division finally broke out through the German lines in May and headed toward Rome. Gray recalled, "Now it was time for the Division to attack. It was to be an all-out effort to take Rome. The men of the Division knew it was going to happen. Just the thought of getting off this beachhead after four months raised the morale of the men to new heights. They would greet each other with, 'I'll see you in Rome.' 'We're going to get the hell out of here!' 'This is it; we're going to Rome!'"

"The attack started with an artillery barrage second to none. The Division artillery opened up, supported by Naval guns from ships off the shore. It was a total effort. The Division moved forward against a strong enemy defense. But it was persistent, and we prevailed. We entered Rome while the other Divisions moved through."

While in Rome, Gray enjoyed seeing some top-ranking people. He recalled, "The next day I got to visit the Vatican. General Clark, head of the 5th Army in Italy, was also visiting the Vatican. He said 'hello' to me and I answered, 'Hello General.' I also was part of an audience with the Pope — his first since the start of the war. It was quite a day!"

COMBAT THROUGH FRANCE

Following the battle at Anzio, the Division spent June and July off the front lines and training for the next invasion — Southern France. Code-named "Operation Dragoon," the mission of the amphibious landing was twofold. First, it was designed to open another front in the battle that would extend and pressure the German forces who were already getting spread thin. Secondly, the operation focused on securing some key ports along the French Mediterranean coast.

On August 15, 1944, Gray and the men of the 3rd Division landed at St. Tropez on the beaches of the Cote d'Azur and began the invasion of Southern France. This time, they were not pinned down for months at the beachhead as they had been at Anzio. Allied air superiority and an expanding French Resistance overran the Germans and sent them on a hasty withdrawal to the north.

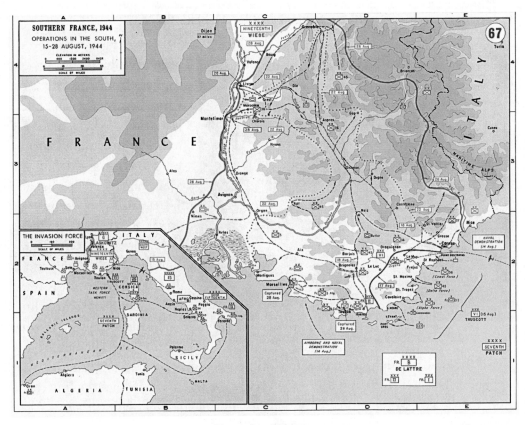

Operation Dragoon.

"France involved going through a lot of medium sized towns and taking one after the other," Gray recalled. "But the Germans defended each one, so it involved combat action."

PROVIDING SECURITY FOR THE LINEMEN

Gray had several memories of his division's movement across France. "A couple times I went out with some linemen in the regiment," he recalled. "It was very important to keep the communications between the regimental command post and the people on the line (battalions and companies). Linemen had to go out rather frequently because the shelling would rip up the lines. So they would travel out to where they were broken and repair them. They would get in predicaments sometimes. Our group provided security. They (the linemen) didn't carry guns because they carried the spools of wires."

THE LOST SOLDIER TURNED LIBERATOR

Soldiers in columns on the move.

Gray also recalled a humorous incident of a lost soldier from his division who became a liberator. He said, "When men are walking in columns, they walk on each side of the road; and they are usually 5-10 yards between each other so that if anything hits, it doesn't hit too many. And they walk along and if the line stops up in the front — that stops the whole line. And what they do is they go into the ditches in the side of the road so that they can catch a little sleep or whatever. And that is what happened. The line stops and everyone gets in the ditch. And when the line starts again they'll say, 'Moving out.' Guys get up and hit the guy behind them, 'We're moving out.' And so it goes down the column. Everyone gets a shot in the ribs and we get up and go."

"Well this particular time, the group I was in was at the end of the column and it was quite long. There was a fellow who was a good friend of mine. The guy in front of him didn't hit him (to wake him), so he is left there (asleep). The whole damn column goes and he is laying in the ditch. Lots of guys fell asleep. You are always tired."

"So he wakes up in the morning and he looks up and sees that he has a comforter on. And there are three ladies sitting there waiting for him to wake up. He wakes up and they explain to him through sign language that the column went on ahead up the road and at the fork in the road went this way. And right over here on the other road going up was a little town, and they were waiting to be liberated. So they persuade him to liberate their town. So, he decided to do it. He went up there with the ladies and the town was waiting for them. The mayor had a big band and the people had hung banners and the school children were out and they all signed the Monsieur as the soldier arrived. The mayor made a big speech and thanked the soldier for liberating the town. And that was it! He then left and caught up with the column the next day."

GRIM PILE OF DEAD

Most of Gray's memories were not of such humorous incidents. Some were downright ghastly. He recalled, "We were in France somewhere when we came across the grimmest thing I think I have ever seen. It was after we had made an attack on the enemy and the enemy had withdrawn and we are moving up to fill that gap. And on the side of the road is a pile of dead German men. It was winter and cold as the devil. And they were all frozen. And here they are piled about 6 feet high. And all I could see were legs and arms all frozen stiff. What a sight that was! When you walk by looking at it, it's something that you don't forget. That's the damn war!"

INTO GERMANY

The 3rd Division moved northward quickly through Southern France. They advanced up through the Rhone Valley, crossed the Vosges Mountains and arrived at the Rhine River at Strasbourg, France by late November. There they took up defensive positions against the German forces there.

BATTLE AT COLMAR POCKET

On January 23rd, 1945, the 3rd Division engaged the Germans again in an effort to clear the Colmar Pocket. Gray recalled, "When we were very close to the Rhine River and all the Germans were being pushed out of France — and how it developed I really don't know — but there was a place called the Colmar Pocket. And that turned into a very big battle. I don't know how many troops were there, but there were quite a few and they still had access to supplies and they were very strong. And the Germans initially prevented us from going up to the Rhine River."

Battle at Colmar Pocket.

"During the battle we came upon a small river or a creek that we needed to cross and there was only one bridge across it. The first of our tanks that tried crossing

17

it broke the bridge. So no tanks could get in there to give us support for that battle. That made it much more difficult for us."

"One thing our unit did that was unique, and I don't think was ever done before, they came in with huge searchlights. They turned them on when it was a cloudy night and they beamed them. They would reflect off the clouds and light up the battlefield. It was amazing, even eerie and spooky. But it did light it up. And they thought they had the neatest invention in the world. There was only one thing wrong with it; the enemy could see us, too. They hadn't thought of that. The lights didn't last beyond a couple of nights."

"The French Government later awarded the Division the "Croix de Guerre" (Cross of War Medal) for its action at Colmar," Gray added.

MOVING ACROSS GERMANY

The 3rd Division reached Zweibrucken, Germany on March 15th and pressed through the Siegfried Line. They crossed the Rhine River on March 26th and proceeded to Nuremberg, where they encountered intense combat. "Nuremberg provided one of the most bitter engagements in Germany," recalled Gray.

Army Forces crossing the Siegfried Line, Germany. September 1944.

During the division's movement into Germany Gray recalled coming up against a special German Division. "This particular time that an attack started," he said, "the Germans threw a division at us called a Herman Goering Division, which was made up of kids that they had raised to become soldiers. They were all pure German, blond hair and blue eyes. They were all young, and you wouldn't trust them as far as you could throw them. You really watched those guys. But they put them into action at the wrong

Battle in Nuremberg.

time. This whole big attack was just starting. And within three hours there was no more Herman Goering Division. It was dissolved. That shows you the power behind these attacks."

By the end of April, the 3rd Division had taken the cities of Augsburg and Munich. Some elements of the 7th Infantry Regiment proceeded to Berchtesgaden and captured the Eagle's Nest, Hitler's mountain retreat. Gray enjoyed the 'fruit' of that triumph. He recalled, "A few of our more aware soldiers had the good sense to liberate a good supply of French Champagne and Hennessey's Cognac from Hitler's Berchtesgaden retreat. To say the least, a good time was had by all. Boy, that Champagne was good!!!"

The division had advanced almost to Salzburg, Austria by the time they learned that Germany had surrendered.

INTERACTION WITH GERMAN PRISONERS OF WAR

Gray had several different experiences with German Prisoners of War. "The prisoners that we would get were regular German Army usually," he said. "And they were not much different than we are. I think half of them were wondering why there were there. And they would be awfully beat up. We threw a lot of artillery at them."

German POWs being interrogated.

"When we received prisoners off of the line, we would contact our interrogators. The theory was, the longer the prisoner had nothing happening he would get a secure feeling. So, if you get a prisoner and get him right to an interrogator you were liable to get more information from him. And it worked pretty well."

GERMAN POW INTO THE DITCH

"One time a German prisoner was in front of me walking on a dirt road — there were always dirt roads. It was night. And a bomber came overhead dropping 'screaming mimis'. It's a big bomb that spins and throws out all the little ones. It makes an ungodly racket. It's an anti-personnel weapon. The bombs started getting closer to us as we were walking on the road. So I got nervous and I dropped into one of the many ditches alongside the road. And I look up, and there is the prisoner, still standing in the middle of the road. So I said, "Get in the ditch." And he gets all nervous and he jumps right in my hole. And we are nose to nose. We just looked at each other and smiled. *(laughing)* What are you going to do? And they kept dropping those damn bombs, which got reasonably close to us. So it was a good thing we got in there."

GERMAN POW WRITES HIS WIFE

"There was a German 'under-officer' they called them, like a top sergeant, that I brought in off the line. Interrogators considered them to be very important because they knew what was going on. They have more information than an ordinary soldier. An ordinary soldier really doesn't know what the hell is going on. He does what he is told. So the interrogator is really working on him, because he knows something but he isn't giving any information. So the interrogator takes a stick and he makes a mark on the dirt and gets a shovel and tells the guy to start digging. It's obviously the shape of a grave. When the prisoner gets the hole dug up to his knees the interrogator comes out again and he tells him, 'That's your grave unless you start cooperating with the interview.' And the German looked at him and then asked for a pencil and paper to write to his wife. And I thought, "'Wow! He's not going to say anything.'"

HOMECOMING

Following the Nazi surrender, Gray's division moved on to Herschfeld (located in central Germany) to prepare for the occupation of Germany. When the war in the Pacific ended, he finally was sent home.

"I shipped out of Marseilles to New York then on to Camp Dix, New Jersey, where I was discharged," he recalled. "A brief train ride to New York City and then a subway to Elmhurst, Queens, New York. I walked a few blocks to 7604 Kneeland Avenue. I rang the doorbell. The door opened, and there stood my mother and father. ... I was HOME!"

As happy as that homecoming reunion was for Gray, it was tempered with an awful realization. "Many more were never coming home," he said. "Many of the gallant line company men would not return. The cost of the Division's journey from North Africa, Sicily, Italy, France, Germany and Austria was a high one. It is recorded forever on a monument in Arlington Cemetery."

U.S. ARMY THIRD INFANTRY DIVISION WWII

5558 KILLED IN ACTION

444 MISSING IN ACTION

18,766 WOUNDED IN ACTION

24,768 TOTAL CASUALTIES

LIFE AFTER THE WAR

After spending two and a half years in the Army (two of those years on foreign soil) and rising to the rank of a Sergeant, Ennis Gray was ready to begin the next chapter of his life.

Gray returned to Fordham University to continue his studies as well as his running. "While there," he said, "I took second place in the National Track Championship, which qualified me for running the Olympic trials at Northwestern University in 1948."

One day, Gray went to visit a friend from Fordham University who was back home in Queens, New York. "So I'm ringing the bell and hoping to see my friend

Ennis and Kay today.

and his sister answers the door," Gray said. "She was wearing her uniform. And that was it! Sixty-six years of marriage now."

The woman who answered the door was Kay. Her uniform was a Coast Guard uniform. She was one of the SPAR's who served in New Orleans and Washington, D.C. during the war. Her story is included in the *Serving On the Home Front* section of this book.

Gray summarized the rest of his life: "I got a job, went to work, got married and raised a family of four children: Dennis, Karen, Jim and Timothy. We had a life together and have been married for 66 years. And that's it."

Today Ennis and Kay live in a retirement community in Carmel, Indiana.

This chapter is based on the author's interview with Mr. Gray as well as Mr. Gray's personal written account of his war experience.

Ennis Gray, in uniform all these years later.

Pushing into Germany
Mortar Man Served in the Army's Blackhawk Division

Manson Eugene (Gene) Groves wanted to follow his older brother Charles into the Army. The elder brother had joined in 1941, as the United States prepared to enter the war.

"As soon as I get old enough, I'll volunteer," he remembers telling his brother.

The Martinsville, Indiana native didn't wait long to fulfill his dream. He left school after the 10th grade and enlisted in 1943 at the age of 17.

"Ma'am," he said to his 10th grade teacher at the end of the school year, "I came to say goodbye. I won't be in school any longer because I joined the Army." She told him he was too young, but he left for military training two days later.

Gene, who was born on March 21, 1926 and was the second born of his father's second wife, was inducted into the Army at Fort Harrison in Indianapolis and then sent to Camp Blanden, Florida for his basic training.

Following his basic training he was sent to the Camp Cooke Army Camp at San Luis Obispo, California where he was attached to the 86th Blackhawk Division and assigned to a mortar team. "We used the 60mm and 81mm mortars," he remembered.

The division was sent to San Diego in the late fall of 1943 for amphibious training.

M2-60mm mortar.

Gene's father died of cancer in 1944 while he was training in California. He went home on furlough for the funeral.

In February of 1945, his division traveled four days across country to Boston and then left for Europe. "We boarded the ship during a winter storm," Gene recalled.

After a 14-day transit across the Atlantic, the 86th Division arrived in France in March of 1945. It joined up with Patton's Army and pushed into Germany near Koln, providing relief for the 8th Infantry Division.

The men of the Blackhawk Division endured 34 days of combat. "You'll never forget when you get your baptism by fire," Gene exclaimed, referring to his first experience with combat as German snipers shot at them.

His mortar section provided fire support to the infantry by launching mortar rounds from a tube that was attached to a plate on the ground. Gene served as ammunition bearer, carrying the mortar rounds up to the gunner. "I carried six 60mm mortar rounds plus weapon, grenades, and gear," recalled Gene.

Mortar Team, 86th Infantry Division.

Each man knew how to do every job within the team in case he had to fill in for someone else.

Gene remembered making a direct hit on the German enemy while fighting on the Rhine River. One of his mortar rounds knocked out a German 88mm antiaircraft weapon that was on the other side of the Rhine shooting back at them.

High explosive 60mm mortar round. (Fort Devens Museum).

The division crossed the Rhine River into Eibelshausen and progressed eastward, crossing several more rivers. "We got to chasing Germans and we crossed six rivers," said Gene. The rivers included the Bigge, the Ruhr and ultimately the Danube.

Gene especially remembered the Danube, as that was the place his unit was pinned down by German tanks. "Patton's troops rescued us," he said. "We were pinned at the river when they arrived."

U.S. mortar team in action.

86th Infantry Division moving across Germany.

Traversing the western part of Germany included some awful sights at a German concentration camp. "We saw the death camps," Gene said. "You couldn't believe how one man (Hitler) could be so cruel. We saw all those dead people lying naked."

Fifty-one years later, in 1996, the U.S. Army's Center of Military History and the United States Holocaust Memorial Museum officially recognized the 86th Infantry Division as a liberating unit.

The division reached as far as the Ruhr Valley in Bavaria when the war in Europe

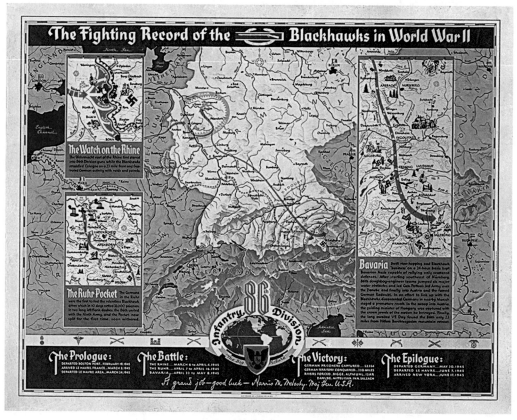

86th Infantry map of movements across Germany.

ended. Following the surrender of Germany, the division assisted with processing German Prisoners of War.

The division returned to the U.S. in June of 1945 and was sent to Camp Gruber in Oklahoma to begin training with new weapons for the upcoming invasion of Japan. By late August, the division had left San Francisco and was heading toward Japan. Their ship got as far as Leyte Harbor, the Philippines, when news of Japan's surrender was received in the aftermath of the atomic bomb.

Instead of proceeding to Japan, the ship landed at Luzon and the members of the division were scattered throughout the island for temporary duty. Gene stayed in the Philippines for a year training Filipino scouts and hauling gravel for road repairs.

While he was there, he had a surprise meeting up with his older brother, Charles, who was passing through the Philippines. "We had a good time hanging around as pals and going to the theaters," said Gene of their two weeks together in Manilla.

During that year he also earned his GED high school degree.

Gene returned to the U.S. in May of 1946. He affiliated with the Indiana National Guard in Martinsville and became the Weapons Platoon Sergeant in his unit, training men on the use of mortars.

"I could get 19 rounds in the air before the first round exploded," he said proudly of his technique.

Shortly after returning from Europe, Gene met Dorothy (Dottie) Kindred at Newbury's department store in Martinsville. He recalled, "I was staring at her and she said, 'If you see something green on me take it off.' I married her six months later."

"My first wife was my M-1 Rifle," he said remembering his early days of military training. He had a much longer and more enjoyable partnership with his 'second' wife.

Gene's marriage to Dottie lasted for 64 years until her death in 2010.

Gene and Dottie were involved in a serious auto accident in 1947. Pregnant at the time, Dottie's unborn child, Paul died from injuries. Two years later, twin boys were born in 1949: Daniel and David. Today the extended family

Technical inspection on 60mm mortars.

Dottie and Gene Groves, 1950.

includes 10 grandchildren and one great-grandchild.

Gene worked for a short time at the Block Plant in Martinsville before landing a job as Assistant Safety Inspector at Bridgeport Brass, where he worked until 1975. In 1971 he started working at the Morgan County Jail as a turnkey, the person responsible for locking down the prisoners.

At the age of 53, Gene attended the Police Academy in Plainfield, Indiana and became a policeman. He worked at the Morgan County Jail for six years, and helped to transport murderer Steve Judy to Michigan City, Indiana for his execution.

Along with his son, he started his own security business, Groves Security Company. He then became a security officer at Fox Cliff Golf Course in Martinsville, where he worked for 40 years before his retirement in April 2016.

Today, the 92-year old continues to work as a part-time security guard at Fox Cliff. In his spare-time Gene enjoys shopping, fishing, and target shooting with his pistol and rifle.

What remains most important to him is his faith in the Lord. "The good Lord saved me during the war, and He brought me home," said a grateful Gene who often wears one or more Christian crosses around his neck. "He took me through a lot of things over there. I would be lying back there if not for Him."

His thoughts return to the men who fought and died. "We honor the men who fought to free our nation. A lot of men made the ultimate sacrifice."

Ultimate sacrifices and blessed freedoms. The two have always been linked together in our nation's history.

Gene Groves.

Beating the Odds
Indianapolis Native Survived a B-17 Bail Out and German POW Camp

Howard Kwitny played bridge each Monday and Friday with his friends at Hoosier Village Retirement Community. Some days, lady luck was on his side and he won. Sometimes, luck was hard to find. The fact that he was playing at all at the age of 91 is a testimony to beating some pretty heavy odds 70-plus years ago.

Howard was born on September 1, 1924 and raised by his parents, Ben and Helen Kwitny. He graduated from Shortridge High School of Indianapolis in 1942 and then attended one semester at Indiana University in Bloomington.

On November 11, 1942 he enlisted in the Army Reserve. Knowing that he was likely to be activated, and wanting to have some time with his parents, Howard transferred to Butler University in Indianapolis for the 1943 spring semester. The Army activated him that May.

Howard completed his 12-week basic infantry training at Camp Wolters near Mineral Wells, Texas. When he learned that the Army Air Force was in need of men to train as pilots and was offering a two-week furlough to anyone who transferred to them, he decided to make the switch.

He was sent to Montana State College in Bozeman, Montana for one semester of College Training Detachment, a prerequisite for pilots before flight training. But he washed out of the program, ending his chances of flying. When he was faced

Waist Gunners on B-17.

with the choice of returning to the Army Infantry or training as a gunner on one of the bombers, he opted for the opportunity of firing a 50-caliber machine gun at 32,000 feet.

Howard attended gunnery school in Kingman, Arizona and armorer school at Lowery Field in Colorado. He became an armorer gunner, specializing in the firing and maintenance of the plane's machine guns. As the armorer, he was in charge of the ordnance on the plane. "I was the one who had to dislodge bombs that didn't drop and keep all the machine guns working," he said.

Howard was assigned to a crew on a B-17 Flying Fortress bomber with the 15th Air Force, 97th Bomb Group, 340th Bomb Squadron. The four-engine heavy bomber built by Boeing was developed in the 1930's. The aircraft was 74 feet long and had a wingspan of 104 feet. It carried a crew of 10 and could travel speeds up to 287 mph. It was used mostly for daytime strategic bombing runs into Germany.

B-17 in flight.

Howard and the newly formed crew trained together for several months in Omaha, Nebraska and Sioux City, Iowa. Howard became the left waist gunner. His crew left the United States on a troop ship bound for Italy at the end of 1944. "I spent my Christmas crossing the Atlantic," he recalled. Their first bombing mission was over Linz, Austria. The target was railroad marshaling yards.

B-17 crew, Howard is kneeling, second from left.

Howard's second mission on February 27, 1945 turned out to be his last mission. It was almost his last day of life as well.

The target was railroad yards in Augsburg, Germany. As the crew approached the designated site, the Ball Turret Gunner passed out from lack of oxygen. Howard, seeing that his crewmember had lost his oxygen, made his way over to him and helped get him reconnected to an oxygen tank, saving his life.

B-17 destroyed by flak.

How To Bail Out of the Flying Fortress

LIFE VEST SHOULD BE WORN UNDER PARACHUTE
HARNESS ON ALL OVERWATER FLIGHTS

TAIL GUNNER
RIGHT WAIST GUNNER
BALL LEFT WAIST GUNNER
TURRET
GUNNER

RADIO OPERATOR
PILOT UPPER TURRET DINGHY CHUTE
CO-PILOT GUNNER
BOMBARDIER NAVIGATOR

As Howard's B-17 dropped its bomb load over the target, the plane was getting pummeled by German anti-aircraft fire at 32,000 feet. The Number 3 engine was knocked out, cutting off all electricity to the plane. Moments later, the plane was engulfed in flames, necessitating the bailout of the crew.

Howard almost didn't make it out in time. The strong centrifugal force of the fast descending plane temporarily trapped him to the floor of the aircraft. "I was pinned and couldn't move a finger," he recalled. "It is a scary feeling to know that you are about to pass out. I prayed for God to help me. And God did help me! It's like he picked me up and pulled me at the waist to get me to the exit door. I jumped, counted to three so that the chute wouldn't get caught in the plane, pulled the cord, and then passed out."

Howard thought he regained consciousness at about 20,000 feet. He recalled he was floating down and that it was hard to catch his breath. "I was scared to death," he said. "From the air I couldn't see any of the other members of my crew. I was all by myself. I saw a lot of flak bursting above me."

As he landed on the ground he felt a sharp pain in his foot. The impact had broken it. Within a short time, some 40-50 Germans (a mixture of civilian and military) had him surrounded. "One of the Germans put a knife to my throat," Howard recalled. "I was hit, kicked and had the

32

heck beaten out of me by some guys, but I didn't feel anything at the time," he said, indicating his state of shock.

He was forced to get up and hurry by foot toward the town. The Allied bomb raid was still in progress, and everyone needed to find shelter. "Fortunately, I was real close to a jail, so I didn't have far to walk," he said.

At the end of the bomb raid, and as he was beginning to exit the jail, someone pushed him down a flight of steps. A German Officer intervened. "I saluted him, and he saluted me back," recalled Howard. The show of respect possibly helped his cause as the officer helped protect him from the crowd that wanted to kill him. "The typical German soldier was a good man," said Howard. "He was there because he had to be."

After a few hours in the prison, Howard and other POW's were transported by truck to another location. While on the truck he was temporarily reunited with the top turret gunner, Bob from his B-17 crew.

What happened next was a long and tiring odyssey of traveling from one POW camp to another. "We walked from Nuremberg to Moosburg, a 12-day march on a broken foot," said Howard. "It was very painful! I had to leave my boots on the whole time for fear of not being able to get them back over my swollen foot if I took them off."

Howard and the other POWs finally settled in Stalag VIIA POW camp in Moosburg, Germany. Located north and a little east of Munich, it was a massive camp of multi-national captives that was originally slated to hold 10,000 prisoners. By the time Howard and the others from his group had arrived there in early 1945, the camp had swelled to over 70,000 prisoners and would soon expand to over 100,000.

While at Stalag VIIA, the POWs focused on survival and waited for a hopeful liberation by the Allied forces, which were slowly closing in on Germany. Howard recalled hearing rumors that as the end of the war approached the Germans were going to march the prisoners toward the Allied front to act as human shields. The International Red Cross convinced the Germans otherwise.

Stalag VIIA.

It was at Stalag VIIA that Howard was also reunited with Al, the veteran right waist gunner from his B-17 crew. "He was on his 45th mission," recalled Howard. The two men helped keep each other alive. "They didn't give us anything to eat or drink," said Howard. "We had to forage for ourselves. We slept together outside to keep each other warm."

In early March, Howard's parents were informed by Western Union Telegram that their son was in a missing status:

```
Washington D.C.—The Secretary of War desires me
to express his deep regret that your son, SGT
Kwitny, Howard I. has been missing in action
over Germany since 27 Feb 45. If further details
or other information are received, you will be
promptly notified.
```

Major General M.F. Twining, the Commanding Officer of the 15th Air Force, wrote a letter to the Kwitny family on March 20th. In it, General Twinning wrote:

Dear Mr. Kwitny:

You are no doubt aware that much of the recent progress of the Allied Armies in Europe is due to the constant pounding of enemy targets across the continent by our Air Forces. On February 27, 1945 your son, Sergeant Howard I. Kwitny, made a vital contribution to the success of this offensive when he served as a waist gunner on his craft in a combat mission to Augsburg, Germany. As the Flying Fortress failed to return to its base, Howard and his crew have been missing in action ever since.

Through our interrogation of returning airmen we have learned that your son's craft was damaged by flak over the target and fell from the formation at once. The stricken bomber lost altitude rapidly but before it passed from view, four parachutes were seen to emerge. Should there be a change in Howard's status the War Department will notify you without delay.

His personal possessions have been assembled for shipping to the Effects Quartermaster, Army Effects Bureau, Kansas City, Missouri, who will in turn forward them to the designated beneficiary.

I am proud to have had your son in my command. It is inspiring to know that men of his courage and ability are carrying on our nation's battles against the forces of tyranny and aggression. Howard won the respect and admiration of all his fellow airmen for the sterling traits of character which he possessed.

Very Sincerely Yours,
N.F. Twining

Howard's parents received a second letter a month later, which had been sent on April 19th. The letter did not give them much more information on Howard, but it did provide contact information for the rest of the crew. This letter was from Major N.W. Reed, Acting Chief, Notification Branch, Personal Affairs Division. Major Reed wrote in this letter:

Dear Mr. Kwitny,

I am writing you with reference to your son, Sergeant Howard I. Kwitny, who was reported by the Adjutant General as missing in action over Germany since 27 February, 1945.

Additional information has been received indicating that Sergeant Kwitny was a waist gunner of a B-17 ("Flying Fortress") bomber, which departed from Italy on a bombardment mission to Augsburg, Germany, on 27 February, 1945. The report reveals that during this mission while over the target at about 12:55 pm, your son's Fortress sustained damage by enemy antiaircraft fire and left the formation. Four parachutes were observed to emerge from the damaged craft, although when last seen it appeared to be flying under control. It is regretted that there is no other information available in this headquarters relative to the whereabouts of Sergeant Kwitny.

Believing that you may wish to communicate with the families of the others who were in the plane with your son, I am enclosing a list of those men and the names and addresses with their next of kin.

Please be assured that a continuing search by land, sea and air is being made to discover the whereabouts or our missing personnel. As our Armies advance over enemy occupied territory, special troops are assigned to this task, and agencies of our government and allies frequently send in details, which aid us in our brining additional information to you.

Very Sincerely,
N.W. Reed

On April 29, 1945, just 10 days after Reed mailed his letter to the Kwitnys, the ordeal for Howard and the other over 100,000 prisoners came to an end as Allied troops arrived at Stalag VIIA. "I watched the 3rd Army take control," said a relieved

Liberation of POW Camp in Germany.

Howard. "I got to see Patton up close personally the next day. Later, I even saw General Eisenhower in France."

Shortly after being liberated, Howard saw the rest of his crewmembers. Amazingly, they had all survived! "The Germans said we were one crew in a thousand that all survived," Howard recalled. "There were so many ways to die after bailing out."

Patton at Liberation of Stalag VII-A.

Howard and the other American prisoners of war were flown to France and taken to Camp Lucky Strike. The men were all offered a two-week pass for some rest and recreation, but Howard declined. "I was so anxious to get home that I turned it down so that I could get home sooner."

He spent a few weeks in France before boarding a troop ship and crossing the Atlantic on his homeward journey.

He was at home waiting to report to the Cadillac Motel in Florida for two months' vacation from military service in August, when he learned that Japan had surrendered and the war had ended.

Howard received his honorable discharge on October 31, 1945. He had earned the POW Medal, Air Medal and a Purple Heart. In a touch of irony, when he arrived home for good, he had to report to the draft board to *register* for the draft.

"I became part of the 52/20 club," said Howard, referring to receiving $20 a week for 52 weeks. It was enough to support him for a year of hanging out with his friends and relatives and playing cards, something he enjoyed doing for the rest of his life.

Following his year of rest, Howard returned to Butler University. "I tried to go back to college for two semesters," he said, "but I couldn't cope with it. I was just too nervous."

He abandoned the classroom and chose instead a career of working with his hands outside. "I did a mess of things," he said, "construction work, roofing, guttering, etc." In 1965, he settled into a job with Alart Construction, selling roofing, guttering and kitchen remodeling materials. He worked at Alart until 1990, when he took a position at AT&T Telephone Company. He retired from AT&T in 1996.

Kwitny family.

In 1952, Howard married Frances Schwartz, whom he had met in Indianapolis after returning home from the war. Howard and Frances enjoyed 25 years of marriage, raising three children: Brian, Cindy and Jill. Frances died from cancer in 1977.

He enjoyed, in his later years, attending reunions with his B-17 crew

In 2006, Howard moved into Hoosier Village Retirement Community in Zionsville. He spent the final years of his life playing cards and enjoying the company of his friends and family.

The life and faith lessons learned from 70 years earlier remained in his mind and heart. "There is a God," said Howard. "That is the sum of all my World War II experiences. Not everyone gets to have the personal experience with God that I

Howard (far left) and B-17 crew at reunion.

did. I knew that He was going to take care of me, and He did."

A winning bridge hand requires luck. A successful life that includes surviving a bail out and being a prisoner of war requires much more than luck. Howard Kwitny was happy to have both the occasional luck of a card game and a constant faith in the providence of God, which sustained him throughout his life.

Howard died on January 15th, 2016. He was 91.

Howard Kwitny.

Memphis Belle Leaves Home for War

WAC Served in Europe and Settled in Indiana

BEGINNING

Eileen (Jones) McClarnon spent most of the years of her youth growing up in Memphis, Tennessee. She loved everything about the city — its people and culture, its warm and sunny climate. She might well have stayed there for a lifetime if it had not been for two things: war and George.

Born in Arkansas on July 17, 1926, Eileen was the youngest of five children born to her parents, Jim and Matilda Rose Jones.

"We moved to Memphis when I was four years old," she wrote in her personal memoir. "I was raised there along the river in what you would call a blue-collar neighborhood. In fact, it was probably more like a 'purple-collar' one because we were so poor."

"Mama was our rock," she wrote. "In spite of the Depression, she always had a little emergency money tucked away in a pocket she had sewn into her bra. She referred to it as keeping it in her 'bosom.' Daddy didn't dare touch it. She worked at a candy factory and was forever bringing home large grocery sacks of candy that had loose wrappers. We had sacks of candy when others did not. However, I dreamed of bananas and oranges. That's what I wanted. Those were treats."

Eileen started school when she was five. Reflecting back on those days in her memoir she wrote, "In Memphis schools, up until high school years, the boys went to one side of the school and the girls went to the other. This was hard on me. I couldn't wait to be older and go to high school. When I finally got there and our classes were mixed, I concentrated mightily upon flirtation."

She also concentrated on dancing. "I loved dancing to Big Band music," she wrote. "They were heaven! I knew that Mama would always have a little money tucked away in her bosom for a new dress so I could go dancing in style when I was invited to the Peabody Hotel. I think Mama lived a little bit through me."

Eileen fell in love and married early in life. "My love at that time was John Tate Morris — 'Booger'," she wrote in her memoir. "He was the football star of Southside High School. After graduation, he was stationed with the Railroad Battalion in New Orleans. I went to New Orleans for a 'three-day sleep over' when I was just eighteen years old, and that's when we were married."

WAR COMES TO AMERICA

"It was a beautiful day in Memphis, Tennessee on December 7th, 1941," Eileen wrote. "A friend and I had been fishing in the Mississippi River. When I returned home, my parents informed me that our naval fleet had been bombed by the Japanese. I had no idea what or where Pearl Harbor was, but I soon learned the devastating details.

"How dare they! That small country! We would destroy them in weeks!

"On the following Monday, our high school was called to assembly to hear President Roosevelt give his 'Day in Infamy' speech. A number of seniors left the assembly hall to join the various military services. Some were never to return."

Two of Eileen's brothers were already serving in the Navy at that time. "One was on a ship off the coast of Iceland and the other on a ship near the coast of Columbia, South America," she wrote.

FDR, December 24, 1943.

Like most Americans, Eileen's family tried to keep up with the news of the war. "We tuned in to the radio for the war news and were horrified to hear of the fall of Luzon, the Battle of the Coral Sea, Guam, Guadalcanal — all falling to the Japanese, that tiny little country."

"My thoughts were consumed by the war. When passing the train or bus station and seeing loved ones clinging to each other in bidding good-bye, I sobbed each time."

Eileen agonized over all the boys that were being killed. She also gave attention to the reports of enemy dead. She wrote, "I would scour the newspaper for the number of casualties that we had inflicted upon the Germans and subtract them from the population statistics to see how many Germans remained. It seems ludicrous now, but then it seemed logical. Also, the brave RAF pilots and later American pilots being shot down over Germany was still so very sad."

Although too young to join a service herself, Eileen got a job at the Air Transport Command in Memphis. "Their purpose was to ferry planes and supplies principally to the China-Burma-India command," she wrote. "I worked there at the Officers' Club for about one year and developed a yearning for far-away places with strange sounding names."

JOINING THE WACS

In March of 1943, Eileen entered into military service. Speaking of her motivation for doing so in an interview she said, "I had watched the German people being taken in by a rogue. We had at my disposal growing up two newspapers, and they would tell about Germany and Mussolini and so forth. And we also had newsreels. I went to the movies about once a week and the newsreels would show them. And I hated to see what these people were bringing about."

Hitler and Mussolini.

She wrote in her memoir, "Still consumed by the war, I stretched the truth of my age by a year and joined the WACs (Women's Army Corps). After basic training at Ft. Oglethorpe, Georgia, I was fortunate to be stationed back in Memphis at the same Ferry Command Base. My job there was to record the flight hours of the officers when they returned from a mission."

DUTY IN EUROPE

Sometime later, Eileen learned that she and other women were assigned to duty abroad. She recorded in her memoir, "What a joy to find that our group of about 40 was being sent overseas. We had no idea what our destination would be, but it sounded exciting. The trip from New York to Liverpool was on a ship called the *Mariposa,* which had been a cruise ship before the war. When we docked in Liverpool and I saw the bombed warehouses and the glass missing from the windows, I was a little less than excited.

"From Liverpool, we were bused to an RAF (Royal Air Force) base in Valley, Wales. As I had not known about Pearl Harbor, I didn't know much about Wales. I was so disappointed. It was an ugly, misty day and the barracks were damp and Spartan with a coal stove at each end of the building. By the next day when the sun came out, I saw and came to love, the beauty of Wales — the entire bucolic scene with the sheep grazing on the green, green grass enclosed in stone fences."

The mission of the Air Transport Command in Wales was delivering planes, mostly B-17s and B-24s, to where they were needed in the theater of operations.

Eileen wrote of her specific job in her memoir, "I requested and landed a job as a

Royal Air Force Ferry Command, 1941–1943.

messenger driving a jeep and delivering mail and messages from one office to another. I also drove to Holyhead, a coastal town about eight miles from the base. I also met the train in Valley to pick up the GI newspaper, *The Stars and Stripes.*"

In addition to delivering messages and newspapers, she also delivered officers around the base. "I drove officers and other soldiers around in a jeep," she recorded in her memoir. "What a great job! I was assigned to a Colonel and to Major Clifford, who favored me."

Eileen not only loved her work, she grew to love the people of England. "I loved and admired the courage of the British," she wrote. "It wasn't until I had children of my own, that I fully understood what it would be like to remove sleeping children from their warm beds to a damp bomb shelter night after night during the blitz. Many of the British sent their children to Ireland to escape the incessant bombing."

"One day, I was on a train returning to Valley from London, and I was seated by a lady who was heading for Holyhead, where she would catch a ship to Ireland to pick up her children. As we visited, she reached into a paper bag for her lunch. It consisted of a sandwich of margarine and watercress. She offered to share. As I declined, I thought of their courage and deprivation and endurance."

While serving in Wales, Eileen met an American officer who changed the course of her life. She described meeting him in her memoir, "The first time I laid eyes on George McClarnon, he was an officer in the United States Air Force in Valley, Wales. I thought he was cute. He remarked to me, 'What do they call you?' I replied, "They call me Rover. What do they call you?" And so, the great romance began.

George McClarnon

The war progressed and the Allied forces moved through Germany. Good news finally came on May 8, 1945. Eileen shared in her memoir, "Rumors abounded that there would be an announcement of Germany's surrender any hour. We waited by the radio and finally President Truman told us the war in Europe had ended. The PX and the Social Room opened and we celebrated until the wee hours."

"There was still much to be done at our base. The many planes were being ferried back to the USA, so we were still involved."

While the Air Transport Command sent back planes to the U.S., the war in the Pacific raged. Slowly but progressively, the Allies defeated the Japanese and leap-frogged across islands; moving ever closer to

The Air Transport Command shipping parts of airplanes.

mainland Japan. And then, suddenly, it was over. Eileen described the elation and the sadness in her memoir, "It was August 1945 when we heard of the A Bomb and Hiroshima. Within a week, this horrible World War was over. We again opened the Social Room and partied, but the joy was tempered by the realization that these wonderful friendships and the camaraderie which we shared must end."

Eileen, center, with service member friends.

Most of the women working in the Air Transport Command were sent to Germany to the occupation forces. But five were selected for a different duty in Paris. Eileen was one of the five. They were sent to Orly Airfield in Paris.

Orly Airfield had been used by the German Luftwaffe after occupying Paris in 1940. The Allies took over the airfield after the liberation of Paris in the summer of 1944.

Eileen had a very different job while assigned to Orly. She wrote, "While there, I worked in the Chaplain's office interviewing soldiers who wanted to go home on furlough and then re-enlist for the occupation of Germany. My job was to ask their motivation for this action. One young fellow who had received a 'Dear John' letter from his wife said that his motivation was to go home and kill his wife and then come back. I think he had a much longer session with the Chaplain than the others."

RETURNING HOME

By early December of 1945, Eileen had completed her assignment and was being shipped home from Le Havre, France. She and the others hoped to be home by Christmas. Five days after leaving France, the ship was caught in a hurricane. Waves grew as high as 70 feet. The ship floundered and last rites were offered to Catholics. The ship survived the hurricane but lost its rudder. Eileen wrote in her memoir, "Being rudderless, we floundered several days until we made our way to the Azores. Our food supply had been essentially destroyed, so we had two very meager meals a day. We had to remain on board because we could not dock at the Azores. After a few days, the Captain informed us that the cruiser, *Enterprise,* would retrieve us in a week or so.

"On the day the *Enterprise* was to arrive, we were up early and on deck waiting for her. We were thinking of the wonderful food awaiting us — the food was so great, the fried chicken… But the most wonderful sight that lingers in my memory was the American flag flying above the *Enterprise.*

"To this very day, whenever and wherever I see the flag is displayed and they play the "Star Spangled Banner," I swell with pride as I relive each and every time the sighting of the flag on the *Enterprise* that day so long ago."

Upon their return home, Eileen and George made plans to meet and resume their relationship. "We both had a difficult task ahead of us," Eileen recorded in her memoir. "We both had old lives to end. But we also had a wonderful one to begin."

NEW HUSBAND, NEW LIFE

That new life began in April of 1946, as Eileen left her beloved home in Memphis and came to Greenfield, Indiana where George lived. Her first experience with Indiana made her homesick. She wrote, "When I came north to Greenfield to meet my new family before George and I were married, the day was grey and there was snow on the ground. I had left beautiful, warm, sunny Memphis and wondered, not for the last time, 'Do I really want to leave Memphis?'"

While she didn't want to leave Memphis, she did want to spend her life with George. They were married on May 12, 1946 in a small church close to Fairland, Indiana.

In 1947, they moved to Indianapolis where George worked at Allison Transmission and Eileen found work as a receptionist and typist at an insurance agency. Their daughter, Melanie, was born that same year. Two other children followed a few years later: Jeff (1953) and Laurie (1954).

After a working a brief stint in Hastings, Michigan with the Swift Company, George applied to Veterinary School at Michigan State University.

Eileen skiing.

Eileen wrote in her memoir, "While we were waiting to hear if George was accepted, he was transferred to my precious Memphis in April of 1949. I was home again! We loved Memphis with its warmth, music, charm and river. We had the time of our lives there. When word reached us that George had indeed been accepted to MSU for that fall term, I was distraught. I did not want to leave my Memphis one more time. I felt like I would rather go to Korea than Michigan…but, when September came, off we went to Lansing and the start of yet another new chapter in our wonderful life together."

Five years later, in 1954, the McClarnon family headed back to Indiana. George had earned a degree in Veterinary Medicine (second in his class!) and Eileen had earned degrees in Philosophy and Religion. "We were broke, but debt-free," she wrote in her memoir.

George opened his own veterinary office on Main Street in Knightstown, Indiana (13 miles east of his hometown of Greenfield).

"And so, we had come to yet another phase of our life," Eileen wrote in her memoir. "We had three growing children, no money, a busy life filled with animals, frantic middle of the night phone calls for help, and the biggest, draftiest, scariest

house in Knightstown. I wondered to myself yet again, 'Dear God, is this it?' I was still longing for my Memphis."

In 1978 George and Eileen built their "beautiful home in the country." "And so our grand adventure began, Bili-Mac farm was born," she recorded in her memoir. They turned their focus to raising and racing horses. "From that day forward, it was a race between the poor house and horse racing," she wrote. "At one time we had 30 horses. They were a joy to us every day."

In 1998 a fire destroyed their home, but not their spirit. She wrote in her memoir, "For five weeks, while our beautiful home was being rebuilt, we lived in a trailer and then finally moved to the tack room in the barn. Those may have been some of my happiest days. The sounds and smells of the barn were comforting to us. On the weekends we moved to the Lee's Inn. I preferred the barn."

When it finally became too hard to get help on the farm, the McClarnon's made the difficult decision to move to town. George was 79. They bought their home in Greenfield, Indiana. In retirement they enjoyed time with their family and traveling in and out of the country.

After struggling with Alzheimer's disease, George died on June 4th, 2011. He and Eileen had been married for 66 wonderful years. Since George's passing, she has found joy in her family and friends. Although, at the age of 91, her good friends have been passing away as well.

Eileen and George.

CONCLUSION

She longed for her hometown of Memphis for most of her life. But Eileen McClarnon longed to serve her country and share life with her husband even more. And that has made the one-time Memphis Belle very happy and blessed.

Such was the sentiment she expressed at the end of her personal memoir. "I guess when it's all said and done, no matter where we have lived, we've had fun. We've been blessed with a family and friends who love us as much as we love them. We have a wonderful story. We have a wonderful life."

This chapter is based on the recording of an interview done by Tresa Strakis as well as from Eileen's personal unpublished memoir.

Eileen and her grandchild.

Basketballs and Bombs
South Bend Native Takes to the Air in World War II

James Louis Powers of South Bend, Indiana grew up in the shadows of a storied football stadium at Notre Dame University, but his preferred domain was the basketball court! Born March 16th, 1925, he attended South Bend Central High School and played forward for the basketball team under an up-and-coming coach named John Wooden.

Coach Wooden's philosophy on living had a profound impact upon Jim, not only during his basketball playing days but also for much of his life. "Make each day your masterpiece" was one of the many Wooden quotes that Jim remembered and sought to implement throughout his life.

In 1943, during the middle of World War II, Jim began to focus on a different 'court,' a different 'team' and a different 'opponent.'

"When you turned 18, you signed up for the draft," he said. "I got a deferment until I graduated from high school. I volunteered to go into the Army Air Force." Having no college experience, Jim was slotted for one of the enlisted positions in the Army Air Forces.

High school basketball team, Jim is standing behind Coach Wooden.

MILITARY TRAINING:

Jim reported to Greensboro, North Carolina in July of 1943 for his basic training. Three months later, he was in Gunnery School in Yuma, Arizona, learning how to fire 50-caliber machine guns. "We had to learn to lead the firing," he said in reference to the discipline of firing ahead of the plane he was aiming to hit while it was flying in the sky.

His next stop in training was Radio School in Sioux Falls, South Dakota. The Army Air Force had decided to train him as a Radio Operator. Jim didn't recall having any say in the matter. "They made so many decisions for me that nothing really stands out," he said. "Somewhere, they must have made the decision that I was going to be a Radio Operator on a B-24. I don't recall making a decision for that. They decided for me."

While at Radio School, Jim learned Morse code. "Oh, that was difficult for me, an 18 year old kid," he recalled. "But I guess I must have passed the test."

It would prove to be a long time before Jim ever used the radio in his assigned plane. "Ordinarily, you would go up with hundreds of planes in a mission," he explained. "The only one that would report anything on the radio would be the radio operator for the lead pilot of the formations."

The final stop before being sent to Europe was Overseas Training in Casper, Wyoming. Here, Jim was assigned to his B-24 plane, flight crew and unit.

Each B-24 crew had 10 men: four officers and six enlisted. Jim's crew consisted of:

OFFICERS:
Pilot: Phil Hamer
Co-Pilot: Steve Ramaley
Bombardier: John Glenn
Navigator: Ray Dengler

ENLISTED:
Ball Turret Gunner: Lenoard Buckheit
Nose Gunner: Karl Lorenz
Radio Operator: James Powers
Engineer: George Marcincavage
Tail Gunner: Burt Mesite
Waist Gunner: Bob Schafer

Jim's B-24 Crew. Jim is standing 3rd from left.

Jim had a somewhat infamous first night with his pilot and crew. "On the first night, the pilot invited us to a get-acquainted party in the hotel room," he recalled. "I remember we were sitting around the room and they had (alcoholic) drinks. I was asked if I wanted a drink, so I said yes. I thought I might as well do that since everyone else was. I had never drank before. (Coach Wooden's strong influence had discouraged this.) I was asked how much I wanted. As I was used to drinking full glasses of milk, I had them fill it. They asked a second time, and I got another full glass.

"The next thing I remember is sliding off the bed and waking up later (on the floor) with the other crew members looking at me and asking me what I had done." What he had done was to drink himself into a bout of intoxication.

Much more than just drinking together, the men trained together. "We gelled together very well as a crew," Jim recalled.

His crew's assigned plane was the B-24 Liberator. The B-24 was one of the most used heavy bombers in the Army Air Forces. Initially built by Consolidated Aircraft

Corporation, the plane had four engines and could carry up to twenty 500-pound bombs or up ten 1,000-pound bombs. It measured about 64 feet in length, had a 110 feet wingspan, and stood 18 feet high. It could fly up to 300 mph for a distance up to 3,000 miles and ascend to an elevation of 35,000 feet. It was basically a beast with wings.

While the plane had room for plenty of bombs, it had no room for creature comforts. There was no heat, no pressurization, no bathrooms, no kitchen and no food storage. Instead, there were plenty of cramped spaces carved out of metal (including the seats) and surrounded by equipment for flying, weapons for firing or bombs for dropping. Since the plane flew above 10,000 feet, the crew had to wear oxygen masks and, because the temperatures dropped to below 40 degrees at 20,000 feet of elevation, they also had to wear protective cold weather gear. But even with all of the equipment to protect them, they still suffered during each flight.

In spite of its lack of comfort measures, there was still much to appreciate about the beast. "I thought the Liberator was a very good bomber," Jim said.

Jim's Liberator became part of the 15th Air Force, the 450th Bomb Group, and the 723rd Bomb Squadron, which was assigned to the Mediterranean Theater. His crew left the United States in December of 1944 and headed off to Italy.

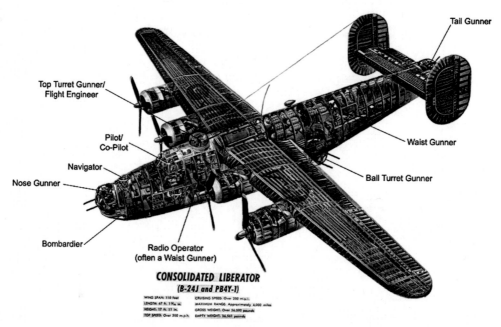

Tail Gunner

Top Turret Gunner/ Flight Engineer

Pilot/ Co-Pilot

Navigator

Nose Gunner

Waist Gunner

Ball Turret Gunner

Bombardier

Radio Operator (often a Waist Gunner)

**CONSOLIDATED LIBERATOR
(B-24J and PB4Y-1)**

WING SPAN: 110 feet
LENGTH: 67 ft. 1¾ in.
HEIGHT: 17 ft. 11 in.
TOP SPEED: Over 300 m.p.h.

CRUISING SPEED: Over 200 m.p.h.
MAXIMUM RANGE: Approximately 4,000 miles
GROSS WEIGHT: Over 56,000 pounds
EMPTY WEIGHT: 36,561 pounds

B-24 Bomber showing crew positions.

BASED IN ITALY

"I was looking forward to getting started," recalled Jim. "It was all a new experience."

Being on a ship was also a new adventure for his crew, and one that was not all that pleasant. "We all got sick," he remembered. "It was a terrible experience."

The crew landed at Naples, Italy and rode in vehicles to Manduria. The airfield that would be their home for the next six months was located 5km north of the town of Manduria, which was located in the heel of Italy's boot, about 390km southeast of Naples. The airfield was used both by the 12th and 15th Air Force and served as the Headquarters for the 47th Bombardment Wing.

The men lived in huts or tents. Each morning the men waited word on whether they would have a bombing mission. Sometimes they had a mission every day. At other times they had days in between missions, largely due to weather conditions over their prospective targets.

When they weren't on a mission, Jim and the other men enjoyed throwing horseshoes.

COMBAT FLIGHT MISSIONS:

Jim recalled flying missions every two days or so. The average duration of a bombing mission was four–six hours. Some missions were up to eight hours.

THE HEATED FLIGHT SUIT

High Altitude Flight Clothing and Body Armor

Flightdak only

1. *A-11 Gloves*
2. *A-4 QAC Parachute Harness (attachable chest pack not shown)*
3. *A-14 Oxygen Mask*
4. *B-8 Goggles*
5. *A-11 Flying Helmet*
6. *B-15 Jacket*
7. *B-4 "Mae West" Life Vest*
8. *A-11 Trousers*
9. *A-6 Boots*

December 2005 (05-4)

B-24 dropping bombs while flying through flak.

Above 10,000 feet the flight crews faced low oxygen and cold temperatures. They used oxygen masks and wore cold weather gear in the non-pressurized and not-heated plane. The clothing and mask were bulky and cumbersome, making it difficult to move around the already confined spaces of the plane.

Most of their bombing targets were in Southern Italy, Southern Germany and Austria; and sometimes the Po Valley in Northern Italy. "In the Po Valley, the German's had their 88s (anti-aircraft artillery) up in the mountains. We wouldn't be that high above, maybe at 12,000 feet," recalled Jim. "If we went to a target, our limit was 24,000 feet. The B-17 could get up to 30,000 feet. So, a lot of time we got the stuffing knocked out of us (due to the lower altitude)."

It was a daily reality for planes to be shot at and lost. There was also a daily need for planes to be fixed up after taking flak. "Every day when we got back, the mechanics patched the holes in our plane from the flak fire," said Jim.

Although Jim's crew was never shot down, they did end up losing a member of their crew when he flew on another plane's mission. He never returned.

In addition to being thankful for making it back alive, there was another benefit to getting back to base after each mission recalled Jim, "At the end of a mission you would report to an area for a debriefing. One thing I remember is you got a shot of whiskey and pack of cigarettes. I didn't drink, so I put the

B-24 after a crash landing.

shot into a bottle. When I got a full bottle I would sell it to my friends and pick up a few extra bucks."

Jim said of the missions, "They were all very serious — life and death. You never think it is going to happen to you, but I was always concerned about it."

UNEXPECTED LANDING

Jim recalled a particular unexpected landing. "On one mission, we did get very heavy flak and it got to the point that we did have to leave the formation. One engine was out, and another was almost running away. The pilot was very concerned. We dropped out of formation, and I tried to contact my unit on radio for an SOS.

"A P-38 fighter came alongside of us and he talked on the radio to us. 'Big bird, this is little bird. We are here to take care of you. We have a friendly air field not too far away, if you can make it.'

"We were throwing things out of the plane. The pilot told us: 'Put on parachutes. If the alarm goes off again, don't stop to ask questions.'"

The bomb bay was already open for the men to jump through. Fortunately, the pilot was able to make an emergency landing at a different airfield. "We were missing in action for two days before we could get on another plane and fly back to base," said Jim.

ANOTHER SCARY EXPERIENCE

There was another frightening moment Jim recalled. "We were on a mission. We always had shrapnel. My job over the target was shoving out the chaff (which looked like Christmas tree tinsel) to confuse the ground artillery.

"I suddenly hear this bang from the explosion of a shell and shrapnel is flying everywhere. I look over at Leonard and I see this red blood across his glasses. And he takes his glove to wipe his face and sees blood. It shook everybody up."

Jim continued, "I unplugged my oxygen mask to see if Leonard was OK and it ended up that when we all came back to consciousness we saw the chaff all over the airplane. The shrapnel had gone through the hydraulic reservoirs of the ball turret and had sprayed the red fluid all over Leonard. He had never been hit."

LAST MISSION

"Our mission was one of the last bombing missions of the European War," Jim remembered. "They sent the whole 15th Air Force up and had the enemy line designated in Germany. We flew in formations of 10. In this particular mission, I remember that before we got to enemy lines these planes all dispersed and went out spreading out as a big line of planes as far as you could see in any direction. American lines lit up flares to let us know where they

B-24s flying in formation.

were and then everybody dropped their bomb load on enemy lines right after passing Allied line. As far as I could see, those bombers were lined up in single file to drop bombs. The next day the Germans surrendered."

Jim (far right) and his crew receiving their Distinguished Unit Citation.

DISCHARGE

With the end of the war, the men turned their attention to getting home. "I needed 50 missions to complete my tour, and I had 45," said Jim. "They asked for volunteers to fly on B-29s, so I decided I would volunteer." Jim was sent home to train on the new plane but, before he could report for training, Japan surrendered.

He received his discharge on October 26, 1945 in South

Dakota. He then hitchhiked home with friend, John Lawton, from Sioux Falls to South Bend, Indiana.

COLLEGE

It wasn't long after returning home before Jim's attention turned back to the basketball court he had loved for so long.

"I immediately enrolled at Indiana University and played on their basketball team," he said. "I was in an accelerated program. But I got ill around Christmas and got further behind in school. When I learned that Coach Wooden got the basketball job at Indiana State University, I decided to drop out of Indiana University and enroll at Indiana State University for the fall of 1946, to play again for Coach Wooden."

Jim was very excited to be reunited with his high school basketball coach. Few men had the privilege, like him, to play for Coach Wooden in both high school and college. Coach Wooden had a life-long impact on Jim's life.

Jim graduated from Indiana State University in 1950 with a Teacher's Degree.

MARILYN & CHILDREN

Jim met his future wife, Marilyn, in 1952. She had graduated from Kalamazoo College in Michigan to be an elementary school teacher, and she was hired at a South Bend, Indiana school. He met her at a teacher's conference at the University of Notre Dame. "She may have turned me down the first time I asked," recalled Jim with a grin.

"Yes, definitely," replied Marilyn, who was likewise grinning.

"My girlfriend and I rode with him up to Michigan for a wedding," she recalled. "We liked his car."

She learned to like him, too. Two years later, she married him. The couple exchanged their wedding vows on November 25th, 1954. "I decided maybe I should get married," she said. "I liked his maturity and that he wasn't a drinker."

The couple soon began building the most important 'team' in their lives — their family. Son Jim was born in 1955. Jeffrey came along in 1957 followed by daughter, Jackie, in 1961 and son, Chris, in 1964.

CAREER

Jim spent his whole career as an educator and coach. He taught physical education, health and social studies at South Bend Central High School from

1950–1969. During those years, he coached basketball, baseball, tennis, and cross country.

In 1969, he took a teaching position at Rochester High School in Rochester, Indiana. He taught there until 1972.

Jim finished his teaching and coaching career at Elkhart Memorial High School in Elkhart, Indiana. From 1972–76, he taught and coached. Beginning in 1976, he took on the position of full-time Athletic Director and served in that capacity until retiring in 1986.

Jim at the end of his teaching career, left. Jim (seated middle) and other coaches including Bobby Knight (back middle), below.

FAMILY TRAGEDY

In 1993, tragedy came to the Powers family. The day before Jim was to be inducted as a coach into the Indiana Basketball Hall of Fame in New Castle, Indiana his daughter, Jackie, died suddenly from a brain aneurysm. She was only 32.

Jim and his family were devastated. Initially, he planned to forego attending his induction in the Indiana Basketball Hall of Fame. But his sons talked him into going, and eldest son, Jim Jr., delivered his father's acceptance speech.

Jackie's absence still pains Jim and his family 25 years later.

RETIREMENT

After retiring, Jim and Marilyn started traveling to Destin, Florida for the winters. There, he enjoyed hitting a smaller ball on the greener 'court' of a golf course.

He and Marilyn moved to Hoosier Village Retirement Center in Zionsville, Indiana in March of 2015 to be closer to some of their family.

HONOR FLIGHT

In September of 2015, Jim returned to the skies for recognition of his military service. He was one of the honored veterans on an Indy Honor Flight, which flies war veterans to Washington, D.C. free of charge so that they can see the memorials erected in their honor and receive expressions of admiration and thanks from grateful citizens

"It was a very, very memorable experience," he said. "It was wonderful. It was really the first time I'd ever given any thought to my military career. It was really, really good. Jeffrey (his son) was my guardian. The World War II Memorial was wonderful and the Changing of Guard at the Tomb of the Unknown Soldier — absolutely fabulous! I won't forget either one. I saw Bob Dole. I had my picture taken with him."

Jim and Bob Dole at World War II Memorial in Washington, D.C.

REUNITED WITH THE B-24

In August of 2016, Jim was reunited with a B-24 Liberator at the airport in West Lafayette, Indiana. "It was memorable," Jim recalled. "It brought back all the vivid memories of missions flown (70+ years ago). It certainly is smaller than what I had visualized. I'm astounded we could get 10 people on that plane."

Jim, Greeted with Kisses after returning from his Honor Flight

Jim in front of the B-24 Liberator "Witchcraft" in 2016. One of the few remaining today, and the only one still flying.

SPEAKING AND SIGNING AUTOGRAPHS

Recently, Jim has begun speaking to civic groups about his military service story, signing autographs, and keeping alive the memories of those who served with him.

Jim Speaking to then Indiana LTGOV Eric Holcomb in 2016.

Jim talking to a fellow Veteran at a military airshow, above.

Jim signs B-25 bomb bay, top right.

Signature on bomb bay, lower right..

Jim standing with a fellow veteran in front of a B-24, showing photos of his service on one.

Jim and Marilyn Powers with their family.

CONCLUSION

Jim Powers.

Basketball remains important to Jim. He watches it on television and still attends some games, but the seasoned teacher and coach knows his priorities. Taking a cue from the life of his old coach, John Wooden, the game that Jim has focused on most is the game of life. And the "team" he has been most loyal to is his family. In the sport of family life, the one-time radio operator and career coach and athletic director is still at the top of his game.

Across Europe on a Motorcycle
Veteran Served as an MP in Europe

Most soldiers of the U.S. Army crossed parts of Europe on foot during World War II. A few rode across the war-torn landscape on the two wheels of a motorcycle. John (Bud) Redmond of Mooresville, Indiana was one of those riders.

Born to Raymond and Florence Redmond on May 30, 1923 in Bridgeport near Indianapolis, he was the youngest of three children. Following his graduation from Ben Davis High School in 1942, he tried to enlist in the Navy and the Air Force. Both declined him because he was blind in one eye. "I was discouraged," he recalled.

But, the Army eventually came calling and accepted him. "I thought they must be in bad shape," said Bud, surprised that they were willing to accept him with his blindness in one eye. Bud completed his basic training in August of 1943 and became a military policeman.

Initially, he reported to New Jersey and did patrols in New York City as part of the Eastern Coast Defense unit. "It was so stupid!" he exclaimed. "We would walk down the streets of New York City to see if military members had their hats on straight."

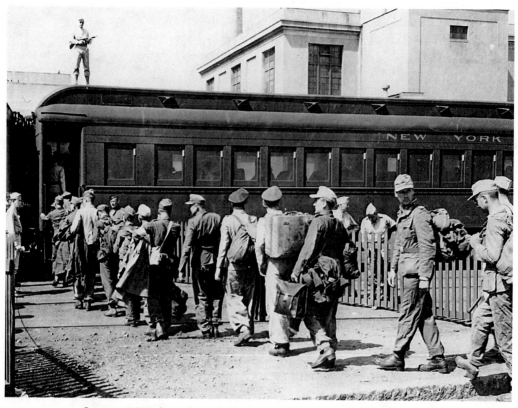

German POWs board a train in Boston. Note MP on top of train car.

More fulfilling duty came along when he started transporting prisoners of war from the east coast to prisons in Kansas and Texas. German and Italian POWs from the battlefields of North Africa were arriving in New York City, and MPs were tasked with escorting them across the Midwest by train to the holding areas out west.

The train trips usually lasted a week. Typically, 6-10 railroad cars were filled with prisoners. Three MPs were assigned to each car. One MP with a Billy club stayed inside the car, another was standing between the cars with a shotgun, and the third MP jumped off at every train stop and watched for any prisoners who were trying to escape, or any civilians who were getting too close. He had a sub-machine gun.

The MPs kept the prisoners close and safe, but they also had some fun at their expense. "We fed the Krauts spaghetti and the Italians sauerkraut," recalled Bud.

He figures he made at least 10 round-trips between the east coast and Kansas or Texas.

One day, Bud saw a poster advertising the need for soldiers to go overseas. Tired of the New York City patrol life, he signed up and became part of the 713th MP Battalion. After a month of additional training on Long Island, his battalion boarded a converted British merchant ship and left New York City on Christmas Day 1943.

It was not an easy crossing of the Atlantic for the convoy of 12 ships. "We had a hell of a time crossing," Bud recalled of the rough seas. "My mess kit would slide down the table when the ship tilted one way and then return to me when it tilted the other way. One time, my tray came back to me and someone had puked in it."

It wasn't just the choppy seas that made life miserable for the men. "The ship was overloaded," Bud said. "There were no bunks to lie down on. We just lay in the aisles."

The ship arrived in Liverpool, England, where the British sailors disembarked. The U.S. troops proceeded to Belfast, Ireland, where Bud and the other MPs got off.

Bud's unit of MPs had seven motorcycles. He volunteered to ride one of them. "Mostly, we would ride down to the dock to give an escort to the convoy of 10 trucks that were taking P-38 planes to an air base in Ireland," he recalled. "It was about a 50-mile trip."

"I liked it all right," he said. "You kind of were on your own. You knew what you had to do and you did it. But you had more freedom."

In May of 1944, just before the Normandy invasion, Bud and his battalion were transported to England and assigned to the 1st Army. They crossed the English Channel to Utah Beach about three weeks after D-Day, and began their movement across France.

For Bud, that meant plenty of riding time on a Harley Davidson 45 that could reach speeds of up to 65 miles per hour. His job was to ride ahead and scout out the roads to see if they were passable for the rest of the convoy.

Bud, left, and friend standing next to one of the motorcycles.

Bud standing beside a truck in Germany.

Bud riding into Berlin.

He saw some interesting sights along the way. One day near St. Lo, France he spotted a dead cow caught 15 feet up in a tree. Its neck was stuck in the fork of the tree. Apparently the impact of a bomb had blown it straight up into the tree. "You see so damn many things, it was just another sight," he said. "Although that was a strange one," he admitted.

The ride was also a dangerous one. Some MPs on motorcycles were decapitated by wires that the Germans had strung across the road. Although the threat was there, Bud said he never felt in danger. What he did feel, however, was cold — especially in the winter. "My hands would get so cold that I couldn't eat after some runs," he said.

Bud's closest call with danger came while leading a convoy up to Bastogne in Belgium, near the Battle of the Bulge. The convoy came to a stop while traveling under darkness one night. Bud was tasked with finding out why. As he rode up toward the front of the convoy, a German plane suddenly appeared from the sky and started strafing the convoy with bullets. "I saw bullets hitting the ground between me and the convoy," Bud recalled. Fortunately, no one was hit.

Patrolling Potsdam.

Following the Battle of the Bulge, the 1st Army Division moved quickly through Germany — at times faster than what gas could be supplied.

Bud was in Marburg, Germany when someone from a Jeep said to him one day, "Hey, did you hear the Germans quit?"

His MP company pulled duty in Potsdam, Germany for the July 17th, 1945 Potsdam Conference with the "Big 3": Truman, Churchill and Stalin, as they met to discuss terms for ending the war.

When Bud returned from the war, he initially used his G.I. Bill to begin the civil engineer program at Purdue University. When that didn't work out for him, he got a job at the Bryant Factory. Most of his professional career was spent at Lily's Pharmaceutical in Indianapolis, where he worked in research for 30 years. He retired from there in 1982.

Bud married Mary Reckord on November 17, 1950. Their marriage was blessed with two children: Mike and Rhonda. Today, their family has expanded to include four grandchildren and one great-grandchild.

The Redmond's continue to reside in Mooresville, Indiana.

Letters From the War Front
New York Native is Injured then Returns to Germany

EARLY LIFE

Francis A. (Fran) Schiffhauer was born on August 2nd, 1924 in Lackawana, New York. He was the oldest of 7 children raised by his parents, Francis Edward and Marion (Murphy) Schiffhauer. "I grew up in the depression when there was no money," he recalled. "I don't state that negatively, it was just an outlook on work."

He graduated from West Seneca and Technical High Schools in New York (just outside of Buffalo) in 1941. At the encouragement of his school principal, he devoted himself to the study of Chemistry and loved it. "It opened my eyes to another world," he said. "I spent all of my time in chemistry and physics."

Following his graduation from high school Fran attended Buffalo Tech, a technical/vocational school in Buffalo, where he entered the chemical analyst program. He also worked at Electro Refractories and Allies in Lackawana as a chemical analyst. "I loved it!" he recalled.

ENLISTMENT

In August of 1942 Fran enlisted in the Army Air Force along with two other high school friends. He wanted to become a pilot. "Every young guy wanted to be one," he said. But it was not to be, as he flunked the Army Air Force physical exam because he was missing a tendon in his right thumb from an accident.

Others from his circle of friends made it into the Army Air Force. His buddy, Peter, became a P-47 pilot. Tragically, he died when his plane was shot down in the Battle of the Bulge. Clarence, another friend, became a navigator on a B-17 bomber. He died in a crash landing. Death was never far away from a man's circle of family or friends during this time.

Fran volunteered for the draft in March of 1943 and selected the Army. "My mother was deathly afraid of the water, and she was afraid I would end up in the Navy," he said. "She agreed to let me sign up for the draft, so I would have my choice. I had grown up on Lake Erie, so I wasn't afraid of water." Respecting the fears of his mother however, he opted for the Army.

TRAINING

Fran did his basic training at Camp Robinson in Little Rock, Arkansas. At some point during the 12 weeks of boot camp, he tried again to pass the Army Air Force physical exam. But once again, he failed because of his missing tendon.

Following his graduation from basic training, Fran reported to Camp Maxey in Texas for two months of advanced infantry training. It was during this time that he was assigned to the Army's 102nd Infantry Division. It was known by the nickname of "Ozark Division" because the division was made up mostly of people from the Ozark mountain ranges in Arkansas, Missouri, and Oklahoma.

ARMY ASTP PROGRAM

In August of 1943, because of his advanced education, Fran was sent to Washington and Lee University in Lexington, Virginia to begin the Army Specialized Training Program (ASTP). The Army had established this program at several universities for the purpose of offering specialized training to recruits

Fran, second from right, as a student at Washington & Lee University, 1943.

that already had some college and might be good candidates to become officers or soldiers with special technical skills.

Fran attended the Army's ASTP program from August of 1943–February of 1944. "It was a great place," he recalled. "It was a beautiful Southern school." The university was named for George Washington and General Robert E. Lee. Lee's body was buried there on campus. Fran took two semesters in the engineering program. He and the other students were kept busy six days a week. Saturday they worked on close order drills.

In addition to giving soldiers specialized education, the ASTP program was also used to delay the build-up of men for the Army pipeline, until the logistical infrastructure was ready to receive the new soldiers and prepared to transport them to Europe. By February of 1944, the Army had shut down the ASTP Program because they were ready to move all the stateside Divisions into the pipeline for embarkation to Europe.

RE-ASSIGNMENT TO THE ARMY'S 102ND DIVISION

Fran was sent to Camp Pickett in Virginia and re-assigned to the 102nd Army Division. He had the unfortunate task of completing another boot camp. "We did

Fran, far right, firing in group at Camp Pickett, VA, 1944.

basic training all over again," he said referring to the February–June timeframe of 1944.

By July of 1944, the members of the 102nd Division were on their way to Camp Dix, New Jersey for final training before deployment. But not everyone in the division landed at Camp Dix right away. The 405th and 406th Infantry Regiments received unexpected temporary orders to report to Philadelphia. The two regiments were assigned the surprising duty of taking over the City Transportation System and making sure public transportation continued to run even though the operators had tried to go on strike.

President Roosevelt had forced the operators to keep working. He allowed no strikes for public transportation during a time of war. The intended strike was a protest over hiring black bus drivers. The racial tension reminded Fran of another discrimination experience he had at the age of five when he witnessed the Ku Klux Klan burning crosses in his neighborhood.

"That was really something," Fran remembered of his temporary duty in Philadelphia. We got on subway trains at 12-midnight and we made them run. It was the funniest duty. We never got to shower or change uniforms. We slept where the busses turned around. There was one of us in the front of each car or bus and one in the back. We carried live ammo. We did it for five days until we were relieved by another division." The two regiments of the 102nd Division performed so well that the city of Philadelphia unofficially adopted the Ozarks as "Philly's Own."

TRANSIT TO EUROPE AND THE WAR FRONT

The 102nd Division was loaded into six ships and departed New York City Harbor on September 15, 1944. The journey across the Atlantic to Cherbourg, France took 12 days. "It was long, and I was sick a lot of the time," recalled Fran. Although he knew he was off to war, he didn't recall being nervous or anxious.

In a letter home to his parents written on May 22, 1945, Fran shared more details of his trip to Europe:

> *We left the states on September 12th and when I was going up the gang plank I was thinking it a coincidence, pop's birthday, your wedding anniversary and my shipping date. We loaded on the ship about 3:00 am in the morning after carrying all our belongings around all night, a very tired and homesick bunch. I just crawled up in the bunk I was assigned to and went to sleep. I awoke about eight in the morning and we were already out of sight of land, so I missed the glimpse of New York and the Statue of Liberty from the sea.*
>
> *We were running on the edge of the hurricane that hit the East coast at that time and for the first few days it was pretty rough sailing, but on the whole the trip wasn't too bad. We were crowded, the chow lines were long, but things weren't as bad as they were supposed to be. It took 14 days for us to hit land again, though we did see the coast of England on the twelfth day. We landed in France on the 26th of September and started our life on foreign soil.*

Upon reaching Cherbourg, the Division hurried off to its designated bivouac area located in rain-soaked orchards near the city of St.-Pierre-Eglise. Fran described in his letter home the horrible conditions of getting to their bivouac and then proceeding across France.

> *On the way to Germany I spent one of the most miserable 5 days of my life. To start out, we walked 14 miles in the pouring rain in muck*

about ankle deep with a full pack. Upon arrival at the end of 14 miles we were loaded into comfortable boxcars for the trek across France. The boxcars are smaller than those we have in the states, about 1/2 as big. They are built for 40 men or 8 horses. The only thing they forgot was that the 40 men had a duffle bag full of equipment besides rifles and packs. Those were 5 cold days and nights with very little sleep and no hot meals.

We got off the train in Belgium and rode our trucks into Germany. When we got off the trucks we walked some more and then we were in combat. This was just a little north of Aachen.

The 102nd had reached the German-Netherlands border. Elements of the division were committed piecemeal to East Holland and West Germany. On October 30th, Fran's 406th Infantry Regiment arrived at Herzogenrath, at the western edge of Germany, near the city of Aachen. The Nazi 30th Infantry Division controlled the area. A faceoff between the two divisions was imminent.

FALLEN COMRADE

After arriving in the area, Fran's squad became pinned down by German fire. Fran recalled that his squad leader told him to make a run for a barn off in the distance. He hesitated for a moment, calculating the danger of being mowed down. While he was thinking, his friend Clooney volunteered to do it instead. "Of the two of us, I'm the faster runner," he said. Fran remembered thinking that no one was fast enough to outrun a bullet. And, sure enough, Clooney was mowed down in the attempt. When the squad leader saw how quickly Clooney had fallen, he radioed in for artillery support. The big guns quieted down the German firing and the squad was able to move again.

WOUNDED IN GERMANY

Fran was wounded on October 31st — the day after his regiment had arrived in Herzogenrath. "The 'Jerries' were really throwing a lot of stuff at us," he recalled. "We were moving up, and we went down a road near the Germany/Netherland border. German artillery suddenly came in, and I was hit by shrapnel in my right leg."

A big piece of shrapnel had penetrated the back thigh of his right leg. Fran continued, "I stood up and said to the guy beside me, 'I think I got hit.' He said I had and told me to sit down while he called for the medic. The medic stayed with me until a Jeep came to take me to the battalion aid station." The rest of Fran's company pressed forward, as they were still coming under some German artillery.

At the aid station, Fran was bandaged up and then transported to the hospital in Liege, Belgium where he stayed for five days. The wound was quite deep. The shrapnel had torn through much of his back thigh and chipped the femur bone. "Twice a day, they unpacked and repacked my wound with Vaseline gauze," he said. "It hurt!" He didn't recall being afraid, but he did get poked a fair share. "I got a lot of needles of penicillin," he said.

From Liege, Belgium he was transported to Paris via a boxcar filled with racks that the liters were placed on. The liters were stacked three high. "It was an interesting and rocky ride," he remembered.

The next day, he was taken by train to Cherbourg, France and then crossed the English Channel on a channel cruiser. The ship docked in South Hampton, England, and he was taken to a surgical hospital to stitch up his leg wounds. "It was like a MASH unit with five or six operating tables," he remembered. "I had Novocain while they stitched me up. I remember seeing the guy next to me getting his leg cut off. It was brutal! I had to turn away, but I could still hear the saw."

His own wound proved difficult to keep closed. "They sewed me up and the stitches didn't hold," he said. "So, they tried heat lamps on my leg to help close the wound. It finally healed over."

While some of the men lost their legs to shrapnel, Fran was fortunate to keep his wounded leg. "I was lucky my wound was not serious," he said. "Fortunately, I was hit in the fleshy part of my leg." A few inches one way or the other and his wound could have resulted in amputation or even death. He remained at the hospital for four weeks.

The next stop on his healing journey was Rehabilitation Center #4 located in Honiton, England (150 miles east and a little south of London). The facility had opened in September of 1944, and had room for up to 3,000 patients. Part of the Convalescent Rehabilitation System of the British Forces, this center had a program to gradually return the injured service member to mental and physical training. The rehabilitative process began while the patient was still confined to bed and progressed steadily toward recreational activities, which strengthened the patient physically and mentally.

The final stage of the rehabilitation program culminated in the patient once again hiking and drilling. The goal was to get the patient back to the fight or back to another form of military service as quickly as possible. On average, the length of a service member's stay at a rehabilitation center was about 18 days.

Fran's body responded well to the rehabilitation regiment. He began to regain his strength through calisthenics, and before long got out on the firing range. Every week, the doctor came to check on him and give him a health status. The goal was to get him back to duty as quickly as possible.

REJOINING HIS UNIT

By the first of 1945, Fran had made enough progress in his rehabilitation that plans were made to get him back to his unit. He rejoined his regiment at the end of February. By that time, the men of the 102nd Division had already crossed into Germany and were pushing eastward.

On March 3rd, Fran's regiment reached the Rhine River in their advance into Germany. The 406th crossed the Rhine on April 9th and engaged the German forces there in fighting.

Fran wrote in a letter to his parents:

> *"When I finally got back to the company after a month of moving, they were on the Rhine River. As you know, I didn't do much actual fighting there — just dodging shells once in a while and making sure the 'Jerries' didn't try to cross back across the river."*

During the next four days, the division covered 150 kilometers. By April 16th, it had pushed forward to the Elbe River, a mere 48 miles from Berlin, where it halted on orders. The fast progress across Germany was slowed only by the large number of German soldiers offering themselves in surrender.

In his letter home Fran reported:

> *We moved from there up north and crossed at Wessel and then started the rat race. We rode trucks for some of the ways, walked and fought. We didn't run into much tough fighting except for a couple days. Most of the time we just had to round up prisoners as the majority of the 'jerries' wanted to give up. We finally reached the Elbe River, and there we stayed.*

Fran, kneeling at far right, April 1945.

Once at the Elbe River, the 102nd waited for the Russian forces to take Berlin and link up with them on the other side of the river. While waiting for the Russians, the division witnessed quite a spectacle on the river. German soldiers and civilians, along with displaced people from other countries, were doing everything possible to convince the U.S. forces to let them cross the river and surrender. They were trying to escape the Russian forces, which were advancing rapidly from the east. The 102nd Division watched as thousands of people attempted to cross the river on whatever flotation device they could find: rafts, debris, wooden planks and even metal washtubs.

U.S. forces link up with Russian forces at the Elbe River.

The meeting of the two Allied forces happened on April 25th as members of the 102nd Division shook hands with the 156th Russian Division. Adolph Hitler killed himself five days later on April 30th. The end of the war was near.

On May 4th, General Eisenhower announced: "German forces on the Western Front have disintegrated. Today what is left of two German Armies surrendered to a single American Division; the 102nd, commanded by Maj Gen Frank A, Keating." Germany officially surrendered on May 7th, 1945. The war in Europe had come to a close.

OCCUPATION DUTY

Fran, sitting on lower part of tank, looking at the camera.

Even before Germany's surrender, the 102nd Division had begun temporarily serving as occupation forces along the western stretch of the Elbe River. At one point, the area of responsibility stretched 50 miles along the river. Fran and others took their turns in patrolling the area, watching especially for any evidence of German arms or ammunition. The division also provided some security around key industrial installations and cultural buildings.

In a letter to his parents, Fran described the division's new duty:

"We started this moving around from town to town as occupational troops. We were up north for a long time, but now we ended up down here southeast of Erfurt (Germany). On the drive from the Rhine to the Elbe we went through Hanover, which was probably the biggest

town you would hear about. When I get home I'll trace the route out on the map."

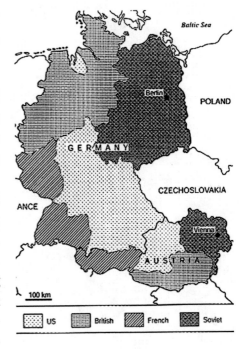

In June of 1945, the Russians insisted that U.S. forces leave the area around the Elbe River, as it was technically now in the assigned Russian zone of occupation per the Agreement at Yalta.

The entire 9th U.S. Army, which included the 102nd Division, crowded the German Autobahn and traveled south to Vilshofen, which was located on the Danube River. Here, they performed occupation duty along 50 miles on the Czech/Russian occupation zone border. In addition to the normal policing role, the 102nd Division was also assigned guard duty at Prisoner of War and Displaced Persons camps. Fran remained in this area until the late fall.

RETURNING HOME

Fran returned to the United States in December of 1945 and was honorably discharged from his 40 months of service.

Taking advantage of the G.I. Bill, he attended Purdue University and graduated from there with a degree in Chemical Engineering in 1950. He went on to work for Allied Chemical, serving many years as a plant manager. He retired in 1985.

Fran married Truth Haase on August 26th, 1950. Their marriage was blessed with eight children: Michael, Matthew, Marian, Daniel, Thomas, Peter, Francis, and Margaret. During their marriage they lived in Buffalo, NY, Wilmington

Fran at Work, 1950

Fran and Truth, 1952

and Newark, DE, Baton Rouge, LA, and Elkton and Baltimore, MD.

In 2009, he and Truth moved to Hoosier Village Retirement Center in Indianapolis, where he was her devoted caregiver until her passing on May, 6, 2016.

Fran volunteered with numerous homeless initiatives and as a Lector at his church. He was an avid vegetable gardener. He took his children camping in the mountains and at the beach, where he also loved to fish. A singer, he performed in church choirs and amateur theatrical groups. In retirement he sang with the University of Delaware Schola Cantorum and the Northern Delaware Oratorio Society. He loved and found comfort in opera.

Following a bout with illness, Fran Schiffhauer died on October 29, 2016 — six months after the death of his beloved wife, Truth. He was 92 years old.

Fran and Truth, 2001.

Fran at the Beach, 2004.

Duty From the Belly of a Bomber
Veteran Served as Lower Turret Gunner on a B-24

Most crewman on World War II bombers flew inside the thin aluminum skin surrounding the plane. But not Rodney (Rod) Sieck of Avon, Indiana. He operated the guns from an outside turret underneath the bomber. While he had a great view of the sky and ground under him, he also had the danger of freezing temperatures and being exposed to enemy fire.

Rod was born on October 2nd, 1925 outside Kansas City, Kansas. "I was raised on a little farm in Shawnee, Kansas," he said. "It was near the Shawnee Indian Mission." His family moved to Bremerton, Washington in 1941, after his sophomore year. His father had secured a job working with sheet metal at the Puget Sound Naval Shipyard.

In September of 1943, at the age of 17 and while still attending Central Kitsap High School in Poulsbo, Washington, he volunteered for the Army Air Force. "My mother wouldn't sign, but my dad did," recalled Rod, referring to the necessary paperwork to enter the service.

"I was just ready to do something else," he said. "I had everything done in school. I wanted to be a pilot. I wanted to be a hot-gun Charlie. The Air Force was expanding and they were taking on thousands of new people, and I was one of them."

In January of 1944 he was sent to Amarillo, Texas for basic training. With the number of applicants so high, he failed to be selected for cadet school. "It was disappointing," he recalled. "I was not surprised because of so many (applicants) coming in. They sent us home on furlough and assigned us to Gunnery school in Laredo, TX."

He spent the next several months learning about aerial gunnery. "I figured I might as well be a gunner," said Rod. "I got to fire a million rounds from a 12-gauge shot gun while on the back of pick-up trucks. And I got to fly all the turrets: nose, rear, and waist."

Following his gunner training he was sent to Nebraska, where he was assigned to a bomber crew on a B-24 Liberator — a four engine heavy-duty bomber. Rod became the crew's belly gunner.

The newly formed crew went to Davis-Monthan Army Air Field near Tucson, Arizona to begin their flight training as a crew. The crew was made up of the following men and positions:

Pilot:	George F. Wieman III
Co-Pilot:	Patrick E. Reithoffer Jr.
Navigator:	Henry T. Donohoe
Bombardier:	Earl Roylance
Engineer/Waist Gunner:	Bruce C. Kirkpatrick
Radio Operator/W. Gunner:	Clarence P. Ebbert
Nose Gunner:	David D. Schaper
Tail Gunner:	Homer E. James
Top Turret Gunner:	Claude T. Roach
Ball Turret Gunner:	Rodney Sieck

By the fall of 1944, the crew picked up a new B-24 in Topeka, Kansas and flew to Grenier Army Airfield in New Hampshire. From there, they departed for their combat tour.

Rod, 3rd from left in back row, and his bomber crew.

Initially they landed in Tunis, French Morocco. "I had my 19th birthday in Tunis," Rod recalled.

A week later they flew to Cerignola, Italy in the southeastern part of the country's "boot heel." They reported to Torretta Field, home of the 461st Bomb Group of the 15th Air Force. Rod's crew had been assigned to the 766th Squadron.

The crews lived in tents at the airfield and flew every three days or so. When they weren't flying they passed the time playing ball.

"One guy we really liked was our bombardier, John Jack Butler," said Rod. "He never made it back from his first combat mission." Rod explained that every crewmember was first assigned to fly with an experienced crew before flying their first mission with their own crew.

766th Squadron headquarters in Italy

Phil Ebbert, David Schaper, Rodney Sieck and Bruce Kirkpatrick.

B-24s on a mission.

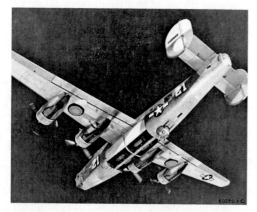

B-24 underside showing sperry ball turret beneath star in tail section.

"Butler hadn't flown yet with an experienced crew," Rod recalled. "So, he looked on a flight roster and discovered another bombardier was scheduled to fly with an experienced crew. He convinced the Commander to scratch that guy and schedule him instead. He went on a mission to Vienna and never came back. He was shot down over Yugoslavia and bailed out." No word was ever heard about whether he survived.

"It was tough," said Rod. "It was sad. We all liked the guy. Of all the officers, we liked him best. He was the most-friendly." (Each B-24 crew was made up of four officers and six enlisted men.)

Butler's death impacted the crew, but it didn't cause more fear. "It didn't make me more fearful," recalled Rod. "I didn't have sense enough to be afraid. I had sadness, but not fear."

Rod's high school class graduated while he was serving in Italy. His mother and sister received his diploma on his behalf at his graduation ceremony.

During his nine months in Italy, Rod flew 34 bombing missions with his crew and seven missions with other crews.

As the belly gunner, he crammed his 5'8" body into a ball turret, which, after the plane was airborne, was lowered hydraulically underneath the plane's aluminum skin.

"It was such a tight squeeze that I couldn't wear my parachute in there," he recalled. "I didn't like to give it up." Rod operated 50-caliber machine guns located near each leg, and he had a tracker above him. He stayed in the turret for much of the flight, which often meant five to 10 hours.

Unknown gunner climbs into a sperry ball turret, like Rod's.

In addition to feeling cramped, Rod also had to endure extremely cold temperatures, which, at times, reached 50 degrees below zero. "You would ice up while you were in there, and it would break off when you got out," he said.

When not crammed into his belly turret Rod operated one of the waist guns. Most of his crew's bomb targets were oil refineries and railways. "It was pretty terrible when you came up to the initial target point," he recalled. "The flak was so black and thick.

"The bulk of our missions were around Vienna, Austria," said Rod. "I flew 13 missions there. Vienna was the most heavily defended target with anti-aircraft weapons. We all groaned when we saw our target was Vienna."

Although never preoccupied with fear, there were many times Rod didn't think his crew would make it out alive. "A lot of times, the flak was so thick and horrid and black that you thought you'd never come back," he said. Many planes never did make it back. He saw plenty of planes go down around Vienna.

While Rod's crew was never shot down and never had to bail out, there were plenty of close calls. "We

Aerial briefing chart for Sortie #20, Muhldorf, Germany.

87

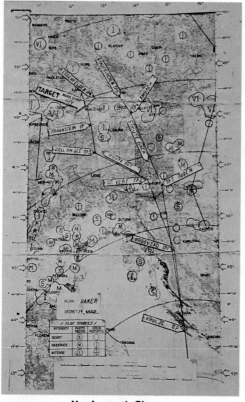

Navigator's flimsy.

got shot up several times and lost engines at other times," he recalled. On one occasion, two of their engines went out and the crew had to make an emergency landing on the island of Vis, located west of Croatia in the Adriatic Sea.

Their plane was unable to take off again because the runway on the island was too short for the B-24. A DC 3 plane arrived later to retrieve Rod's crew.

Two of Rod's crewmembers almost lost their lives on one of the other missions. Flak hit the plane near the upper turret and disconnected the oxygen lines used by Hank and Mike. Unable to breathe, they quickly took off their cumbersome heated flight suits and tried to make it to where the small emergency oxygen bottles were kept.

Muhldorf before Sortie, left. Muhldorf after Sortie, right.

Both passed out before getting to the oxygen. Unprotected from the bitter cold air and without oxygen, they both would have died in moments. Fortunately, when they did not respond to a radio request, the pilot sent back another crewmember who found them and got oxygen to them just in time.

Damage to Marshaling Yard in Muhldorf, Germany.

Rod had better luck than many. "I flew all the missions over there and never had a scratch," he said with gratitude.

Rod recalled that his crew's farthest mission was Blechammer, Germany, where the Nazis had chemical plants and POW camps. The flight time to that location was nine and a half hours. "Pretty scary," he said, "because it was so far out and there was lots of flak."

The average duration of a mission was seven hours or so. The bomb loads were usually dropped at 21,000 feet.

While in Italy, Rod received a letter from his mother informing him that his dad had almost passed away from a heart attack. "I went to the Commanding Officer and asked if I could fly extra missions to get home to him sooner," Rod said. By that time in the war, a crewmember had to fly 35 sorties of 50 missions before he could go home.

Rod flew seven extra missions in an effort to get home sooner. "Dad survived and didn't die until seven or eight years later," he said.

After Germany surrendered in early May of 1945, the 461st Bomb Group crew waited for word on when they could return home. The men got occasional three-day air passes to visit Rome, Florence, France or Genoa.

Dave Schaper and Rod.

Rod and Edna Mae.

Rod's crew left Italy together on their plane and headed for the United States in June of 1945. After a stop in Africa, they flew into horrible weather on their way to South America. "We had seven Army officers with us," Rod recalled. "We entered the worst storm in our lives from Natal to Brazil. Worst weather ever. The Army officers were terrified. It was pretty horrible, but we kept it hidden."

Rod received his honorable discharge five months later, on November 2nd.

He spent most of his civilian career working in sales for several firms as a manufacturer representative, eventually becoming Vice President of Sales with Honeywell. He worked until he was almost 80 years old.

Rod married Edna Mae on September 1st, 1950. The couple raised two daughters: Judy and Susie.

In 1954, the Sieck family moved to Evansville, Indiana where they spent the next 20 years. They relocated to Kansas City in the mid-'70s, when Rod accepted another job.

Rod and his wife were married for almost 60 years before her death in May of 2010.

Rod moved into a retirement community in Avon, Indiana in April of 2016 to be closer to his daughters.

The 92-year-old veteran recently took to the skies again with Indy Honor Flight. He enjoyed his trip to Washington, D.C. to see the World War II Memorial and other sights. And best of all, he didn't have to squeeze into a turret beneath the plane, endure extreme temperatures or watch for enemy aircraft.

40th Reunion with bomber group. Rod and Edna are on the far right.

Mr. Rodney Sieck
Apt 108
182 S County Road 550 E
Avon, IN 46123

Rod at the WWII Memorial.

A Forgotten Christmas & Uncertain Future

Veteran Spends Christmas as a POW in Germany

As he looks back over his 92 years of life, Scott Thompson has many warm and wonderful memories of Christmases with his family. "We had very little for Christmas," he wrote in his diary as he reminisced of his childhood. "But I don't remember them as being unhappy. And later I remember many happy Christmases when we all went home for Christmas."

There is, however, one Christmas that especially sticks out in his mind; not because of the memories of family and holiday traditions but rather because of the lack of those memories — or really any memories.

It was the Christmas of 1944. "This is a story about a Christmas that I really don't know what I was doing," he wrote in his diary.

Christmas of 1944 was filled with obscurity and uncertainty for Scott and thousands of other captured U.S. and British soldiers languishing in a German POW camp. They wondered whether they would live or die and whether they would ever see home or family again.

Scott Thompson was born to Harvey and Vandilla Thompson on May 9th, 1924 in Owen Township of Warrick County, Indiana; which is about 30-miles northeast

of Evansville. He grew up on a farm and later attended Folsomville High School, graduating in 1942.

Scott enrolled at Evansville College (it later became the University of Evansville) and began classes with the intent of majoring in Social Studies Education.

And then the Army draft came a calling in the spring of 1943.

Scott, age 19 at the time, reported to the Fort Benjamin Harrison Reception Center in Indianapolis for processing. He spent 30 days there.

He then reported to Camp Wheeler near Macon, Georgia where he completed his 13 weeks of basic training. "It was extensive and hard training for an infantryman," he recalled during one interview.

Being more of a private person, he didn't care much for the communal living in the barracks.

Following basic training, he reported to the Army Specialized Training Program (ASTP) at the University of Alabama, where he took two semesters of pre-engineering courses.

Scott was then assigned to the Army's 106th Division under the leadership of General Allen Jones. The 106th Division consisted of troops, many of them from Indiana and other Midwestern states, who were slotted to be replacements for combat in the European theater.

The 106th Division had been activated in March of 1943 at Fort Jackson in South Carolina. The Division was made up of three regiments, each regiment consisting of three battalions. Scott was in Company F of the 2nd Battalion, 423rd Regiment.

New division members reported to Fort Jackson, South Carolina in early March of 1944. After participating in the 2nd Army Tennessee Maneuvers, the division relocated to Camp Atterbury in south central Indiana, where it remained from March–October of 1944, preparing for deployment to Europe.

In November of 1944, the division was sent by train to Boston, reporting to Camp Miles Standish. On November 10th, the 106th Division, consisting of some 15,000 men, boarded the troop ship, *Queen Elizabeth* and departed the U.S. on their way to Europe.

The ship arrived at Greenock, Scotland on November 17th. The 106th then boarded trains for southern England, near Cheltenham, where they trained for a few weeks.

On December 6th, 1944, six months following the invasion at Normandy, the division crossed

Camp Atterbury.

the English Channel and arrived in France at the port of Le Havre.

The division quickly made their way across France by trucks and proceeded into the Ardennes Forest of Belgium. By December 11th, the division had relieved the 2nd Infantry Division and taken their position along the Schnee Eifel line, a 26-mile long front in a heavily wooded, mountainous forest close to the German border. By Army Service Manual standards, a division would normally be responsible for no more than five miles of a front in combat operations. Division Headquarters was at St. Vith.

Shortly after arriving on the front line, the 106th Division began sending out scouting parties to watch for enemy presence.

Scott, who by this time had become a messenger for the Division, recalled one occasion of being out on scouting duty. "I remember going out on one scouting report. And we didn't go far until we ran into Germans. Of course, we weren't supposed to engage. I guess we were lucky they didn't see us. We came back and reported the sighting."

All was quiet on December 11th. Deceptively so! Although German forces had previously retreated into Germany to defend their homeland, many of them

106th Division in Ardennes.

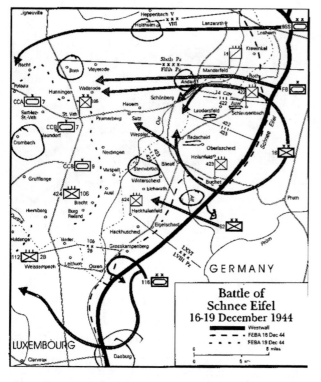

Battle of
Schnee Eifel
16-19 December 1944

had been making their way silently into Belgium for a surprise attack. Allied forces were gathering along the line to prepare for an offensive into Germany. But it was Germany who would launch the surprise and last-ditch-effort offensive to attempt pushing back the Allies.

On December 16th, just five days after the 106th division arrived on the front lines, Germany attacked with a major offensive. The offensive became known as The Battle of the Bulge.

Scott described the attack in his diary: "The Germans attacked at 5:30 a.m. on December 16th; turning their guns on the 14th Calvary (armored) which was attached to the 106th Division and then on the field artillery battalion."

Shortly after the German offensive had begun, Scott was involved with helping to transport a wounded platoon commander, Lieutenant Patton, to the hospital. He had been shot. (The Lieutenant was no relation to General Patton.) He recalled,

Battle of Bulge.

"We loaded him onto the Jeep and took him to the hospital, which was near the headquarters. While we were going, he showed me a pearl handled 45mm gun he carried, and told me, 'My Daddy gave me this when I graduated from West Point (the Academy). I know we are going to be captured and I don't want them (Germans) to get this gun. I want you to take it.' So I took the gun and carried it with me. And later on, when our unit surrendered us, I buried it. So, that gun is buried somewhere in the Ardennes Forest."

Scott never made it back to his unit after taking Lieutenant Patton to the hospital. He remained with the Division Headquarters. "I remember taking cover at Division headquarters," he said. "I had worked all night digging my foxhole. When the shooting started, I found an officer had crawled into it. I told him it was my hole and he got out."

Things went from bad to worse for Scott and the regiments of the 106th Division. "After three days of fighting, the 422nd and 423rd Infantry Regiments were decimated," recalled Scott. "We were struck really hard by the Germans and just collapsed. We were cut off and ran out of supplies. The weather was bad and no support was possible from the air."

As disheartening as it was to consider, surrendering seemed to be the only logical choice for the Regimental officers of the 106th. "We were ordered to surrender," Scott recalled. "I was probably captured on December 19th along with several thousand others."

Allied soldiers surrendering to the Germans.

In all, almost 7,000 personnel surrendered to the Germans and became prisoners of war.

Scott didn't remember being scared during his capture, but he did recall feeling numb. The numbness blurred the passing of time. Christmas Day came, barely noticed by most. "On Christmas Day, we were prisoners and we were put on trains to be taken back to Germany," he said.

"The Germans marched us to the nearest railroad and loaded us on 40x8 boxcars," he said. "We waited, but no locomotives were available. The weather had cleared and the American Army Air Force had begun attacking all German trains. Our boxcars were actually strafed, and I remember looking out the boxcar window and seeing bullets striking the ground as close as 30-40 feet from us. We (both prisoners and Germans) piled out of the cars and formed a huge human cross to show we were prisoners. I guess the guards let us do this because they didn't want to be shot at either."

A touch of irony, the attacking aircraft may very well have been the P-47 Thunderbolt; many of which had been made in Evansville, Indiana, close to where Scott had grown up.

"We then were marched a long distance into Germany and crossed the Rhine River at Kohlenz," Scott recalled.

He added, "I had saved my heavy wool overcoat, while most of the men had discarded theirs. Two buddies and I slept under it. I don't really remember what happened to it after that."

He did, however, remember seeing some sights of beauty in the midst of the carnage of war. "The German countryside was beautiful, and the large churches dominated the small towns," he recalled. "I remember them resembling St. Joseph's parish in Jasper, Indiana."

An imposing German Stalag awaited Scott and the thousands of other Allies who had been captured or surrendered. "After marching a good distance into Germany, we were placed on trains to a German Stalag and processed," Scott recalled. "The camp was really run by British officers captured earlier in North Africa. We finally ended up at Stalag IVB in East Germany."

Stalag IVB, one of the larger German prisoner of war camps, was located in the Province of Saxony about five miles from the town of Muhlberg.

Stalag was a shortened form of the German word Stammlager, which means main camp. Most all of the prisoners at Stalag IVB were Americans. At its peak,

Stalag IVB.

it held over 30,000 prisoners of war in crowded conditions meant for far fewer prisoners.

Although a few prisoners talked of escape, there were no successful attempts. The prison was far into East Germany, and few of the men knew German to ask for any assistance from anyone.

They worked during the day and slept at night. "Being Privates, we were sent to Zeitz, Germany near Leipzig to dig air raid shelters," Scott recalled. "As workers, we got extra rations which consisted mostly of heavy dark bread and thin soup."

It was never enough food to stave off hunger. "We were hungry all the time," Scott said. "We were not physically abused by the German guards, but there was a deplorable lack of food and clothing. But it was true for the Germans as well."

The POWs in Scott's group received only two partial Red Cross packages during their time at Stalag IV-B. "The cigarettes and coffee we traded to the German civilians for food," he recalled.

Scott figured he lost 30 pounds or so during his four months of imprisonment. "I remember saying if I ever got out that I would never again be hungry or cold," he said. "I've kept my thermostat at 73 degrees and have had three meals a day ever since."

He wrote two letters home during his imprisonment — one to his mother and the other to his sister. "They got those letters before they were ever notified that I was a Prisoner of War," he said. "The Army informed my parents by telegram dated January 10, 1945 that I was missing in action as of December 21, 1944."

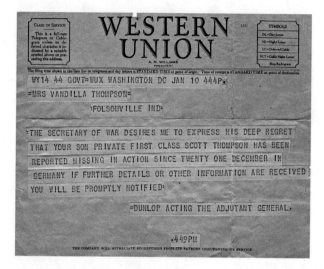

Ironically, his parents didn't find out about him being a prisoner of war until after he was liberated. "My parents first learned that I was a prisoner of war from a card that I wrote to them on January 10, 1945 — they received it on April 13, 1945," said Scott. "The War Department notified my parents that I was a prisoner on April 19, 1945. We were probably liberated about that time."

Although the prisoners were permitted to send mail, Scott didn't recall the prisoners ever receiving any mail from home.

A little more than four months into their imprisonment, the prisoners began to hear the sounds of liberation. "We could hear the Americans approaching from their gunfire," Scott remembered.

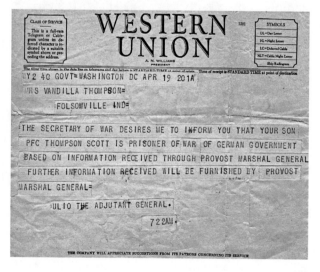

Stalag IV-B was actually liberated by Russian forces from the east on April 23, 1945. Scott recalled, "We were very close to where the Russians and American Armies met at the Elbe River on April 25, 1945."

Upon his release, Scott and the other prisoners were marched to another town to become officially liberated. "We were turned over to the group that took care of POWs," he said.

Scott's combat was officially over. "I never got a scratch," he said. "And I never shot anyone."

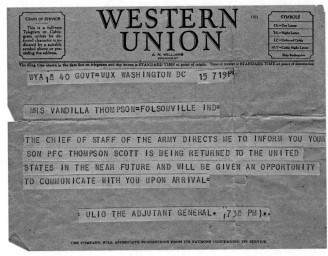

Following his liberation, Scott was evacuated and transported by plane to a hospital in Rheims, France.

The Germans surrendered a short time later. "I was in an American hospital in Rheims, France on Victory in Europe Day, May 8, 1945," he said. "I remember the day well because May 9th is my birthday."

He was later transferred to another hospital in Lyon, France.

"A Medical Doctor came and examined us," recalled Scott. "He said, 'I can get you back to the U.S. sooner by labeling you for malnutrition'. But it wasn't straight away. The Army never goes straight away."

After his recuperation in the hospitals, Scott enjoyed a day leave in Paris (he got up in the Eifel Tower) before continuing on to Le Havre, France to board a ship and head back to the United States. He landed at Newport News, Virginia on June 18th, 1945. After a furlough at home in Indiana, he was sent to Miami Beach, Florida for further rest and recuperation.

Scott finished out his time of service at Fort Benning, Georgia, where he worked in the motor pool. In a bit of irony he said, "I was assigned to the motor pool, and I didn't even drive yet."

Scott, who by that time had reached the rank of a Corporal, was honorably discharged from the service on December 11th, 1945.

His Separation Qualification Record summarized his military service with the following:

Scott with relative.

Scott, Patricia and Jane Ann.

"Served with the 423rd Infantry Regiment, 106th Infantry Division in England, France, Belgium, and Germany for a period of 8 months. Arose to the position of assistant squad leader in rifle squad of 12 men. Directed fire upon enemy foot troops, installations, and vehicles. Lead patrols into enemy lines. Performed duties under all types of enemy fire. Was POW for 4 months."

Scott met Patricia Hickman after the war. Both of them were teachers at an elementary school in Evansville. They married in 1953, and their marriage was later blessed with a daughter, Jane Ann. The couple enjoyed 53 years of married life together before Patricia's death in 2016.

Scott completed his Bachelor's Degree in Social Studies Education at Evansville College in 1948. He later earned a Masters' Degree in Education at Indiana University in Bloomington.

He enjoyed a 35-plus year career in public school education, teaching junior high social studies at Newburgh Elementary for two to three years before moving over to Harwood School where he taught for the next 32 years, retiring in 1989.

"I enjoyed most being with the other teachers," he said looking back.

Scott belonged to the Methodist Temple, the Evansville Retired Teachers Association, and the Indiana Retired Teachers

Association. He was also a lifelong member of NEA. For many years, he was an active member of Washington Avenue Presbyterian Church (now closed), where he served as both a Deacon and an Elder.

In retirement, he and Patricia enjoyed traveling together. Their traveling came to an end, however, when both of them were diagnosed with cancer.

Scott died on December 20th, 2016, three months after his wife's death. He was buried in Sunset Memorial Park Cemetery in Evansville, Indiana.

In the 73 years since his forgotten and uncertain Christmas of 1944 in Germany, Scott enjoyed many Christmas celebrations with his family. And he found peace in

Scott Thompson, 2016.

knowing that both his country and the world are better places because of his and others' sacrifices in World War II.

Portions of this story and quotes came from a video interview for the Freedom Heritage Museum in Evansville, IN, conducted by Richard Litov on March 29, 2014.

Landing Troops All Around Europe
Naval Officer Served on a Landing Craft, Infantry

John (Jack) Welsh was born on September 10th, 1921. He was raised in Greenfield, Indiana. What follows, with my editing for length and section headings, are his own words from his personal unpublished memoir regarding his World War II experience as an officer in the Navy on board Landing Craft, Infantry ships.

On Saturday, December 7, 1941, I was in a movie theater in Terre Haute, Indiana when the management of the theater stopped the movie. We heard President Franklin Roosevelt's voice say over the public address system that Pearl Harbor was being bombed by the air force of Imperial Japan and that it would go down in history as "A day of infamy." He said that as of the time of the bombing of Pearl Harbor, a state of war existed between the Government of Japan and the United States.

ENLISTING IN THE U.S. NAVAL RESERVE

I was a junior at Rose Polytechnic Institute (near Terre Haute, Indiana) in mechanical engineering. I volunteered when I did, because I wanted to have something to say about the branch of the service I would be in and what I would be doing. My choice was the Navy. I loved the water and ships, and I wanted to be an officer. Since I was a junior in engineering school, I saw a way to serve my country, be on ships, and further my career as well.

In February 1942, I enlisted in the U.S Naval Reserve in the V-7 program. Under this program, I was actually in the U.S. Naval Reserve, but on inactive duty. My active duty would begin when I graduated from college, and my first assignment would be in Officer's Training School in New York City.

ON THE *USS PRAIRIE STATE*

On February 22, 1943, I reported aboard the *USS Prairie State*, which was moored alongside the dock on the Hudson River in New York City. It was a part of The U.S. Naval Reserve Midshipman's School in New York City, which was at Columbia University.

Although it was the old Battleship *Illinois* (launched in 1901), the guns and superstructure had been removed and replaced with a big ark-like structure where we all assembled for our classes and drills.

We reported to classrooms that were built around the periphery of the covered deck and learned about engines, boilers, steam systems, fresh water generation systems, gunnery, navigation, signaling, rules of the road, etc. We were required to quickly learn all of the things needed to make us into naval engineering officers. The engineering courses were very difficult because we had to cover so much

USS Prairie State, **Midshipman's School, New York.**

territory in a short time. We were tested after one month and, on March 16, 1943, I was promoted to Midshipman.

On June 15, 1943, we received our commissions as ensigns in the U.S. Naval Reserve and, a day later, graduated from Midshipmen's school.

ASSIGNMENTS

My first orders had me reporting to Com 12 in the Ninth Naval District in San Francisco on June 30, 1943. My assignment was in the Federal Building downtown and my duties were to dispatch the large flying Navy Seaplanes bound for Hawaii and other Pacific destinations. I carried a packet of orders and other information to the airplanes and handed it to the captain.

I was detached from Com 12 in San Francisco on July 28, 1943 and ordered to report to Diesel School at the General Motors Institute in Flint Michigan on August 9, 1943. Diesel school was very interesting to me, and since I had worked on my old Ford many times, it was fun to work on the big diesel engines. We learned to tear down and rebuild the G.M. 671 engines, which we would have on the LCI (L)'s (Landing Craft Infantry Large) and on the big 12-cylinder engines, which were used on the LSTs (Landing Ship, Tanks). After eight weeks, we graduated from G.M. Diesel School.

My next assignment was at the Amphibious Training Command in Solomon's, Maryland, where I reported on

THE POWER TO WIN

September 19, 1943. Here we learned about the amphibious Navy and practiced landings.

LANDING CRAFT INFANTRY, LARGE

My group was assigned to the LCI(L)s, (LANDING CRAFT INFANTRY, LARGE) which were seagoing vessels about 165 feet in length, 28 feet beam, and 460 tons. They had quarters for four officers and 26 crewmen and could accommodate 280 troops. The ship was equipped with bow ramps, one on each side, which could be extended, and the forward end lowered into the water for the troops to go ashore on the beaches.

The ship was controlled by the officers operating from the conning tower at the top of the ship. Underneath the conning tower was the pilothouse where the quartermaster and another seaman normally steered the ship and regulated the engines by the engine telegraphs.

The LCI(L)s were an ideal means of transporting troops quickly at sea and were easily maneuvered into position in harbors and landing beaches. After a few weeks in class, we began going to sea on the LCI(L)s. I was surprised at the speed of these ships. They could cruise at about 13 knots (about 15 land miles per hour), and flank speed was about 17 knots (about 20 land miles per hour).

The training cruises at first were in the Bay and then soon we began going into the ocean. One of the first training exercises in the ocean was beaching practice

USS LCI(L)-551.

on Virginia Beach. This beach, we learned later, was a lot like Omaha Beach in Normandy, France, where we would be going in the invasion on D-Day.

There was a lot to learn about beaching the ship in a way so that the troops would be able to walk down the side ramps and step into the water, where it was not too deep. We had to learn where to drop the stern anchor so that it would hold and would be able to help pull us off the beach, through the surf, and back out into the ocean; so that then we could pull up the anchor and turn around and head out to sea.

The ship was armed with five 20 mm automatic guns; one mounted on the bow and the other four on the top deck. There were depth charges mounted on the stern for protection against submarines. We learned how to operate all of these and to go to our battle stations when General Quarters sounded. We had a general audio system, which could be heard all over the ship; except in the engine room when the engines were running fast.

The ship had no fresh water generator, so all of the fresh water had to be stored in tanks in the bottom of the ship. The diesel fuel for the engines, steam generator, and galley range was stored in other tanks in the bottom of the ship. Additional tanks in the bottom of the ship could be filled with sea water to trim the ship fore and aft as needed for beaching operations and to give the ship more stability during rough weather.

The officers controlled the ship from the conning tower, which was the highest part of the ship. It had no cover over it. We were always at the mercy of the weather while in the conning tower. The officers in the conning tower would speak through a voice tube to the people in the pilothouse and say "heading 92 degrees and engines at standard speed." Then, the person operating the steering lever would move the rudder so the ship would come to 92 degrees and then move both engine telegraphs to standard speed. The engine telegraphs in the engine room would show standard speed, and the men in the engine room would move the engine throttles to obtain the proper shaft rpm for standard speed, etc.

When we were at sea, we trimmed the ship to be nearly level and kept the tanks full so the ship would be more stable. When we were loaded with troops and were going to go into the beach we trimmed the ship so that the bow would be as high as possible so that we could bring the troops up close to the beach. When we did it right, we could back off the beach after the troops left. We knew that if we became stuck on the beach during an invasion we would be sitting ducks for the enemy gunners and bombers.

ASSIGNMENT TO LCI(L) 517

On Dec. 5th, after about ten weeks of this training, we received orders detaching us from the Amphibious Training Base at Solomon's, Maryland and directing us to report to The Commanding Officer, Receiving Station, Pier 92, New York, NY on December 13, 1943 for fitting out LCI(L) 517. Our ship was not yet completely finished, so we were able to see it in the shipyard as it was finished; and then to see it launched and commissioned.

It was very exciting for us finally to have our own ship. It is doubtful whether many would have called it a beautiful ship, but it looked great to us. Our quarters inside were really quite good. I had a stateroom with a porthole, two bunks, a desk, file cabinets, and closet. I was assigned to this ship until September 1945, when we were in Pearl Harbor, Hawaii.

The three officers were the Captain, the Executive Officer, and myself, the Engineering Officer. There were about 26 enlisted men and non-commissioned officers.

The group for which I was responsible included the motor machinist's mates, electricians, oiler, and others for a total of 13. It was called "The Black Gang". My first duty was to organize my group to function efficiently in operating the ship. Everything had to be in top operating condition at all times, no matter where we were. So, I selected the leaders, assigned duties, and saw to it that orders were

LCI 517 being scraped and painted by crew in Falmouth, England, 1944.

followed and that the jobs got done. Also, I made up the watch lists each week.

Since there were only four officers, each of us, except the skipper, was required to accept other duties in addition to our primary assignment. In my case, in addition to being the engineering officer, I was also supply officer, and commissary officer. That meant that I was responsible for keeping a full inventory of supplies aboard and being responsible for the ship's store.

For the next several weeks, we were busy getting supplies in, getting everything running, and learning to operate the ship. We went up the Hudson river to calibrate the compass, took a three-day shake-down cruise on the ocean, cruised down to Virginia Beach for beaching practice, and generally got used to working together.

Jack Kneeling, left, with Officers of LCI 517.

LEAVING FOR ENGLAND

About February 20th, 1944, we received our orders to join a convoy bound for Falmouth, England. There were ships of all sizes and types including tankers, freighters, and some Navy Cruisers and Destroyers for our escort. The German submarines were very active in the Atlantic at that time, so we did a lot of watching for periscopes. The North Atlantic in February is usually very stormy, so our crossing for the most part was very rough. We liked to get in the lee of a big tanker and use it as our breakwater, which helped a lot. One day,

Atlantic Convoy in WWII

LCIs in convoy to England.

when we were in the lee of a big tanker in a particularly bad storm, the tanker blinked, "Please drop back. You are making us seasick."

Our routine at sea was very tiring. Each officer had to take his turn as Officer of the Deck, who was the one in charge of operating the ship. The Officer of the Deck stayed in the conning tower, which was the control center and the highest part of the ship. Two enlisted men were in the pilothouse just under the conning tower, and two men were in the engine room. With everyone else asleep at night, it was up to those on watch to keep the ship operating properly, and to keep our station with the other ships.

The Officer of the Deck was the only one outside and, at night, he was the only one who could see beyond the ship. We were at war and always ran without any running lights. We could not use the radio. When we were in a convoy, or running with a group of other ships, we kept our position by following a dim night light on the stern of the ship in front of us. When we were in the lead, we were responsible for setting the proper course and speed.

During the daytime, we used signal flags and semaphore code along with our searchlight as a blinker to communicate with the other ships. At night, we used a small spotlight with a directional hood to communicate with the other ships.

Often in the north Atlantic the seas were very rough and, with the lack of sleep and the need to hang onto the guardrails to keep from falling overboard, we were tired all of the time.

TRAINING IN ENGLAND

We sailed into Falmouth Harbor. Falmouth was our base for several weeks. By now, it was about March 15th. Falmouth has a large harbor, which is at the mouth of a deep river. Several times while we were in Falmouth, the German bombers flew over and bombed the fuel stations and waterfront. They usually came in at night.

We practiced beaching on the English beaches. We were issued sealed orders each time we went to sea, and they were not to be opened until we were 10 miles at sea. The orders told us the course we were to take and the beach we were to land on. Often, we took troops aboard so that the practice would be for both the navy and the army. Actually, we were not sure whether it was a practice run or the real thing until we opened the orders. We continued this type of operation all along the southern coast of England.

When we arrived at Southampton, we thought we were getting close to the point where we would depart for the invasion, but we did not know when or where

Practice landings at Slapton Sands in England.

and, thankfully, neither did the Germans.

As we went from port to port along England's southern coast, we frequently heard and then saw the German V-1 and V-2 jet propelled bombs. The V-1 bombs sounded like outboard motors as they flew along. They were only about five hundred to one thousand feet high so were very visible from the ship and from the countryside. As

V-1 flying bomb on display, Putnam County, Indiana.

long as the bombs kept going, we knew we were safe. However, when the engine stopped, the bomb, which looked like a small plane, went down and exploded. I am sure that they did quite a lot of damage and killed many people, but we usually did not see the newspapers so we did not know how many people were killed or how much damage was done. Thankfully, none of them dropped on us. The V-2 bombs flew faster and higher and made a larger explosion when they fell.

On June 3rd, 1944, troops from the First Infantry Division of the First Army came aboard our ship. We sensed that this might be the big operation because

Landing troops in Normandy, France on D-Day.

the troops seemed to have more equipment than before but, of course, we were not sure.

A big storm had just hit, and there was a lot of wind and rain. We heard that the Channel was very rough. We all anchored in the center of the Southampton River in a long line as far as we could see. We were not allowed to go ashore. It was close quarters with about 280 soldiers plus our crew aboard for several days while Eisenhower and his staff and the British were deciding what to do. I remember two of my friends who were also engineering officers on sister ships rowed over in their ship's dinghies and we played monopoly while we waited.

Finally, on the evening of June 5, we received orders to move out. We got underway and started down the river. It must have been about 5 p.m. We passed the Isle of Wight and headed out to sea. It was a huge mass of ships as far as we could see; landing craft, troop ships, battleships, cruisers, destroyers, tankers and it seemed every kind of ship that existed.

Our LCI(L)s and troop ships carried the troops and the LSTs (Landing Ship, Tanks) and LCTs (Landing Craft, Tanks) carried tanks, trucks, guns, and supplies. When we opened our orders, they announced the "Great Crusade" on which we were embarking. It was called Operation Overlord. Everyone aboard received a copy of Eisenhower's letter. We were to land on Omaha Beach in Normandy.

LCI Convoy crosses the English Channel.

As it was just beginning to get dark, we saw the big bombers flying over going the same direction we were. They were flying to bomb the areas where we were to land, and other targets. Later, we could hear the C-47 cargo planes full of paratroopers and pulling gliders full of paratroopers flying over.

We were at general quarters, manning all of our guns and depth charges. It was one huge convoy stretching over an area much larger than we could see, and it moved quite slowly, or we would have arrived in France too early.

We kept going all night and, just after daybreak, we could see the coast of Normandy. All of the landing craft were moving in an endless column. We passed between the big battleships and the shore. The battleships were firing their large 14 inch and 16 inch shells over our heads toward the land to destroy the gun emplacements on the bluffs behind the beaches. The bombers had already been on their bombing runs and, when the battleships stopped their shelling, the large British landing craft carrying thousands of rockets began firing them at the beach. It was a steady roar for at least five minutes.

The beach was all-ablaze. The first wave of LCIs, LSTs, LCTs, etc., went in toward the beach at 6:30 a.m. The Germans had not yet been able to man their guns at 6:30 AM, but soon they had their 88 mm artillery weapons trained on the beach, and they began hitting the ships and troops on the beach.

Our Flotilla of 36 LCI(L)s headed toward the beach at 10:30 a.m. The ships would sail along in a column and, upon the signal to turn, we would all turn in

LCI 517 underway.

toward the beach at the same time, like a "right face" as if we were marching. As we got closer to the beach the Germans were hitting more and more of our landing ships, so our Flotilla was ordered to stop and unload into LCMs (Landing Craft, Medium boats), which were much smaller and harder to hit.

By then, we were probably within 150 yards off the beach and shells were falling all around us. I remember the LCMs following along as we kept going. Thankfully, none of the ships in our group were hit, although we saw many more that were hit. As soon as we were unloaded, our orders were to rendezvous about 10 miles off the beach.

Our group had no way of knowing that, as large as it was, the Omaha Beach Invasion was only one of five great invasions taking place at the same time; although ours turned out to be the largest. The U.S. 1st and 29th Infantry Divisions of the U.S. First Army landed on Omaha Beach. It was too big to describe; almost too big to comprehend. However, we did not know all of that at the time. We could only see our operation on Omaha Beach, and it alone was by far the biggest operation we had ever seen or heard of.

We soon received orders to get underway and proceed to Brighton, England. By now it was dark and as we were cruising along all at once we sighted about four German fighter-bombers. We came to general quarters at once and the German planes dropped several bombs, but thankfully they didn't hit anything. We wanted to shoot at them with our 20mm guns but were ordered not to because we had tracer shells loaded and other German planes would be likely to see us.

The next day our ships were loaded with British troops. We sailed back across the English Channel to the newly built temporary harbor at Omaha Beach and tied up at one of the floating docks. While we were back in England, our Seabees and the British engineers and ships had towed the floating docks over from England and built the temporary harbor out from the beach in France. The troops could now walk off the ship and onto docks.

As I remember, we loaded Scottish Highlanders aboard with their bagpipes and bicycles. They were big jolly fellows, and we liked them at once. I have wished many times that I could have learned where all of the men we took to the beach ended up. The Scottish Highlanders went ashore with their bagpipes sounding very impressive.

After our trips to the beaches were completed we went to the British Naval shipyards in England for some repairs.

INVASION OF SOUTHERN FRANCE

Our next orders directed us to proceed down the coast of Europe into the Mediterranean Sea and report to the U.S. Naval Base at Bizerte, Tunisia.

Allied leaders had decided that an invasion into Southern France between Toulon and Nice on the French Riviera would enable the Allied forces to advance toward the north and cut the supply lines to the German troops on the Cherbourg peninsula.

Bizerte, Tunisia was the selected port from which this invasion would be launched. It had a good deep-water port, but the Germans had sunk many ships in the middle of the channel. Our navy had cleared a narrow space through this channel through which we could thread our way into the port.

Harbor in Bizerte, Tunisia.

117

Loading Troops for invasion of Southern France, 1944.

We loaded up with American troops in Bizerte and headed for the designated landing beach in Southern France. We kept watch for submarines and bombers but saw none. On the morning of August 15, 1944 we sailed carefully up to the beach near Ratatouille between Toulon and Nice, extended our ramps, and the troops waded ashore. We did encounter shelling from the German shore batteries, but no bombers or fighter planes appeared. We then headed back to Naples and returned to Bizerte.

Our officers had to take turns standing watch at night because we were moored alongside the dock. We had heard about the huge rats, so we were very careful with the rat guards on our mooring lines. And we did not leave the gangplank in place when we were not using it. We kept the ship about three feet from the dock. We had our 45 mm automatic pistols on our belts in case of trouble. I did see some of those rats, as large as dogs, scurry along when it was very dark and quiet.

French Moroccans with big handlebar mustaches came aboard. They looked mean but were a fun loving group. We arrived at the beach the next morning, lowered our ramps, and the Arabs walked down the ramps. Again, there was no trouble from the German Air Force. The shore batteries were in our hands by now.

Soon, a large group of German prisoners came aboard our ship, and our orders were to take them to Naples, Italy. The prisoners were made up of old and very young

German POWs aboard LCI 517 en route to Naples, Italy, 1944.

Germans, and there were others from Austria and other European countries. They were very friendly and had absolutely no interest in fighting Americans. American Military Police were in charge of them. The prisoners said they wanted to help, and asked what they could do. Well, by now our troop bunks were quite dirty after being used many times, so we asked if they would clean them. They seemed happy to be doing something useful, and soon we had the cleanest troop bunks in the whole flotilla.

We took that load of prisoners back to Naples, which was where they definitely did not want to go. They had always considered themselves superior to the Italians, and here they were going back as prisoners. However, we had our orders, so back they went.

LANDING TROOPS IN LEGHORN, ITALY

We stayed in Pozzuolli, Italy for some time. Then we returned to Naples and loaded up with American troops. We sailed up the Italian coast to Leghorn and entered the harbor. The port was in the hands of the U.S. Army, so there was no

Naples loading American troops for end run in Leghorn, Italy, Aug. 1944.

trouble from the Germans. This time, we came alongside the docks and the troops walked ashore.

I think we brought troops to Leghorn two more times. After these trips, we headed back down the coast to Naples and Pozzuolli.

While we were in Pozzuolli, we had to change one of our main engines. It had broken down while on our way back from Leghorn. We had a spare engine on the well-deck. It was an arduous task with nothing but chain falls to move the old engine out of the compartment and the new engine into place.

BACK TO THE U.S.

In mid-December we were ordered to return to the U.S. We headed west toward Norfolk, Virginia. I remember as we were heading out through the Straights of Gibraltar, we heard on the radio the sobering news that President Roosevelt had died. He was our commander-in-chief and had led our country for so long. Harry Truman, who was Vice-President, became President.

We had an uneventful, cold, voyage across the Atlantic and arrived in Norfolk about the middle of January 1945. We had been gone almost a year. We were granted leave and most of us headed home for a visit.

TO SAN DIEGO

After a welcome time at home in Greenfield, I took a train back to Norfolk and arrived on my ship. We received orders to report to the U.S. Navy Base in San Diego, California via the Panama Canal.

We arrived at San Diego the middle of March. We learned that our ship was to be converted to a gunboat in preparation for the invasion of Japan. All of this required at least eight weeks, so we had time to enjoy San Diego.

When our ship had been refitted, we had beaching practice on Catalina Island and other beaches. The seas are much higher in the Pacific than they are in the Atlantic. We had to learn how to get back off the beach and through the heavy surf without being stuck on the beach.

On May 8, 1945, while we were still in California, Germany surrendered and the European War was finally over. We were docked in the Navy shipyard when Victory in Europe (VE) Day was announced. There was a big celebration at the Navy base and in the city.

On July 12, 1945 we received orders to proceed to the port of San Pedro to await our turn to get ship modifications done at the U.S. Navy Shipyard at Long Beach, California. While we were in San Pedro, I received my promotion to Lieutenant (Junior Grade).

On August 15, 1945, the Japanese surrendered. We were very relieved of course, because we knew that the casualties would be very great on both sides if we were to invade Japan. I will always remember the huge celebration of the end of the war in the San Diego harbor. It was much larger than the one for V.E. Day. As night fell, there was a huge fireworks display, and many of the warships in the harbor fired tracer bullets into the sky. It went on for hours. Most of us went ashore and helped celebrate that great event.

TO THE PACIFIC, AND A NEW SHIP

We soon received orders to report to the commanding officer at the Naval Station in Pearl Harbor, Hawaii. We sailed out of the San Diego harbor and headed for Hawaii.

While in Hawaii I took a dinghy out and sailed around Pearl Harbor. I cruised way down the harbor until I found the big battleships, cruisers, and destroyers. I remember finding the battleship Arizona which had been torpedoed by the Japanese on December 7, 1941. Only part of the superstructure was above the water, and oil was still bubbling to the surface.

On September 23, 1945, I received orders detaching me from the LCI(L) 517 and assigning me to AD COMPHIBSPAC, Pearl Harbor, Hawaii. In all, I had served 23 months on LCI(L) 517, 10 months as engineering officer and 13 months as executive officer. I packed up my things, said goodbye to my shipmates, and moved into some officer's barracks on the Naval Base. It was an emotional time for me since I had been assigned to the 517 for almost two years and had been through so many experiences with most of the same crew.

THE SOUTH PACIFIC AND LCI(L) 698

After a week or so, I received orders to report to a different ship — LCI(L) 698, located in Kwajalein within the Marshall Island chain in the Pacific. The engineering officer on that ship had fallen down the passageway to the engine room and injured his back. He was sent to a Navy hospital, and a replacement engineering officer was needed. On October 3, 1945 I was assigned to the 698.

Jack, far right, and crew on LCI 698 in Kwajalein Harbor with homemade Christmas Tree, 1945.

I boarded a plane and headed to Kwajalein. When I found the LCI(L) 698 and went aboard I found the officers and crew to be very likeable. The 'black gang', as the engineering group was called, treated me with some suspicion at first, wondering what kind of a boss I would be. As I got to know the men they soon accepted me and we got along fine.

Duty on the 698 consisted of sailing around the Marshall Islands carrying passengers, freight, mail, and anything else anybody needed delivered. It was almost ideal duty, sailing around the South Sea Islands. We would load up in the morning and sail for a few hours to another island, unload our cargo, stay overnight, load up again in the morning, and do the same thing again. The weather was hot, of course, but we soon got used to that.

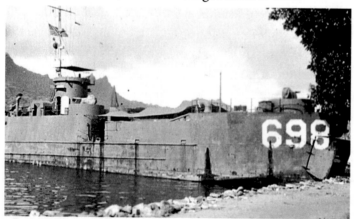

LCI 698.

One of our assignments was to sail to the Caroline Islands, which were very near the equator, and pick up natives who had been displaced during the war. We returned them to their home islands. They would crowd onto our decks with their chickens, pigs, goats,

122

and their possessions. The ship always had a coconut oil odor after they had been aboard.

After several weeks of returning the islanders to their home islands, we returned to Kwajaleen.

BACK TO THE U.S.

On January 14, 1946 I received orders to report to COM 12, San Francisco, California. I flew from Kwajalein to Pearl Harbor and, a

Native islanders in a village on Ponape, Caroline Islands.

few days later, boarded an aircraft carrier bound for San Francisco. I had never been aboard a carrier before and was very impressed with its size and the nice quarters.

On February 26, I was assigned to the 19th Fleet to assist in laying up ships of the line, which were no longer needed during peacetime. The ships had to be treated in such a way that corrosion would be at a minimum while they were laid up.

To do this, the engines and other working equipment was

Jack on carrier back to the U.S., 1946.

coated with grease, and the compartments were sealed with the closed hatches. Then, high-pressure blowers pumped dehydrated air through every part of the ship by means of the pipes of the fire protection sprinkler system. My job was to help oversee this work. It was kind of fun, going aboard all of these ships and setting up these operations. About that time, I was promoted to Lieutenant, U.S. Naval Reserve.

On April 2, 1946, I was detached from COM WEST SEA FRONT in San Francisco and ordered to report to the U.S. Naval Separation Center Great Lakes, Illinois. On April 16, 1946, I received an honorable discharge from the U.S. Navy and received a very nice letter from President Harry S. Truman thanking me for my service, and another from Secretary of the Navy, James Forestall.

THE SECRETARY OF THE NAVY
WASHINGTON

May 31, 1946

My dear Lieutenant (jg) Welsh:

I have addressed this letter to reach you after all the formalities of your separation from active service are completed. I have done so because, without formality but as clearly as I know how to say it, I want the Navy's pride in you, which it is my privilege to express, to reach into your civil life and to remain with you always.

You have served in the greatest Navy in the world.

It crushed two enemy fleets at once, receiving their surrenders only four months apart.

It brought our land-based airpower within bombing range of the enemy, and set our ground armies on the beachheads of final victory.

It performed the multitude of tasks necessary to support these military operations.

No other Navy at any time has done so much. For your part in these achievements you deserve to be proud as long as you live. The Nation which you served at a time of crisis will remember you with gratitude.

The best wishes of the Navy go with you into your future life. Good luck!

Sincerely yours,

James Forrestal

James Forrestal

The campaign ribbons that I had received were, World War II Victory Ribbon, American Campaign Ribbon, European-African 2 Stars, and Asiatic-Pacific Campaign.

This time, when I went home to Greenfield, Indiana; it was for good.

CONCLUSION

This story, about a very important part of my life, is to help my family understand what it was like to live through this very profound part of history. In looking for a way to conclude this story, I can say that it has become a labor of love. To grow up in that time period in America was to be profoundly affected, first by the Great Depression, and then, to be involved in one way or another in the war.

Overall, it was a great experience and a very formative one for us all. I was very fortunate that I was never injured nor had a serious sickness. Many were not so fortunate. However, to have the intense training that we had, and to be assigned to ships, which would take us halfway around the world when we were in our late teens and early twenties, is a priceless experience. We knew that we would be in many life threatening situations, but somehow we took it all in stride, followed our orders and, thanks to excellent leaders, plenty of resources, and the grace of God, we prevailed; and the world was changed forever. It has been a pleasure to tell this story.

— Jack Welsh

POSTSCRIPT:

After coming home from the war, Jack met and fell in love with Norma Lewellyn. They married on August 24th, 1946.

Jack worked many years for Eli Lilly and Dow Chemical Companies in Indianapolis before starting J.W. Welsh Engineering Consultants at age 52 with his wife, Norma; a company they successfully grew until his retirement at age 68.

Forever a man of the water, he enjoyed sailing, fishing and simply puttering with anything connected to boats or the water. He also enjoyed golf, a pastime he shared with his wife while living at The Pointe in Bloomington, Indiana and Ft. Myers, Florida.

Jack Welsh with his family.

John (Jack) Wilson Welsh passed away peacefully on October 28, 2015, in Indianapolis surrounded by his loving family. He was 94.

Norma, his loving wife of 69 years, died two years later on November 24, 2017. She was one day shy of turning 91.

Surviving Jack and Norma's deaths are their two children Susan Marr (Jeff) of Indianapolis and Doug Welsh (Joan) of Cincinnati, as well as seven grandchildren and eight great-grandchildren.

CHINA-BURMA-INDIA

Traversing the Dangerous 'Hump'
Veteran Recalls Adventures in a C-46 Transport Plane

Ralph "Duane" Collings knows a thing or two about Morse code and radios. He was a radio and Morse code operator in World War II and then spent almost 40 years of his civilian life using the same on the railroad.

Born to Boyd and Fannie Collings on November 11, 1924 (Veterans Day) in Parke County, Indiana, Duane was the youngest of 4 children.

He graduated from Mecca High School in Parke County, Indiana in 1942. He didn't attend the ceremony. "I missed graduation from high school due to a bad case of strep throat infection," he recalled in his personal memoir. "My classmates brought to our house my diploma and awards; although I was too sick to care."

Following high school, he and two buddies hitchhiked to Chicago and worked at the stockyards delivering messages. They returned home after a few months. Duane found a job as a busboy for a short time at Turkey Run State Park. There he met his future wife, Pauline Gooding, who was also working there as a server.

MILITARY TRAINING

One day Duane and a buddy decided to go to the recruiting station and join the Navy. His buddy passed the physical and left for Chicago. Duane failed the physical exam because he had a punctured ear drum.

Duane, lower right, and siblings.

Undeterred, he tried enlisting in the Marines; but he was turned away for the same problem. He received treatment for his ear from a doctor in Rockville, Indiana who used silver nitrate. His ears improved some.

On November 11th, 1942 he turned 18, registered for the draft and volunteered for military service through the draft board. This time, he passed the physical and was accepted. And this time he chose a branch of service that didn't reject him, the Army Air Force.

Duane was sworn into the Army Air Force on February 10, 1943 at Fort Benjamin Harrison, outside of Indianapolis. He wrote in his memoir: "On arriving at Ft. Benjamin Harrison, earlier arrivals were out policing up the grounds around the gate and greeted us with, 'You'll be sorry!'"

He and the other new arrivals continued to receive unsolicited guidance by the more "experienced" men. Duane wrote, "The next advice we heard was, 'Don't volunteer for anything!' This advice was very faulty, for a few nights later we were ordered to 'fall out' and asked by the duty Non-Commissioned Officer for three volunteers. We all looked at each other and smiled. Then he said, 'If I don't get three volunteers, I'll choose them myself.' He told the three he selected to go back to bed and sent the rest of us to all-night KP (kitchen patrol) duty. Live and Learn!"

During their time at Ft. Benjamin Harrison the new Army enlistees had to take a battery of tests. One of them was an auditory test. Duane wrote, "We were also given a radio code test which was given in a large room and consisted of a series of two sounds, some of which pairs were alike, and some different. Because all of us had colds, you might hear one sound and coughing would drown out the other. So, I gave up and finished marking my test by guessing and sat waiting for the test to be over." He passed.

Duane was then sent by train to St. Petersburg, Florida for his basic training. He recalled that the base was a swamp area that was known as "Tent City." In addition to learning the basic disciplines and skills of military service he was subjected to another auditory test. "As before, I had to guess because of the coughing," he wrote.

He then added parenthetically: "Don't laugh, but this got me into radio operators school."

HAMMER FIELD, CALIF
FRESNO 1943

CROWLEY - DYSART - ME

Duane at Hammerfield, CA, 1943.

Following graduation from basic training, Duane reported to Signal Corps Radio School near Joplin, Missouri. Here he studied Morse code. "I thoroughly enjoyed Morse code," he wrote. "And in the nine weeks of schooling I became proficient enough to be asked to stay on as code instructor, but I declined."

His next stop was Hammer Field in Fresno, California for Overseas Training. "We lived in tents," he wrote. "There was lots of physical training and hand-to-hand combat training in the mountains. I learned judo. It was very, very hot! Temps were 120 degrees in daytime. At night, from my cot, I never saw so many shooting stars in my life!"

Duane learned that the Army Air Force was in great need of volunteers for aerial gunnery. That sounded like good duty to him. So, he signed up, was accepted, and began his training at Kingman Arizona Army Air Field.

It was here that his eardrum problem resurfaced. Duane wrote, "During the physical, they re-discovered my punctured ear drum and, to be accepted to fly, I needed to sign a waiver that stated the government would not be held responsible if I later had hearing problems. I signed."

Duane found gunnery training to be exciting. "We began training on the 50-caliber machine guns and, being a radio operator, I was trained in the belly ball turret in the B-17s," he wrote in his memoir.

He quickly discovered that shooting moving targets while flying at fast speeds in a plane was not all that easy. "I learned that I was not a very accurate shot when shooting free-style 50s (50-caliber machine guns) from the waist doors at targets towed by B-26 planes in the distance," he wrote. "But I was deadly from the ball turret where you only had to track the target a few seconds, and the turret gun sight moved the 50s to lead the target enough to the intersection of paths."

Duane graduated and became a bona fide aerial gunner on December 4th, 1943. By this time, he had risen to the rank of a Sergeant.

Duane and Pauline.

GETTING MARRIED:

Meanwhile, back home in Indiana, Duane's former girlfriend had begun writing him. He explained from his memoir: "Pauline Gooding, whom I had dated at Turkey Run State Park, was riding with her Uncle Ralph on the way from Russellville to Waveland and got hung up in a snow drift. They walked to the nearest house, where my sister Marilyn and husband Ed Fowler lived, to use their phone. While Ed got the tractor and pulled Ralph out of drift, Pauline noticed my service picture and got my address and wrote to me."

The reconnection having been made, Duane resumed dating Pauline while he was home on a short leave between training schools. The couple was married on May 21, 1944.

Pauline accompanied Duane out to Sioux Falls, South Dakota for Radio Operator and Mechanic's school. He graduated on August 18, 1944 and then sent Pauline back home to Indiana, as he knew he would soon be assigned to a cargo crew and be headed to war.

C-46 CARGO PLANE

Duane reported to Bergstrom Field in Austin, Texas for training as a radio operator/mechanic on a C-46 cargo plane.

The Curtis C-46 Commando was a twin-engine transport that was used extensively in the China-Burma-India (CBI) theater of operations. It was the aircraft of choice for making the dangerous flights over "The Hump", as the Himalayan Mountain Range came to be known. It was used to transport vital supplies from India to military forces located in China.

Curtiss C-46 Commando.

The C-46 proved to be the most effective transport aircraft in handling the heaviest loads at the highest elevations, all while enduring the most tumultuous weather.

While it had a good record of success, the plane was never far from succumbing to the dangers of flying in such harsh conditions — something that Duane and his crew experienced soon enough.

CREW TRAINING

Duane wrote in his memoir, "We were appointed to four-man crews and I was radio operator/mechanic." The pilot, co-pilot and crew chief were the other members of the crew.

Duane soon learned that his pilot was not all that experienced at the controls. "One of our first flights together was on a bright sunny day; the kind of day you would love to fly," he wrote in his memoir. "We flew through our various appointed headings and on our return leg to base both pilots noticed that white, puffy clouds had drifted in under us and obscured the ground. They nearly panicked, and were talking back and forth how they would get down through the clouds and land. How was I to know they hadn't been instructed in instrument flying? Nevertheless, they decided to just dive through and hope they weren't really low clouds. We made it in OK — but the gray hairs were starting!"

The four men graduated from crew training on November 14th, 1944 and were sent to Baer Field in Fort Wayne, Indiana for overseas preparation. From there the crew took a train to Miami, Florida to begin their trek eastward toward combat duty.

ARRIVAL IN INDIA

On January 29th, 1945 the crew was on their way. It was a long journey. Duane recalled in his memoir, "We flew by four-engine plane via the Azores in the Atlantic (a small island with mostly mountains, but one side was flat with a runway), where we landed, refueled and then flew on to Africa's Gold Coast. We flew over deserts and flat-topped mountains to Karachi, India. There were no seats; we sat on the floor of the plane using our bags for pillows."

They remained at Karachi for a few days. While there, Duane witnessed an explosion that wasn't due to combat but rather stupidity. He wrote, "We used one of their newly built latrines, which had about 8 or 10 holes. It was ventilated by screen-wire around the building near to the top of building. A sign outside said 'Absolutely no smoking'. I had just come out and headed away when a bomb went off behind me. I turned around and a G.I. came running out. The screens and side of the latrine were blown out. He had thrown a lit cigarette butt down the hole and fumes from the chemicals caused the explosion!"

Duane and his crew were flown next to Chittagong, India, which became their home base for a time. They arrived there on February 7th, 1945 and were assigned to the 4th Combat Cargo Group of the 13th Combat Cargo Squadron based at Chittagong, India in the China-Burma-India Theater. Often referred to as the forgotten theater of World War II, the China-Burma-India (CBI) Theater included combat drama, logistical challenges and success stories similar to the more well-known European and Pacific theaters.

FLIGHT MISSIONS

The seriousness of flying cargo planes in a combat theater and maintaining plane security quickly became real to Duane and his crew. He wrote, "Once we started flying overseas out of Chittagong, India in all kinds of monsoon weather, we were told if we ever had to bail out and by chance got back to base we had better have the crystals out of the Command Radio set or there would be hell to pay."

He soon learned that the planes had higher priority to the Army Air Forces than the men that flew them. "We were told that we were expendable, as they could get millions more men; but planes and equipment would be very difficult to replace," wrote Duane.

"OLD 7910" IN BURMA 1944-45

He and his crew were expected to fly, regardless of weather conditions. As he recalled in his memoir, "We in the Combat Cargo Command were told we would fly in all types of weather when demand was made for supplies."

Even when the weather was decent, the landing strips in Burma rarely were, as Duane remarked in his memoir, "We flew sorties over the Chin Hills into Burma, landing at dirt airfields in support of the British 14th Army. Most airfields were bulldozed and packed dirt. Some were taken over by the Japanese by night, and run out by the British by day so we could land. We flew in ammunition, food, bridge sections-anything the British said was needed. We flew in all kinds of monsoon weather — combat cargo crews had no excuses not to fly!"

CREW ACCIDENTS

Unlike most other crews, Duane's crew never flew together after arriving in India. "On arriving in the theater, my crew never got to fly together even once as a unit because of a serious accident that our pilot had," Collings wrote in his memoir. "He was flying touch-and-go instrument landings with a Major instructor in the co-pilot seat. A cover was placed over the windshield and side windows so you couldn't see out. They would circle around a landing pattern, land on instruments and, as soon as the wheels touched down, the pilot would advance throttle and take off again. They had made several landings and take-offs, and on one, the Major pulled up the landing gear before the plane had reached a speed to keep it airborne. The plane sank back down to the runway and when the props hit the runway one blade came thru the side of the cockpit cutting off one of the pilot's legs. I never saw him after we reached Chittagong."

"Our co-pilot, crew chief and I were ordered to fly (with other crews) anytime there was a shortage of crews and a plane was available. Our paths never crossed, and we never flew together again."

The pilot's accident wasn't the only mishap to one of Duane's fellow crewman. A crew chief he often flew with had a fatal mishap. He wrote, "While operating the ramp vehicle which pushes and pulls planes around, he was airing up a tail wheel tire on a plane and mistakenly connected the "high pressure" hose to the tire instead of the 'low pressure' hose and was decapitated when the tire and rim blew up. I was flying in Burma when it happened and only heard of it when I came in that night."

One of the missions Duane flew on involved picking up sections of a bridge for transport. He recalled, "I volunteered with a crew to fly steel bridge sections badly needed by the British in Burma. They were loaded in the plane, and I remember only having enough room to crawl over top of the load and dragging my parachute to get to the cockpit."

Tragedy occurred while the steel sections were off-loaded into British trucks. This time, it was a Burmese man who was the victim. Duane wrote, "Some Burmese were unloading the sections into a British truck (Lorry). They had about seven or eight sections in the truck and, in sliding out the next section, the front edge of it hung up on the top section of the one in the truck. So, finally a little guy jumped down into the hole between the steel braces, knelt down and lifted up the top one while the guys in the plane shoved; and it took off and pinned his head and neck to the brace behind him, killing him instantly! This seemed to be the most hilarious event the Burmese crew had ever seen, as they stood laughing and pointing at him! Go figure!"

Bridge sections weren't the only odd cargo Duane saw loaded in one of his planes. He wrote, "I volunteered to fly with a crew to Dum Dum Airport in Calcutta to pick up a partially dismantled helicopter and fly back to Chittagong for the Air & Sea Rescue Service. Pilots used a slide rule to figure the weight in each section of the fuselage while loading to ensure that the plane was not tail or nose heavy. But there was no way to figure the weight distribution of a helicopter fuselage and detached props, etc. It was loaded finally and we taxied out for take-off. Down the runway we were picking up speed at full power, but the tail wheel would not lift from the runway. Soon, it was too late to abort take off. The pilot & co-pilot both pulled back on the steering columns, and the plane finally shuddered off the runway, just barely clearing some trees a short distance from the end of the runway.

Personally, I don't believe we would have made it if not for me pulling up so hard on the backs of their seats!"

TENSIONS WITH A PILOT

Cargo was the least of Duane's problems when he flew with one particular pilot. He felt his life was in jeopardy every time he went up in the air with the man. He described two incidents in his memoir and the fireworks of tempers that flared up between him and the pilot.

C-46 in flight.

"I had problems with one pilot I flew with quite a few times. He was a good pilot, but I thought he had bad judgment and tended to make too many instant decisions. We had flown a sortie to a new field carved out of nothing, which had been flown into enough to make the dirt a light, fluffy, powdery dust. We were circling in the landing pattern following another plane that was landing ahead of us. When this plane landed, it immediately disappeared in a huge cloud of dust, and we were heading in behind him. I suggested we go around again and land when the dust settled, but the pilot ignored my advice (naturally) and landed on the first tip of runway and immediately into the big dust cloud from the first plane. We didn't go very far before their tail just missed the co-pilot's side of the cockpit and embedded into our right wing & engine. The other plane had stopped as soon as he could, not being able to see. So, two planes were shot! Luckily no one was injured. We had to hitch-hike back to Chittagong on one of our other crew's planes."

"The last sortie I flew as a member of his crew was into central Burma. After being unloaded by the British and Burmese, we made a "short field" take-off, which means taxiing to the end of the dirt runway and lining up with a runway for take-off. Both pilots stand on the brakes, give the engines full power, release the brakes, and after a short start retract the landing gear and head for the sky. Japanese small arms fire was all around our air strip."

"As we flew north at a pretty low altitude, the pilot got a radio message request to land and pick up a wounded British soldier at a dirt strip. So, he cut around and made ready to make a direct head on landing. We were under strict orders not to do so, which I reminded him along with the co-pilot. But he headed in on direct approach, landed, and suddenly pitched nose down into a large bomb crater in the middle of the runway. The plane sunk into the mud!"

C-46 stuck in mud.

"Luckily no one was hurt and, as it was nearly dark, the pilot assigned me outside of the plane to stand guard until midnight, at which time the crew chief would take over. All four of us carried .45 caliber automatics in shoulder holsters and had very little ammunition. Anyway, I was certain we would soon have company if any Jap troops were close, as they would have heard us land and knew we hadn't taken off again."

"The night passed and no attack came, so we took turns listening for planes overhead so we could radio to them and report our condition."

"After being relieved from my first night of guard duty, I woke the pilot up and gave him a cussing out; calling him names and telling him how stupid he was and that I would never fly with him again, even if I got court martialed! He told me if we got back, the first thing he would do would be to file insubordination charges against me. And I told him to file and be damned!"

"On the second or third day, a British group moving south came by, so we walked and at times rode one of their jeeps until we arrived at an airstrip where we could be picked up. The British sent a cablegram to our base advising what was necessary to float our plane out of the mud. Eventually, we were picked up by a plane from another squadron in our Combat Cargo Group and flown back to Chittagong."

"The first thing the pilot and I did on reaching Chittagong was what we both threatened each other. I was never reprimanded because of this, partly because our Commanding Officer was steamed by the fact that the pilot had lost another plane! I never flew with that pilot after that."

"But when the war ended, he came to our basha (hut tent) from their officers' camp and begged me to volunteer to go to China and fly with him. He said the Chinese were offering pilots $25,000 and other Non-Commissioned Officer crew members $15,000 per year. That was loads of money back then. But I told him to shove it and get out!"

BIRTH OF A SON & STRUGGLE WITH PREMONITIONS

Some good news finally reached Duane in India when his wife, Pauline gave birth to their first son. Duane recalled in his memoir, "It was during these times I was hoarding my monthly allowance of beer (two six-packs and cigars) as Pauline was expecting and I needed to celebrate when I received word. Gary Duane Collings was born on April 21, 1945, and I received a rush V-mail notification about two weeks later. It was a happy time but also a very sad time. During our weather and flying problems I had grown into a frame of mind — a premonition maybe — that I would not survive to ever return and enjoy my family. It was not anything that I dwelt on continually, but it was hidden in the back of my thoughts as I realized we were taking too many risks that outweighed our odds of survival."

Like many of the crew, Duane sought to soothe his nerves from his harrowing flight experiences. He wrote, "While we were in Chittagong and Myitkyina and when we came in late from flying, we would be met by the Flight Surgeon, and he would give us a shot of whiskey. When I got to know him better I could talk him into 2 shots. On an empty stomach, I sometimes felt as though I was floating over the footpaths on the levees back to our basha. But it did help us relax and GOD knew we needed that."

"In fact, GOD knew a lot of things about us over there. I'm sure there were prayers streaming towards heaven night and day! And I consider myself very fortunate that mine were answered at the time. 'God Is My Co-Pilot' is not only a book title; it was a fact of life."

WAR ENDS, BUT NOT FLYING

Duane survived the war, thanks to God's protection and the surrender of the Japanese following the destruction of the atomic bombs dropped on Hiroshima and Nagasaki. The end of the war, however, did not bring an immediate end to flying for Duane; but it did change the types of flight missions. He recorded in his memoir, "At the end of World War II, our flying to support troops in Burma ended, and we soon were committed to 'Flying the Hump' to support Chiang Kai-shek in China."

"We settled into tents at South Myitkyina, which is pronounced "Mission Aw," on the banks of the Irrawaddy River in northeastern Burma. The gossip was that we were to be sent home, but our Commanding Officer, Lieutenant Colonel Lucian Rochte, volunteered our Group because he wanted more time in the China-Burma-India Theater to make full Colonel. Anyway, we were soon flying into China

C-46 unloading in China.

delivering supplies of all kinds, and any bathing we did was in a swift and a mostly muddy river."

"I thought life had been very hazardous while stationed at Chittagong, and it was," Duane wrote in his journal. "But the Hump was a totally different experience. Flying in all kinds of weather as before, but at higher altitudes! Airfields in China were mostly located in low places with tall mountains encircling them; making for hairy approaches and landings once you got over the Hump. Very few times could you land and take off in good weather on either side of the Hump."

C-46 flying over the "Hump."

Duane's son, Gary, added his own description of the danger his father and others experienced when "Flying the Hump:" *"The Hump was also known as the 'Aluminum Trail,' so-named for the planes that never returned from their flights over the Himalayan Mountains.*

His aircrews did not encounter the enemy in air combat. Their 'enemy' was the Himalaya Mountains

when shrouded in low clouds and/or dust storms from monsoon winds that stirred the dust to low or no visibility. Many planes did not clear the imposing mountaintops and crashed in the jungles inhabited by cannibals. The fleece-lined, leather flight jackets of the crewmembers had a large circular patch sewn on the backside with inscriptions in a few dialects of the so-called friendly tribes, urging the return of any surviving crewmembers to a military base if they were fortunate enough to be found by them. So many planes crashed on the mountains that they were aptly dubbed the 'Aluminum Trail' because of the scattered wreckage of downed airplanes.

"Their planes would often leave in decent weather, clear the mountains, and drop the cargo, but the weather would drastically change on the return trip. Dad described standing between the pilots on many flights, desperately searching for a 'hole in the clouds' that would show they were clear of the jagged mountaintops.

Downed C-46 along the Himalaya "Hump."

The pilots would then dive the aircraft to lower altitudes to search for the dirt landing strip.

"The WWII airplanes were not pressurized, so crewmembers wore their flight jackets for warmth and were required to strap on oxygen masks at an altitude of 10,000 feet. Dad was reminded of this altitude limit during his first trip by automobile on routes through the Rockies Mountains at elevations over the airborne threshold."

While in India, Duane did get to see some of the treasured sights there, including the Taj Mahal and the Old Fort. Writing in his memoir he admitted, "They were outstanding, but never really appreciated by a bunch of 21-year-olds until many years later."

He also saw some of the worst sanitation conditions. "Appalling to see the open sewers with the bodily waste floating in them," he wrote.

[Duane, seated second from left, with buddies at the Taj Mahal.

HONORABLE DISCHARGE:

After accumulating the required 600 flying hours, Duane was sent back to the United States. "I was in one of the first groups to get to return to the states because of the point system used," he wrote. "My awards, having a wife and son, and a number of flight hours boosted my total."

Duane, by now a Staff Sergeant, was honorably discharged on November 24, 1945 at Camp Atterbury in Indiana. He was awarded the Distinguished Flying Cross and Air Medal with two Oak Leaf Clusters along with the Central Burma Battle Star, Good Conduct Medal, and Burma-China Offensive Campaign Battle Star.

The citation of his Distinguished Flying Cross and Air Medal reads as follows:

The Distinguished Flying Cross is hereby awarded to the following named office and enlisted men of the Combat Cargo Group, for extraordinary achievement while participating in more than one hundred hours of aerial flight over territory in Burma where exposure to enemy fire was probably and expected. These missions were accomplished in unarmed cargo type aircraft bearing troops, supplies and heavy equipment over hazardous mountain terrain into the forward areas. This display of a devotion to duty and a degree of efficiency above and beyond that normally expected reflects credit on these pilots and these crew members and on the Army Air Forces of the United States.

Duane, Pauline, Gary and Steve Collings.

LIFE AFTER THE MILITARY

Upon his discharge, Duane hitchhiked home from Camp Atterbury to Waveland, Indiana where his bride and a six-month old son, Gary were waiting for him. A few years later, in 1949, his second son, Steve was born.

Shortly after returning home, Duane found work on the B & O railroad at Russellville, Indiana as a Morse code telegraph operator. He worked for the railroad for 39 years, retiring as a station agent in 1985.

He and his wife, Pauline, celebrated 69-1/2 years together before her death in December of 2013.

The Collings' extended family has grown over the years. His two sons, Gary (Kathy) Collings of Westfield, Indiana and Steve (Susie)

Duane and Pauline, Sept.1985.

Collings family multi-generation, Dec. 1980.

Collings of Micanopy, Florida had families of their own. Duane is the grandfather of four children and the great-grandfather of five kids.

Following retirement, Duane's background in telegraphy led him to an interest in basic computer programing. He was fascinated with the advent of computers and their programing. He typed his memoirs on one of his early computers.

HONOR FLIGHT

Duane took his first jet plane trip and last flight on his 64th Wedding Anniversary (May 21, 2008) as a member of the Boone County Honor Flight group, whose members were flown to Washington D.C. to view the World War II Memorial.

Both he and son, Gary were overwhelmed emotionally by the honor and response which included a water hose tribute. Duane didn't feel well, but he kept up. The pilot invited him up to the cockpit to take a look. He couldn't fathom the plane being at 35,000 feet. He remembered he had to don oxygen at 10,000 feet while on the C-46.

Reflecting back on the trip he said, "I had the most fantastic and (humbling) day. I have never felt as though I was a hero, just a very average Joe trying to do what was expected of me. But this trip was so very eye-opening as to the depth of emotion some people have for veterans."

Gary and Duane on Honor Flight plane.

EPILOGUE

Today, at the age of 93, Duane lives in an assisted-living retirement community in Carmel, Indiana. His older sister, Marilyn Fowler, is a resident there as well; and they enjoy visiting with each other.

Duane remains a member of the Morse Telegraph Club (Terre Haute Chapter) and the Roachdale, Indiana VFW Post 3284.

Looking back over his full life he reflected in his memoir, "At times I reminisce and wonder why I was spared and some of my buddies weren't. Did God have plans for me in the future?' All I know is, I came back from overseas, hired on the railroad in 1946, and Pauline and I spent 39 years railroading while raising two of the finest sons who, in turn, raised the finest families. I pray that is what God had in mind for us to do."

It appears that was exactly what God had in mind for him.

Here, There and Everywhere

Indiana Farmer Served In All Three Theaters of War

BEGINNINGS

William (Bill) McColgin grew up on a farm in Indiana. He had a special bond with the Indiana soil.

World War II introduced him to the soils of distant countries in three different theaters of combat: Europe, India and some of the Pacific islands.

Born on August 13, 1918 on a farm in Greenwood, Indiana, Bill was the middle child born to Claude and Lottie (Green) McColgin.

The farm had a water line coming into the home but not plumbing for a bathroom. Bill did not experience indoor plumbing until he was married.

As he grew up he worked on the farm and was given special responsibility in caring for the tomatoes. He participated in 4-H in the crops and garden category.

Bill graduated from Whiteland High School in 1936 from a class of 24. "I took as much math as possible, as I wanted to become an engineer," he told Douglas Clanin with the Indiana Historical Society in an interview with him in 1994.

Following high school, Bill enrolled at Purdue University and began working on a civil engineering degree. He took the required two years of ROTC (Reserve Officer

147

Training Course). Illness interrupted his education and training. "I got typhoid fever during the fall semester of my sophomore year and missed that semester," he said.

While recovering from his sickness at home, he decided he would seek a commission in the Army, because he saw that the war was coming. He was accepted into the advanced military training program and signed a contract to serve in the Army.

The summer between Bill's sophomore and junior years he attended a surveying camp for civil engineering. The following summer, he attended military camp at Fort Knox, Kentucky where he spent six weeks living in tents, eating from a field mess and practicing with the 75mm artillery gun and howitzer.

Bill graduated from Purdue University in June of 1941 and was commissioned as a 2nd Lieutenant in the Army. But he didn't want to stay with the artillery. "As a civil engineer, I wanted to get in on the construction of the camps," he said, referring to the new bases that were being built around the world as the United States prepared for war. "So, I asked for a transfer to the Quartermaster Corps. It came through in July of 41. I went into the service as a Quartermaster." He was called up to active duty that August.

A year later, the Army turned over all of the maintenance functions to Ordnance; so Bill was automatically transferred to Ordnance.

TRAINING

Bill reported to Quartermaster School in Camp Lee, Virginia. "We were assigned to companies of black (enlisted) troops being trained in the Quartermaster Corps," he said during his interview. "We experienced training them and, at the same time, we went to school half the day for eight weeks getting training with maintenance, shoe repair, clothing, laundry and so forth."

"I was there when Pearl Harbor was attacked on Sunday afternoon, December 7th. I knew things had been changed because my original orders had called for one year of duty, after which I would return home. And, it was quite obvious, it wouldn't work out that way." It didn't.

Bill left Camp Lee around Christmas time of 1941 and headed for Fort Harrison in Indianapolis, Indiana. He was assigned to Company A of the 5th Quartermaster Battalion. "They were in automotive maintenance," he said, "and I thought that was really good to get sent to Fort Harrison, having ties with my girlfriend and home in Greenwood. But I was only there for a week, until I got orders to Camp Tyson in Tennessee."

The camp, a barrage balloon training center, was near Harris, Tennessee. From there, Bill reported to another Quartermaster School — this one was at Camp Normoyle in Texas, just west of San Antonio.

The school was supposed to be for eight weeks, but the training was compressed to four weeks instead. The newly trained officers traveled to Charleston, South Carolina from where they would deploy overseas.

OVERSEAS

On May 27th, 1942, Bill and others boarded the *SS Mariposa* and departed for an unknown destination. The *Mariposa* was a luxury ocean liner. This was the first-time it was used as a troop ship. Thus, there were some nice accommodations for the officers, "We ate off of a hotel-like menu most of the time," said Bill.

The ship was at sea for most of 52 days. Sometimes it was in a convoy and, at other times, it was sailing independent and zigzagging to avoid enemy submarine attacks. The *Mariposa* arrived in Karachi, India (today, it is in Pakistan) on July 23rd. Bill recalled rough seas when the ship went around the horn of Africa. It was the only time that he recalled being seasick.

Bill in India, Christmas 1942 with flowers given by natives.

INDIA

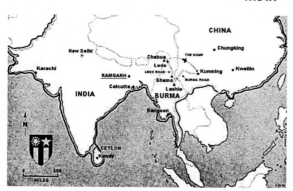

"We were stationed at Karachi for four to five months, and we were assembling vehicles," Bill recalled during his interview. "All the vehicles that came off the ships went through our unit. We serviced them before any of the companies could get them."

Prior to falling into Japanese control in 1942, the British used the Burma Road to move shipments of supplies from England to China to support the government there. Once the Burma Road could no longer be used by the Allies, England sent their supplies to India and stored them in various places throughout the country.

"There were hundreds and hundreds of trucks boxed from Britain that we assembled and turned over to the British in India for their use," said Bill. "And the whole purpose of being in India was eventually they (The Allied Forces) intended to build a road from India through Burma and into China."

Bill soon moved across to the eastern tip of India. He shared in his interview, "After four months of being in Karachi, I was sent to Ledo, Assam; that's up in the northeast corner of India, right on the Burma border. I took the train clear across India." He went there to prepare for the arrival of the 85th Quartermaster Company, which he would be leading temporarily while his Captain was away.

"After a few weeks, the company was called up to Ledo," Bill said. "We had to load all of our equipment on the India trains. We got halfway across India, and then we had to transfer everything to narrow gauge. So, we had to unload everything off one flat car to put it on the narrow gauge cars. The last few miles, we went on the road by way of convoy."

Upon arriving in Ledo, the company found favorable quarters. Bill shared, "And we were assigned an area that was an Indian tea garden. It was owned by the British. We took over the tea garden house, which was elevated. You could drive the jeep underneath it. The (enlisted) men had bamboo huts, and we had a big bamboo dining hall. And all of this (construction) was done by Indian labor, under the reverse lend and lease. The British had Indians build bamboo huts for us in exchange for what supplies we were sending the British at that time."

Enlisted quarters, Ledo, India.

Bill's unit also helped supply the Chinese who were in the mountains. He explained, "About 30-40 miles west of us was an American airfield. The Chinese had outposts on those mountains. I furnished nine or 10 men who worked with the Air Force and the quartermaster and packed bags and threw them out by parachute to feed the Chinese that were on various outposts between China and India. The only way they could get supplies was when we would fly over and throw out the bags. I got to make one of those trips one day, which was pretty interesting to fly over on a C-47 with no doors on it and kick out the parachutes. "

Bill got a firsthand look at the construction of the Ledo Road project. "The Ledo Road was being built by this engineer battalion we went overseas with," he said. "And it was right through the jungle. There was no gravel. They took stones out of the river and crushed it. And they hired a lot of the natives to help dig the ditches alongside." Bill remembered that the Indians used baskets on their heads. "They filled the baskets, carried them on their heads and dumped them at the designated spots for fill. So they had hundreds

C47 dropping supplies.

of laborers that were helping to build this road." [Bill on Ledo Rd with Sign] [Bill on Ledo Road]

Bill provided vehicle maintenance support to the workers on the Ledo Road. "I had to split the company and move part of them up into the jungle because they had finally gotten 40-50 miles away on that road," he recalled. "I sent a platoon of men up there to work in the jungle, and they lived up there for a while."

The Ledo Road, also known as the Stilwell Road after General Stilwell who was responsible for the whole theatre, was completed in late 1944 and stretched for 478 miles across mountainous terrain. It connected Northeast India to the Burma Road in Burma, allowing a continental route into China. The first supplies brought by truck reached China in early 1945.

Bill's unit provided critical maintenance of military vehicles. He recalled, "While we were in India, we had two big shops and they were about like our pole barns. They had metal roofs with steel frames. And that is where they dried the tea leaves. They had layers of tea. We took out the framework and we were able to pull all of our trucks and everything under the cover to work on them."

Vehicle maintenance area in Ledo, above.

Inside vehicle maintenance shop, Ledo, left

Bill remembered having access to many different supplies at military warehouses in India. Some items had been designated for China but, since there was no way to get the items into China, the supplies were given to units in India. Bill was able to even secure some "toys" for his men. "At one time, we had about 20-30 motorcycles for a company of 120 men to play with because there was no way to get them into China at that time."

Bill on Ledo Road with sign.

One Sunday, Joseph Stilwell, the Army General in charge over the China-Burma-India Theatre, made an inspection visit at Bill's company. He was impressed with a grease rack the men had made, but when he saw some tires lying out under the sun he said it was a "disgrace" because of the rubber shortage back home. He didn't say another word about it and left shortly afterwards.

The tires were designated for trailer beds that were going to be pulled by Jeeps and driven along the railways, but the

Bill on Ledo Road.

trailers were not yet built because the materials for building them had not yet arrived. Bill called the men together right after the General left and had them gather all the tires and bring them under the shade for storage.

"So, I had the tires all under cover and about two hours later, unannounced, came General Stilwell with his driv-

Trucks on the Ledo Road heading to China.

Bill, left, in India beside a bear.

Bill with elephant in India.

er and no one else with him. He drove up to the spot, looked around and said, 'Nice job, Lieutenant.' And he left. You could see he was pleased because he had come back to make sure they had been take care of. He wanted it done immediately, and he didn't give me any more than enough time to get it done. But we had it done, so I was real pleased."

Concerning General Stilwell, who was also known as 'Vinegar Joe' for his sometimes sour disposition, Bill recalled, "He was highly respected by the men. He didn't ask them to do anything that he wouldn't do himself, I'm sure."

While in India, Bill witnessed a dogfight between a Jap plane and an American fighter. On another occasion, he saw a Japanese plane get shot down. "I got up to the mountains from base HQ to help recover the bodies," he said. "I've still got four live ammunition shells from that plane on my back porch. And I have a cup that came out of the plane and says 'Made in Japan.'"

RETURN TO THE U.S. FOR FURTHER DUTY

Bill left India on August 16, 1943 and headed home via a hospital ship. He arrived in the states on September 14, 1943.

He explained during his interview the reason for the Army bringing him back, "They had decided to bring a few cadres back from overseas to help form new units. I picked 13 men from my company to come back as a cadre."

Bill took leave and returned to Indiana to marry his fiancée, Helen Carey, on September 26, 1943. Helen then returned with him to California. They enjoyed their first few months of married life as Bill waited for a new Army unit to be organized.

General Stilwell eating Christmas Day C-Rations, 1943

NEW UNIT

By spring of 1944, the 379th Ordnance Medium Automotive Maintenance Company had been formed. The unit was assigned to Camp Howze, Texas (close to Gainsville). Bill was promoted to Captain at this time.

Shot-down Japanese fighter.

Bill, left, in Ledo.

The newly formed company then went to Fort Polk, Louisiana for maneuvers and had additional training at Camp Jaffey, Oklahoma and Fort Smith, Arkansas before moving on to Fort Rucker, Alabama to make final preparations for deployment.

Bill's unit left the States on February 27 of 1945 to go to Europe. They landed at Camp Lucky Strike (close to Normandy, France) on March 17. "We were in tents and wondering where we were going to go," said Bill.

A 2nd Lieutenant Bill had known from earlier duty approached and asked if Bill wanted to be assigned to Germany as part of the occupation forces. "We need somebody to do our maintenance," said the 2nd Lieutenant.

Bill replied, "It sounds good."

The 2nd Lieutenant said reassuringly, "We'll be in the back, and we will just maintain Army HQ vehicles."

Bill and Helen, 1943.

Bill was pleased with the mission for his unit. "I thought you couldn't be any luckier than that," he remarked.

MAINTAINING VEHICLES IN OCCUPIED GERMANY

"So, we were moved forward to a German shop that they captured," Bill said, "and we moved into a hotel in the city of Appel (south and east of Hamburg). We could

Bill Sitting in a German car repaired in his shop in Germany.

hear the gunfire (from the front). We were only about 10 miles from the Elbe River. We could hear everything up at the front, but we were far enough behind that we were real safe.

In addition to maintaining vehicles, Bill's unit also collected weapons that were turned in by German soldiers who had surrendered. "It was a real nice assignment, if you had to be there," he recalled. "And we were lucky. We got to visit various places around."

Germany officially surrendered on May 8th.

THE PHILIPPINES

The war in Europe had ended, but Bill's time in service was not yet completed. He still had one more theatre of war to experience, the Pacific.

"When the war was over in Europe we were assigned to go to Marseilles (France) and take off for the Pacific Ocean," said Bill.

His unit departed from Europe on June 21, 1945 on a Navy troop ship. They went from Marseilles to the Panama Canal. "Once we were across the Panama Canal," he recalled, "we had to travel with lights off because the Japanese still had subs that were active in the waters."

The company landed at Manila in the Philippines on August 6, 1946 — the same day the U.S. dropped its first atomic bomb over Hiroshima.

"We had some old wrecks of buildings for headquarters," Bill said.

The city of Manila was in ruins from the prolonged combat that had taken place there. Bill recalled, "You would see one hotel in complete shape with no damage and half a block each way everything was wiped out. The story was that Gener-

Bill in Manila with "War Over" news.

al MacArthur owned that hotel. A few big buildings were untouched, but everything else was blown to pieces. It was filthy."

Bill's auto maintenance unit settled in Niigata, just south of Manila. "We set up a base there and serviced automobiles," he said. The 379th Ordnance Medium Auto Maintenance Company remained in the Philippines until after the Peace Accord was signed in mid-September.

Following the surrender, Bill made it into Japan. "We went up in LSM's (Landing Ship, Mediums)," he said. The men could still see the Battleship *Missouri* in the harbor, where the peace treaty had been signed. They also got a close look at the menace of a storm. "We were in Yokohama Harbor during the typhoon," he said. They rode out the storm in the harbor.

Bill got on Japanese soil and saw a few sights. Although he didn't get to Hiroshima or Nagasaki, he did see some of the cities that had been firebombed.

Devastated downtown Manila, 1945.

While he was in the Pacific, Bill received some good news from home. "I was overseas when my boy (William Carey) was born," he said. "About two weeks after he was born, I got word from the Red Cross that I had a son. I couldn't get any mail because I was on the move."

On one occasion, Bill was actually on the same ship for a day as his younger brother Hugh, who was in the Navy. Neither of them knew it and they never saw each other. They learned about being on the same ship only after coming home from the war.

TRIP HOME

On November 22, 1945, Bill departed from Japan for the United States. He was the last of his original cadre of 14 men to leave the Philippines. He boarded a Navy Headquarters ship and headed home. Stopping in Hawaii, he rode the rest of the way to San Diego, California on an escort aircraft carrier.

Bill in Japan.

He reported to Camp Atterbury in central Indiana and got home just before Christmas, 1945. Helen had already returned to live with her folks in Indiana after Bill had gone overseas again.

Bill was finally discharged on March 22nd, 1946 and officially became a Major the next day. He remained active in the Army Reserve through 1952.

During his active duty in the Army, he served for almost five years; over two years of which was on foreign soil in three different combat theatres. He had earned the following medals: Philippines Liberation Medal, American Campaign Service Medal, American Defense Service Medal, European African Middle East Service Medal, Asiatic Pacific Service Medal and the Victory Medal.

"I felt fortunate that most of my duties were combat-free," he said as he reflected upon his years of service. "It was miserable in India. We had malaria and all kinds of problems. But still, it was safe."

He benefitted from his Army service. It fostered a high sense of responsibility in Bill, which he used the rest of his life. And, equally important, he learned to gain the respect of many of his men.

Bill and Helen, 1996.

AFTER THE WAR

Before leaving for military service, Bill had worked six weeks for the Pennsylvania railroad in Wilmington, Delaware in 1941. He returned to work with the railroad from 1946–52.

During those years, he moved his family to Ohio, New York, Pennsylvania, and Warsaw, Indiana. He worked his way up to supervisor of track in the mountains of Pennsylvania. "I enjoyed most of it," he said. Although he was on the staff, he had to do physical work at times. "They expected you to wear a suit coat and tie regardless of what the job was," he said. "Almost every day, I had some damage to my clothing." Bill got called out on every accident to examine the track to see what happened.

The job was hard on his growing family, which soon included three more sons: Robert Wayne (1948), James David (1951), and Jerry Lee (61). He had to move his family frequently and with very little notice — sometimes only a day or half a day, and he wrestled with some of the ethics in protecting the railroad.

In 1952, he left the railroad and returned to his childhood work of farming. He farmed 450 acres in Westfield, Indiana (north of Indianapolis) owned by his father-in-law (Lowell Carey) or rented out. He bought adjoining land and raised hogs, beef cattle, and grain (wheat, oaks, corn) and hay.

He raised his boys on the farm and they all worked together. He made sure they became involved in church camp, scout camp, and 4-H camp. And three of his four sons became Eagle Scouts. The other one was only one merit short of the goal.

Bill made a woodshop in the barn and dried wood and made furniture pieces: tables, entertainment center, end table, etc.

He stopped farming in 1988 when he was in his early 70s. His farm of 227 acres is still owned by his family today and farmed by his youngest son, Jerry Lee.

Bill maintained a strong Christian faith all his life. He and his family were active members at Sheridan Christian Church, where he served as Elder and Chairman of

The family clan.

the Board. He was also active in the Lions Club in Westfield in his retirement.

In 2006, Bill and Helen moved to Hoosier Village Retirement Center. Helen died on January 22, 2015. They had enjoyed 71 years of married life together.

Bill died on February 8, 2018. He was 99 years old. He lived a long and full life. He served his country and saw the world. And, most importantly, he survived the war and returned to his native Indiana soil and the family he treasured for a lifetime.

Bill McColgin, 2016, holding his wartime diary.

This chapter is based on a recorded audio interview done by Douglass Clanin, Editor at the Indiana Historical Society, on September 27, 1994 and from personal visits that the author made with Mr. McColgin.

PACIFIC THEATER

Combat in the Pacific with the Marines
Veteran Served for 27 Years, Two Wars and One Missile Crisis

Most people in the Armed Forces serve for one or two terms of enlistment and then return to civilian life. Not Robert Anderson! The Indianapolis native served in the Marine Corps for over 27 years — a span which included two wars.

Bob was born in Indianapolis on March 29, 1919. Following his graduation from Shortridge High School in 1937, he enrolled at Purdue University and pursued a degree in engineering and economics. He graduated in June of 1941 with a Bachelor's Degree in Economics.

Initially, Bob wasn't much interested in the military. "I didn't really like the military then," he recalled.

But he didn't have much choice in being exposed to it. Reserve Officer Training Corps (ROTC) was a requirement for all male college students during their freshman and sophomore years. While in ROTC Bob received artillery training.

Eventually Bob decided to enlist in the Marine Corps. He reported to the Marine Officer Candidate School at Quantico, Virginia in October of 1941 — just a few months before Japan bombed Pearl Harbor. Because of his artillery experience in ROTC at Purdue University he was selected for Field Artillery Training with the Marines.

At the completion of his training he traveled across the country and reported to the 2nd Battalion, 10th Marine Regiment, an artillery unit located at San Diego, California. "They used the 75 mm M1 Pack Howitzers," said Bob. "You could tear them down, break them up and carry them across streams and rivers or put them into trucks." He was assigned to be the Executive Officer of E battery, which consisted of 6 pack howitzers and the 141 men who were assigned to fire them.

The Pack Howitzers, which could also be transported by animals, were considered to be short-range weapons in the Marine Corps arsenal. Fired projectiles had an effective range of 7,200 yards.

COMBAT DUTY DURING WORLD WAR 2

In October of 1942, the 10th Regiment set out for New Zealand along with elements of the 2nd Marine Division, which included the 2nd, 6th, 8th and 10th Regiments. They all participated in combat training from November of 1942 — January of 1943. "That was a wonderful country," remembered Bob. "The people, the greenery, the mountains ... and it was a good training area." The training was designed to prepare them for combat on the Island of Guadalcanal.

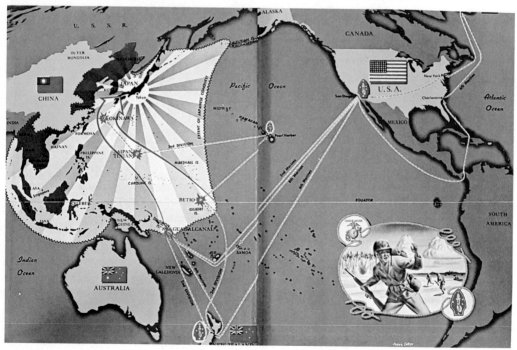

GUADALCANAL

Arriving in January of 1943, Bob and the Marines of the 2nd Division came into the tail end of the battle for Guadalcanal. The landing had initially begun in August of 1942 as one of the Allies first major offensives in the Pacific. By early 1943 the Japanese had been mostly defeated, and only pockets of resistance remained. At the end of February, the remaining Japanese troops withdrew from the island.

Training on 75mm on New Zealand.

"It wasn't too bad at all," recalled Bob of his battalion's initial combat experience. "The Japanese didn't have too much artillery, so we didn't have many bad days. We supported the 6th Marine Regiment."

Although they avoided the worst of combat with Japanese forces, many of the men were not

able to avoid the other enemy on the island — mosquitoes! Malaria was rampant on the island. "Those men that were stricken the worst were sent home," said Bob. Others, including Bob, suffered with the disease but recovered on Guadalcanal.

With Guadalcanal safely in Allied control, Bob's regiment returned to New Zealand for more combat training. The malarial attacks inside many of their bodies went with them. Recalled Bob, "I started shaking so badly during the Easter Mass that they sent me to Wellington (site of Division Headquarters) for medical treatment."

TARAWA

The invasion of Tarawa was 2nd Marine Division's next combat objective. The Marine forces conducted their amphibious landing on November 20th, 1943. Initially, things were going poorly enough in the invasion that some artillery units were called forward to augment the infantry. Bob's unit was put on notice that they might be used for infantry as well. But that changed when they received orders to move to a different location all together. "We were ordered to go to the next Atol (Bairiki) and fire across the water on to (Betio) Tarawa," he said. "We fired for only

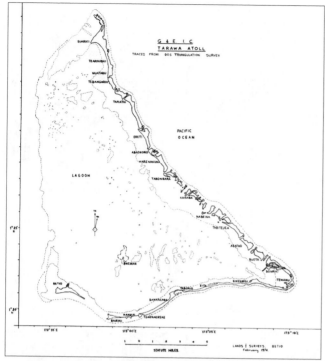

Pack Howitzer.

half a day because the fighting on Tarawa was so close you couldn't shoot without hitting your own men. So we stopped that." Fortunately, Japanese forces weren't on that atoll as the 2nd Battalion, 6th Marine Regiment had driven them off earlier. So, Bob and his unit were not fired upon.

The fight for Tarawa lasted four brutal days. At the end, the Allies took control of the island, but at a sharp cost of 3,166 causalities, of which 978 were deaths.

Following the victory at Tarawa the 2nd Division returned to Hawaii and settled at "Camp Tarawa" on the northern part of the big island. There they rested, replenished their equipment and supplies, and retrained from January — May of 1944.

SAIPAN

The island of Saipan, in the Northern Marianas, was the 2nd Division's next combat objective. They left Hawaii on May 24, 1944 and arrived at Saipan for the invasion on June 15th.

"It was a little rough," recalled Bob of the assault, "because I was Liaison Officer with the 8th Marines; and they made the assault."

As the Liaison Officer it was Bob's duty to remain with the Regimental Commander at all times. "The Liaison Officer kept track of the Forward Observers which were assigned to the infantry companies to direct fire, and advised the Regimental Commander as to how to best use his artillery assets," he explained.

The battle on Saipan was fierce! "We took quite a beating over there," he recalled. "The Japs defended Saipan at the beach, as opposed to Okinawa when they waited until forces came inland and then fired at them from the caves. There was lots of artillery on Saipan. They had the high ground and were firing down upon us. Fortunately, they didn't have too many artillery guns. Once we got over the mountains it was all downhill from there, and the infantry began moving real well."

Combat on Saipan.

Saipan came under Allied control on July 9th, following three weeks of heavy combat. Out of the 71,000 troops from the 2nd and 4th Marine Divisions and the 27th Army, 2,949 were killed in action and another 10,464 were wounded.

TINIAN

The island of Tinian was close to Saipan and was the next objective for the 2nd Marine Division. Bob recalled making the amphibious landing on that island in a Landing Craft Vehicle and Personnel (LCVP), specially designed vehicles that could ride through the water and up to the shore. They were also known as Higgins' Boats.

LCVP.

The primary focus of the battle of Tinian was securing the airfield from which the American B-29 Super Fortresses would be able to reach mainland Japan. It became the busiest airfield in the war from that point forward. The fighting on Tinian was fortunately light — the battle was over in less than a week - and the men soon found themselves with an earned period of 30 days leave from which to go home for a visit.

Bob flew home close to Christmas of 1944 and enjoyed a 30-day reunion with his family.

OKINAWA

At the end of his leave, Bob returned to the Pacific theater for more combat operations. The next objective was the island of Okinawa, where Bob would spend the next seven months of duty.

Okinawa was located 340 miles from mainland Japan and was the desired real estate for a major build-up of Allied forces in preparation for the planned invasion of Japan. But securing that island took a massive effort. The campaign was the largest amphibious landing in the Pacific. It took 82 days (April 1st–June 22nd, 1945) to secure the island.

The whole 2nd Division went in for the amphibious landing. But Bob's regiment pulled back and went around to the other side of the island to make a feint landing there. The intent was to cause a diversion and drive some of the Japanese attention away from the main landing. Following the feint tactic, Bob's regiment landed a few days later on Okinawa at the main invasion point. They stayed on the island for the rest of the campaign and prepared for the invasion of mainland Japan.

While on Okinawa, Bob was reunited with E Battery and served as their Artillery Officer. "I was awfully fortunate to stay with the 2nd Battalion, 10th Marines when I joined it in San Diego all the way through the time on Okinawa," he said. "That didn't happen with too many people (officers)."

It was while Bob was on Okinawa that the Japanese surrendered and the war ended. "Rumors of the war's end were all over during that time," he said. "You didn't know which ones to believe and not believe."

Looking back on all the combat he experienced, Bob gave high praise to the Marine Reserve Forces. "I was a regular Marine, not a reserve," he explained. "Most all of the fighting was done by reserve forces. They did a wonderful job! You couldn't tell the difference (between the reserve and active forces)."

After over 27 months of combat duty, Bob finally returned back to the U.S. in the fall of 1945. His career with the Marines, however, was far from over. In fact, he had just begun a stretch of military service that would last for another 23 years.

OTHER POSITIONS/UNITS

Bob's other jobs during his long Marine Corps career included the following:

- A short stint of recruiting duty in Fargo, ND for a few months, but he didn't care much for it.

- Instructor for the Naval ROTC at the University of Kansas for two years. "That was good duty," he recalled. "The Navy always treated me just wonderful."

- Student at the Army's Advanced Artillery School in Ft. Sill, Oklahoma for nine months. "There were 7 Marines and 250 Army Officers," he recalled. "Tremendous sized classroom. We (Marine Corps Officers) were outnumbered. It was an excellent school."

- Instructor at Marine Corps Officer Candidate School in Quantico, Virginia for 1 year. He took over an artillery battery used to demonstrate artillery tactics to the Marine Corps Officer Candidates.

- Commanding Officer of 2nd Battalion, 10th Marines at Camp LeJeune, North Carolina from 1949-1951. "That was interesting because that was the outfit I had joined as a 2nd Lieutenant and then later took command of it," he said. "It was an awful period because of the shrinkage of the reserves."

Artillery crew in Korea.

- Commanding Officer of the 1st Battalion, 11th Marines (artillery) in Korea from 1951-53. "We weren't doing much fighting at that point," he recalled. "We were supporting the 8th Marines, and they were blocking the entrance from North Korea to South Korea into Seoul."

- Aide to Vice-Chief of Naval Operations in 1954. "It was the same year they dedicated the Marine Corps Memorial in Washington D.C.," Bob remembered.

- Gunnery Department on a Navy Cruiser. "I sailed with the Navy when I was with the Commander Cruiser Force Atlantic Fleet," said Bob. "I had 2 six month tours on the Navy vessels on the cruiser division staff."

- Planning Officer, Fleet Marine Force in Norfolk, Virginia.

- Advisor on the *USS Canberra* in the ship's gunnery department. He served during the Naval blockade of Cuba with the Cuban Missile Crisis in October, 1962. "Russia was bringing over missiles for Cuba," explained Bob. "As

USS Canberra.

a ship in the task force we blockaded the island around Cuba and shadowed the Russian Missile Force." The blockade and further international negotiations helped deter the Russians from installing the missiles on Cuba. "At the same time as this was going on, I received a transfer to the Fleet Marine Force Atlantic's

Planning Station under General Lucky" recalled Bob. "Their mission was to support the US troops on Cuba and Guantanamo Bay. So I had experience both with the Navy and the Marine Corps during this blockade effort."

- Marine Corps Attache' for the U.S. State Department in Bogota, Columbia, 1963-66. The attaché collected intelligence information for the Department of Defense and helped maintain good communications with the host country and the United States military.

- Commanding Officer, 1st Battalion, 11th Marine Regiment, 1st Marine Division in Camp Pendleton, California.

RETIREMENT

Bob retired from the Marine Corps as a full Colonel in 1968, having amassed 27 years of military service. "I had wonderful duty," he said, looking back. "If I had been able to pick out my duty stations I wouldn't have been able to do a better job picking. And the Navy treated me the best."

Following his retirement from the Marine Corps, Bob became a bank branch manager with Indiana National Bank, where he worked from 1968–1980. He retired in 1980.

WIFE/FAMILY

Bob met his wife, Virginia Mennel in high school and dated her while they were in college. She was enrolled at Butler University and he was a student at Purdue University. They married on February 21,

Anderson and his wife, Virginia, at the MC Ball.

1942, after he was commissioned in the Marine Corps. The couple remained married for 60 years, until her death in 2001.

Their marriage was blessed with a daughter, Carole Bland, in 1945. The family eventually expanded to include one granddaughter, Michele, and three great-grandchildren.

Following his retirement in 1980, Bob spent more time with his wife. In her later years she developed leg problems. "The last 6-7 years I was pushing her in the wheel chair," he said. "She was a great gal. She stayed with me for two wars and moved all around with me. Still today when I have a decision or problem I ask myself what would Virginia have done?"

Robert Anderson died at the age of 97 on October 8th, 2016. He was buried in Crown Hill Cemetery in Indianapolis.

Finding His Way Through the Pacific

Navy Navigator Turned Preacher
Has Traveled Around the World

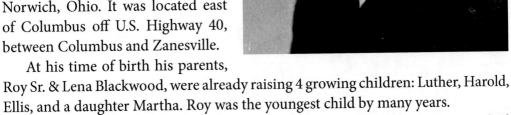

Joining the Navy often meant experiencing the adventure of traveling to new places. That was true for Roy Blackwood. World War II introduced him to many exciting new locations. And in every place he found God beside him.

Later in life he introduced his family to the adventure of international travel by taking them on a year-long trip around the world.

BEGINNINGS

Roy Blackwood was born on February 7th, 1925 on a farm in Norwich, Ohio. It was located east of Columbus off U.S. Highway 40, between Columbus and Zanesville.

At his time of birth his parents, Roy Sr. & Lena Blackwood, were already raising 4 growing children: Luther, Harold, Ellis, and a daughter Martha. Roy was the youngest child by many years.

Eldest brother Luther once said to the youngest Blackwood, "Roy, we had cleared out of the baby business, and then you were born."

More often than not, young Roy found himself getting "in the way" of his family as they frantically performed their farm tasks. "Get out of my way!" was an all too often refrain when Roy was seeking the attention from his siblings.

Blackwood family farm near Norwich, Ohio.

Roy's mother, Lena died when he was just 3 years old. Roy's father, a veterinarian who owned 2 farms, was in no position to take responsibility for the care of his youngest son.

Roy's father called his sister, May Blackwood, who was teaching school in New Castle, Pennsylvania. He asked her to come back to Ohio and help take care of Roy Jr. Ms. May was a single woman who, at the time, had been teaching in the public school and in a Reformed Presbyterian Church in New Castle. She accepted her new caretaking role.

Initially Roy and his Aunty May lived in the Blackwood Home on 106 East Main Street in New Concord, Ohio where Roy Sr. and May's mother (Roy Jr.'s grandmother) was living. The home was owned by Roy Sr. Blackwood and his brothers. It provided older family members with a good place to stay when needed. As Roy explained, long before there were social services offered by the federal government, extended families took it upon themselves to provide their own form of security for older family members in need. Roy Jr. benefitted greatly from that provision.

The Blackwood brothers came into town from their farms each weekend, bringing food for the family members living with Grandma Blackwood. They went to church together and had dinner together there every Sunday.

Roy and his Aunty May Blackwood.

"We watched the cars go by on Highway 40 and visited on the porch," said Roy Jr. with nostalgia. "It was just good times."

Following his Grandma's death and about the time Roy was heading off to high school, Aunty May bought a home of her own at the west end of High Street in New Concord. She and Roy moved into it.

Aunty May and Roy went to Florida during the winter months. Her doctor had suggested the warmer climate for her health. Aunty May homeschooled Roy during those months they spent in Florida. "She taught me how to study," Roy said. She had learned that fishing is what Roy enjoyed most, so she motivated him for studying by saying that they would go fish when his lessons were done.

Aunty May taught more than school subjects. She taught her nephew to nurture his faith life as well. "She recognized my loneliness and my penchant for getting 'in the way' and taught me to memorize Scripture, and thus get 'in the way of God,'" said Roy. "Fifteen years later those verses were the means of my salvation," he added. Looking back, Roy could see that God was already preparing him for a lifetime call into the pastoral ministry.

During the winter of 1938, Roy, age 13, caught a prize fish on a fishing boat off the coast of Palm Beach. The fish was a giant 212-pound hammerhead shark. The shark measured over 8 feet in length and dwarfed the boy standing next to it when it came time to capture the Kodak moment. His photo next to the shark along with its dimensions appeared in the local newspaper.

Roy's love for water and fishing eventually played a role in determining which branch of service he would select when war came to the United States.

April 13, 1938
Two wild ducks are staying at City Park Lake, in contrast to tame ducks already there. Roy Blackwood Jr., 13, New Concord, is pictured in the Jefferson today holding up a 212-pound hammerhead shark he caught off the coast of Miami. He was visiting Florida with his aunt, Miss May Blackwood, New Concord.

ROY CHOOSES THE NAVY

Roy attended New Concord High School in New Concord, Ohio through his junior year. The breakout of a world war caused him to skip his final year of high school and enter college early.

He recalled of that time, "The night of Pearl Harbor (December 7th, 1941) I was in the Prince of Peace State Speaking Contest being held in a large church in Zanesville, Ohio," explained Roy. "I was reciting the speech 'Peace in Flames' by Russell Holloway, and I won the state contest that night. We came back to the Blackwood home and the neighbors converged on us. 'Have you heard what happened today?' 'What do you mean?' Then they told us about Pearl Harbor, which had taken place at the very time I was speaking my oration." Roy's oration ironically proclaimed a peace that had just been taken away by the hands of the Japanese.

Roy tried to get into the Navy right away. "No doubt, I wanted the Navy," he said. "It was my love of ships and fishing on the open water!"

He met resistance, however, when he tried to enlist at the recruiters' office. "They laughed at me and said I was too young and to come back when I was older," he remembered.

Undeterred, Roy asked them what he would have to do in order to get into the Navy and to fly planes. Although he loved the water, he sought the vantage of the sky for his role in the war. The recruiter told him he needed to be older and needed to get some College-level math.

Roy then talked with his high school speech coach to see if there was any way he could go directly to college without graduating from high school. His coach, who also happened to be the local college registrar, helped Roy enroll at Muskingum College, which was located in his hometown of New Concord. Motivated to join the Navy as quickly as possible, Roy skipped his senior year of high school and enrolled at Muskingum College in the fall of 1942.

In the meantime, a neighborhood friend of Roy's from New Concord had joined the Marines right after the attack on Pearl Harbor and had learned to fly a plane. His friend's name was John Glenn, the man who would one day become a famous astronaut. "I played some ball with John, who was ahead of me by a few years," said Roy.

Wanting to follow John's example, Roy devoted himself to his studies and kept his focus on getting into the Navy.

ENLISTMENT AND TRAINING

Following his year at Muskingum College, Roy entered the Navy. For the next 18 months his life consisted of military training, flight schools, navigation training and additional college.

His first stop was Midshipmen's school at Columbia University in New York City. The Navy had begun the Midshipmen Schools in June of 1940 to train more men to become Naval Officers as the U.S. was building up its forces in preparation for war. Roy spent 16 weeks there learning about military bearing and being an officer.

He spent the next six months at Flight Preparatory School in Florida, where he had his first experience in flying solo in an open cockpit, single engine Stearman biplane that was used extensively for training pilots during World War II. "I loved to fly!" he exclaimed. "It was one of the first privileges from graduating from midshipmen's school."

Following Flight Preparatory School, Roy was sent off for more college instruction in Illinois as part of the Navy's V-12 program. While at the college he was timed running the mile and astonished his coaches by running an under four-minute mile. Some of the Navy's top brass heard about the speedy young man and had scheduled a visit to the college to see Roy run. But the day Roy was going to be timed again for his mile run in front of the Navy's top officers he received his official orders to report to an escort carrier called the *USS Petrof Bay, CVE-80* which was in port on the Southern California coast of San Diego.

Stearman biplane like the one Roy flew in training.

SERVICE ON THE USS PETROF BAY

The *USS Petrof Bay* was one of the Navy's escort carrier's in the Casablanca-class of ships. She had been commissioned in February of 1944 and was assigned to the United States Pacific Fleet.

At 512 feet in length, the ship was longer than one and a half football fields. She could travel over 19 knots and carried a complement of 860 officers and men. When the squadron of 28 planes and pilots were on board she added another 56 people, pushing her to just over 900 personnel while underway.

USS Petrof Bay.

The escort carriers in this class of ships were all named for bays in Alaska.

Roy reported to the *Petrof Bay* in the summer of 1944.

The Commanding Officer of the ship, Captain Joseph "Paddy" Kane, knew of Roy's credentials as a midshipman with navigational training. "Welcome aboard the *Petrof Bay*, Mr. Blackwood," he said as Roy boarded her for the first time. "I'm appointing you to be the navigator of the *Petrof Bay*."

While the appointment was an honor for the young man from Ohio, it also meant accepting restrictions from flying while the ship was underway. It was the Captain's orders that ship's staff were not permitted to fly while the ship was out to sea. Roy's flying was limited to the times that his ship was in port and he could get to a Navy airfield.

Ensign Roy Blackwood.

But the restriction also opened up opportunities for Roy to fly more than one type of plane. "That was a great thrill," he recalled of taking to the air from various Navy air fields around the world! He took every opportunity he could to get back inside a cockpit because he had to fly a certain number of hours each quarter to keep his flight status and pay.

As the ship's navigator Roy was responsible for knowing and charting his ship's location on the sea at all times. He was involved in planning the course and keeping the ship's commanding officer informed on the progress of the journey. He also maintained the navigational equipment as well as the charts and publications. "The Captain was impressed with the accuracy of my work," said Roy.

Ship navigator using a sextant.

"The *USS Petrof Bay* didn't have any of the new electronic gadgets for navigating in those days," recalled Roy. "I had to calculate our position wherever we were in God's world by (1) identifying the three stars I was using for that fix (usually the sun or moon was one of them), (2) measuring the exact angle between us and each star (with a sextant), and (3) noting the precise time. Where these three 'Lines of Position' crossed each other on our chart was our exact location. With that information, we could place the ship anywhere in the Pacific Ocean within a half mile."

His work as a navigator reminded Roy of God. "My aunt had taught me to memorize Scripture by whole chapters," said Roy. "The 19th Psalm proved to be crucial to me while on the aircraft carrier:

> *"The heavens declare the glory of God; and the firmament showeth His handiwork. Day unto day uttereth speech, and night unto night showeth knowledge. There is no speech nor language where their voice is not heard. Their line is gone out through all the earth and their words to the end of the world.*   (Psalm 19:1-4, KJV)

"Those words came to have particular meaning for me on board the Petrof Bay as navigator," he said.

Those words also reminded Roy that Japanese enemies, looking at the same firmament of God, could also navigate their courses. "And I couldn't do anything about that," he said.

Roy's appointment as navigator also made him a department head on the ship with supervision over others. It was quite a learning opportunity for the young Naval Officer. "Being commander in the Navigation Department gave me new responsibility," he said. "I was able to learn how to be head of a division of men. One of the great problems was that many of the men in the division were old enough to be my father. It was very hard for those men to accept me as their commander. But

Petrof Bay with camo paint.

we learned to get along and they learned to respect me. I learned to respect them, too."

The crew of the *USS Petrof Bay* was sent to the Pacific theater of war where they were involved in these combat operations:

Invasion of Peleliu (Sept. 15–29, 1944)
Battle for Leyte Gulf (Oct. 24–28, 1944)
Invasion of Iwo Jima (15 Feb.–7 March, 1945)
Invasion of Okinawa (April–May 1945)

While supporting the invasion of Okinawa the *Petrof Bay* came under attack by Japanese Kamikazes. Roy got a firsthand look at how the ship avoided the path of the suicide pilots' diving planes. "I remember when we were under attack from the *Kamikaze* (Divine Wind) suicide pilots flying explosive-filled airplanes to sink our ship," recalled Roy. "Our captain would take over the wheel and the throttle, and we would see the Kamikaze plane crash just to our port, or to our starboard side, or overshoot us. He showed me how to throw the ship into reverse at full speed or turn to starboard or port, causing the Kamikaze to miss the ship. The amazing thing was that we were one of the only carriers that was never hit. I look back now and see God's Providence over the last 90 years, and it adds new meaning to the verses of Psalm 19 that I had memorized as a boy."

The ship was on its way to Pearl Harbor in August of 1945 when news of Japan's surrender reached the crew.

Years later, on a trip around the world, Roy stopped at Pearl Harbor to show his family the sunken ships. "I remember seeing the bubbles still coming up from the sunken ships," recalled a somber Roy. "I wondered about the men still trapped there."

Following the surrender of the Japanese the *Petrof Bay* was used to bring veterans back home in what the men referred to as 'magic carpet trips'. Officially called "Operation Magic Carpet," the War Shipping Administration was given the responsibility for bringing military personnel home from the European and Pacific Theaters. All types of ships were used, including Navy vessels.

From October 1945–February of 1946 the *Petrof Bay* kept busy shuttling troops back to the U.S.

"I enjoyed seeing the men getting back on their way home," said Roy.

The *Petrof Bay* reached the end of her official active service with the Navy in February of 1946. Recalled Roy, "The last time we came back through the Panama Canal we went clear up (the eastern seaboard) to where the ship was put out of commission (in Boston Harbor). The Captain put me in charge of a lot of that. That was a sad experience putting that ship out of commission after all we had gone through on her."

For her service during World War II the *USS Petrof Bay* received a Presidential Unit Citation along with five battle stars.

MEMORIES OF HIS SERVICE

Of all his experiences in the Navy, the responsibility of serving was what Roy remembered most.

"I enjoyed it, but the responsibility was very great. I grew up fast. I was in charge of the Navigation Division. I felt responsibility for them. I wanted them to respect me, and they did."

Roy's other recollections included:

"I don't remember much about the different ports. I was too busy as the navigator to get the information for coming into and out of each port. When we were underway, I was busy with keeping track of where we were."

"The Captain taught me how to drive that ship in the way it had to be driven."

"I saw many planes go down and into the ocean."

"We were shot at many times."

"I was frightened at times but too busy to think about it."

Roy and Margie on a motorcycle in Scotland, 1950.

DISCHARGE

During his almost 4 years of service in the Navy, Roy was awarded the American Theatre Medal, the Asiatic-Pacific Theatre Medal, and the Victory Medal for World War II. Roy was officially and honorably discharged from military service at the end of August of 1946.

COLLEGE AND MARGIE

When Roy returned home to Ohio to begin the next chapter of his life he decided to resume his college education. His great-grandfather had helped build Geneva College in Beaver Falls, Pennsylvania. "I knew I would attend there," he said. He enrolled and began his studies there.

Geneva College gave Roy not only a fine education; it gave him the opportunity to meet his future wife, Margie.

"That first evening at the dining room four of us veterans were eating and there was this beautiful dark haired girl who went to the piano and began playing the songs we liked. 'Who is that', I asked? 'That's Margaret Margie Graham', someone said. She was a daughter of a pastor. We all sought her attention, and I ended up with her. I began dating her."

Roy graduated from Geneva College in the spring of 1948 and immediately set his sights on another degree. He had spent 4 years serving his nation in the Navy. Roy now wanted to spend the rest of his life serving the Lord in pastoral ministry. He enrolled at the Reformed Presbyterian Theological Seminary in Pittsburgh, Pennsylvania while Margie began teaching at a nearby elementary school. He graduated from seminary in May of 1951.

MARRIAGE, MORE EDUCATION & FAMILY

Margie's father, also a pastor, married Roy and Margie at his church in Ambridge, Pennsylvania on November 20th, 1948 while Roy was studying at the seminary.

Shortly after graduating from seminary a classmate friend of Roy's and his wife went to Scotland to begin working on a doctorate degree. Roy and Margie decided to follow them there. Roy enrolled in the doctoral program of Theology at the University of Edinburgh.

While they were living in Scotland Margie became pregnant and gave birth to a son William and later a daughter Beth.

The Blackwood family returned to the United States in the early 1950s. Roy began serving a Reformed Presbyterian Church in Bloomington, Indiana.

He and Margie had a third child, Bob. (Roy and Margie lost an infant in childbirth after Beth; a death that still saddens Roy to this day.)

Roy and family during a trip to Scotland.

Roy and his family returned to the University of Edinburgh in the early '60s so that Roy could complete his doctorate degree in Theology. He graduated in 1963.

MINISTRY CAREER

The family then came back to Indiana where Roy resumed his ministry as a pastor. Roy had a long and fulfilling career as a pastor, church planter, teacher and mentor in the Reformed Presbyterian Church. He served as pastor of churches in several Indiana cities including: Bloomington, Columbus, Lafayette and Indianapolis. God also used Roy to start new Reformed Presbyterian congregations.

Roy was also active in building influential relationships with community and state leaders. He knew and gave counsel to state legislators and governors. He was even given the honor of being named an honorary Secretary of State by Ed Simcox in 1982.

Roy, retirement years.

FAMILY HIGHLIGHT

While raising their family, Roy and Margie had considered two prevalent approaches to rearing children. One approach was to hold the kids close at home and protect them from the dangers and evil of the world. The opposite approach was to let the kids go as soon as they were independent. Roy and Margie decided on an approach that was somewhere in the middle. And they chose an around the world family trip to implement that approach. "The purpose of the trip was to take them out and show them the world and let them know that wherever they were, Jesus was with them," said Roy.

In 1974 Roy and Margie took them around the globe to demonstrate that Biblical truth. Their son, Bill had already begun college, and the other two were about to do the same. The family drove out east on Highway 40 and then flew to Germany. Roy bought a Volkswagen camper in Germany. He used it to drive his family eastward across Europe and Asia. When they arrived in Japan he shipped the Volkswagen to California. The family then flew to California and returned to Indiana along Highway 40, completing their circumnavigation of the world. It was the trip of a lifetime!

Blackwood extended family.

RECENT YEARS

Roy's son, Bill, and his wife live in Scotland, as do Roy's daughter, Beth and her husband. The youngest, Bob, and his family live in Fort Wayne, Indiana.

On November 16th, 2011 Roy's beloved wife, Margie died. They had been life partners and soul mates in marriage for over 63 years.

Today, at the age of 93, Roy lives at a Hoosier Village Retirement Center in Zionsville and enjoys making new friends, sharing his faith and continuing his own study of the Scriptures. He still attends worship services at the 2nd Reformed Presbyterian Church in Indianapolis. And he enjoys spending time with his children, grandchildren and great-grandchildren.

Although he doesn't get to travel much anymore, he is anxiously awaiting the trip in the future that will surpass his family excursion around the world. And that is the trip to Heaven won for him through Jesus Christ!

CARROLL BOTTOM
SIGNAL MAN , *USS FRANKLIN, USS LEXINGTON*

1942-1947
"BIG BEN"
THE SHIP THAT
WOULDN'T DIE

Signaling on the High Seas

Indianapolis Veteran Served on Two Carriers in the South Pacific

Communication between ships out at sea has always been important. During World War II, that communication was vital. And much of it happened through the work of Navy signalmen who stood on a special bridge and used signal lights and flags to send out their messages to other nearby ships.

Carroll Bottom of Indianapolis was one of those signalmen. He had the distinction of serving on two Navy Aircraft Carriers during the tumultuous years of combat in the South Pacific.

Born October 21, 1925 in Mackville, Kentucky, he was the only child of his parents Ray and Una Bottom. Following his graduation from Mackville High School in 1943, and with the war in full swing, he enlisted in the Navy.

He completed his boot camp at Great Lakes Naval Training Center in December and then was sent to signal school at the University of Chicago, graduating from there in March of 1944.

Carroll was then transported to the west coast where he jumped on a troop transport and headed for Hawaii. He spent a month at Ford Island before being assigned as a signalman on the aircraft carrier USS Franklin (CVS 13), nicknamed 'Big Ben'.

USS Franklin, 1944.

The ship, named for founding father Benjamin Franklin, was in the Essex class of carriers. It was 872 feet long, had a beam of 147 feet and could reach speeds up to 33 knots. It carried a crew of 3,448 and had room for up to 100 aircraft.

The *Franklin,* which had been commissioned just a few months earlier, headed to the North Pacific in June of 1944. For the next five months the Franklin provided critical combat support for operations in the Bonin and Mariana Islands, Peleliu, and Leyte.

Carroll's job as signalman involved sending and receiving visual messages from other ships in the area using signal lamps, flag semaphores, and flag hoists.

"I liked it — sitting in the nest and sending messages to all those ships," said Carroll. "It was a lot of responsibility. You knew you were important."

Some of that communication was also sent to war planes coming back from their missions. Carroll recalled, "When the planes came back from bombing runs the Captain of the ship would tell the signal bridge to give them a 'C' (Charlie) to land. (The "C" was transmitted via the use of the signal light.) The pilot then dipped his wings to register receipt of the message."

There were some scary moments in watching the planes land. "When the planes don't come in right, they crash onto the ship's flight deck," said Carroll. "It appears like they are coming right at you."

It wasn't just flags and lights that Carroll raised. On one occasion he participated in a burial detail for sailors killed in action. It involved raising the planks that the dead bodies were resting on and releasing the sailors into the ocean for final burial.

Fortunately, life wasn't always about combat. During days that there were no combat operations, Carroll recalled enjoying some of the 'creature comforts' of life on board ship. "It was a big ship," he said. "I always had a place to sleep and something to eat. We even made our own ice cream."

Life out at sea on the largest of Navy ships offered more than food and sleep, it offered some spectacular views. "It was beautiful and relaxing to watch the calm seas at night," recalled Carroll. "It provided an opportunity to reflect and think of loved ones back home."

It also provided an opportunity to appreciate the circumference of the earth. "It was 11 miles to the horizon," Carroll remembered. "It was neat to see a ship approaching and only see the top of the mast at first."

But danger was never far away. Calm gave way to fear, chaos and death when the *Franklin* came under a Japanese air attack in October of 1944. Three Japanese bombers attacked the ship off Leyte, killing 56 and wounding 60. The *Franklin* became the most heavily damaged Navy Carrier to survive combat. Fortunately Carroll Bottom survived the carnage.

Damaged *USS Franklin*.

USS Lexington CV 16.

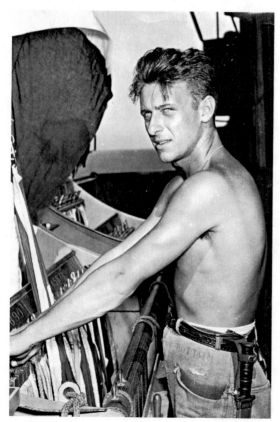

Carroll setting up flag hoist on *USS Lexington*.

Instead of returning with the *Franklin* to the United States for repairs, Carroll arranged to stay in the theater of combat and was transferred to the *USS Lexington,* another aircraft carrier that was in Ulithi.

The *Lexington,* nicknamed the "Blue Ghost," was named for another carrier with that name that had been lost in the Battle of the Coral Sea earlier in the war.

Although he was on a different ship, Carroll soon experienced a similar fate that he had on the *Franklin.* In early November of 1944, shortly after the Battle of Leyte Gulf, the ship came under attack by Japanese kamikazes. A Japanese plane crashed into the ship's superstructure. Once again, Carroll was spared injury. But others were not so lucky. "I saw a bomb flash that melted the binoculars to a signalman's chest," Carroll recalled. "About 75 sailors died."

The surviving carrier went on to provide fire support for the Marines invading Iwo Jima in mid-February of 1945.

By mid-summer, the carrier was participating in the final barrage of air strikes against mainland Japan, just prior to her surrender on August 15th. Although at the time the carrier was 40-50 miles out to sea from mainland Japan, Carroll recalled hearing the explosion from the atomic bomb over Nagasaki. The Captain of the Lexington announced through the ship's sound system, "The noise you just heard was the atomic bomb exploding over Nagasaki." Expressing his reaction to the news Carroll said, "I thought it (the bomb) was great because it would help the war come to an end."

Carroll didn't get to go home immediately after the war. "The married men got to go home first, and then single sailors later," he recalled. "We weren't crazy about that."

After Japan's surrender, the Lexington continued to fly air patrols over Japan and drop supplies to prisoner of war camps. It remained at sea for another 60 days.

By January of 1946, Carroll had returned to the United States via the port at San Diego. He was honorably discharged in March of 1946, leaving military service with 5 campaign ribbons and 8 battle stars.

HOME AGAIN

He returned home to Kentucky and attended Bryant & Stratton Business School in Louisville for a year. He then worked for a year in the accounts payable office for an auto dealer in Mt. Washington (near Louisville) and drove a school bus.

In 1949, Carroll enrolled at the University of Louisville and began work on a marketing degree. He transferred to the University of Kentucky a year later to take advantage of lower tuition and graduated from there in 1953 with a B.S. in Commerce.

Following graduation he worked for two years in the sales department of Ford Motor Company in Louisville before taking a job with the Commercial Credit Corporation in Evansville, Indiana.

In 1956, he transferred to Fort Wayne, Indiana where he met his wife, Aileen Vodde, at a local restaurant. "When I saw that woman and she looked at me, I knew I was going to marry her," he recalled. "And that is exactly what happened. There may have even been some divine intervention there." They married on February 23, 1957

Carroll and Aileen, celebrating their 50th anniversary.

and enjoyed raising two children (Jeffrey and David) and spending 51 years together.

In 1957, Carroll transferred to the Commercial Credit Corporation office in Indianapolis. In 1962 he started selling insurance with Commonwealth Life Insurance.

Carroll took a position with Transport Life Insurance Company in 1964 and worked for 19 years with the Motor Carrier Trucker's Industry. After some bouts with cancer and open heart surgery, he retired in 1983.

In the 1970s and into retirement, Carroll enjoyed getting back on the water — not as a sailor, but as a fly fisherman. He began making his own flies and rods. "I taught myself how to do it," he said.

Carroll's custom-made flies.

Carroll was a long-time active member of Indy Fly Fishers Club and, in addition to the Central Indiana streams, fished streams in Missouri, Kentucky, Florida, Tennessee, Illinois and Minnesota.

In 2007, his beloved Aileen died from colon cancer. "I think about it every day," he said concerning a future reunion with her in heaven one day. And, with regard to his own death, he added: "I'm ready."

Carroll took to the skies in September of 2015 as a participant in the Indy Honor Flight trip to Washington, D.C. Along with 180 other veterans, he got to see the World War II memorial erected in his honor.

At the age of 92, Carroll feels good about the life he has been blessed to live. "I've lived a peaceful

Carroll and Aileen.

life and have enjoyed the fruits of my labor. I've thanked God for my life and for him dying on the cross. I pray every day. I even pray for Democrats," he added with a smile.

The one-time signalman now waits for a final signal from his God to call him home for the great reunion with his wife and his great entrance into heaven.

Carroll Bottom, September 2015.

Surviving Combat in the Philippines

Rifleman Served in Guadalcanal
and Bismark Archipelago campaigns

William (Bill) Gabonay wasn't much interested in the military or the World War raging half a continent away in 1941. He would have rather not been part of it. Nevertheless, he soon found himself as a rifleman in the Army, serving in dangerous and steamy places about as far away from Indiana as one could get.

Bill was born on May 28th, 1917 in Clinton, Indiana, a community of 7,100 located in the western edge of central Indiana, just north of Terre Haute and close to the Illinois border. The fifth of eight children, his parents were Margaret and Joseph Gabonay, first generation Americans who emigrated from the region around Bratislava, in what is now Slovakia.

He had a normal childhood consisting of school, chores, and playing with his friends.

The Gabonays' were devout churchgoers. "Every Sunday our family walked the three blocks to Sacred Heart Roman Catholic Church," he wrote in his spiral-bound unpublished memoir, *My Life*. "Hardly anyone had a car."

During his senior year at Clinton High School, Bill worked in a grocery store and a bowling alley, setting up pins and being a line referee on league bowling nights. He graduated in 1935.

Bill as a Junior in high school, 1934.

After graduation, he worked in a shoe repair shop before enlisting in the Civilian Conservation Corps (CCC) where he helped build roads in Shakamak State Park, 45 miles south of his hometown of Clinton. He enjoyed his time in the corps.

Following his service with the CCC, Bill moved to Indianapolis to look for work. During the next several years he worked half-a-dozen different jobs including making ladies stockings, crafting Venetian blinds, filling orders in a custodial business, attending a machine shop course and loading engine bell housings with International Harvester.

He felt capable of working better jobs and tried to secure one; but he found it hard to land one, as many prospective employers were concerned that at the age of 24 he would soon be drafted. It turned out that they were right.

Bill Gabonay entered military service on October 2, 1941. "What a sad day that was," he wrote in his memoir, summing up his feelings about being drafted into the Army. He was 24 years old and the first among his five brothers to be drafted. "The idea of going into combat against another human being wasn't something I really wanted to do," he wrote. "Of course, when the Army called, I had to give my time to Uncle Sam."

Despite his lack of enthusiasm and reservations Bill Gabonay, like millions of other men in the United States, accepted his responsibility to serve his country and devoted himself fully to this next chapter in his life.

Bill, center, in group shot during training.

TRAINING

Bill was sent to Camp Wolters in Texas for his basic training. Both the extreme heat and the distance from home made it hard on him. He admitted in his memoir he was "homesick, depressed and 1,000 miles from Indianapolis, with only a furlough at Christmastime to look forward to."

But alas, when Pearl Harbor was attacked on December 7th his furlough was canceled and he was not able to return home. Instead of heading north back to Indiana, Bill headed west to Fort Ord, California in early January of 1942 for additional infantry training. "Twenty-plus mile marches every Thursday without fail," he recalled of the training in his memoir.

From there, he transferred to Camp San Luis Obispo in California and was assigned to Company F of the 185th Infantry Regiment, which was mostly made up of National Guardsmen from California, Nevada and Utah. The regiment became part of the Army's 40th Division, known also as the 'Sunshine Division'.

From May—August of 1942 the Division relocated to Fort Lewis, Washington for some final training before being shipped out. Bill was among 20,000 other G.I.s getting ready to ship out for combat. "I and others wondered if we would ever get back to our homes in Indiana and elsewhere," he later wrote.

OFF TO HAWAII

In August of 1942, the ship carrying Bill Gabonay and his regimental comrades set out to sea from San Francisco. Their orders initially had them heading to the Philippine Islands. The destination changed about a week into the trip, as Bill explained in his memoir: "Nine days after leaving San Francisco, packed like sardines on the troop ship, U.S.S. Grant (a relic of World War I), plans changed, the ship diverted, and the troops off-loaded at Honolulu where they boarded another ship for the island of Maui."

Maui proved to be a long stop. "We did some training (jungle warfare)…strung barbed wire by the shores …and spent some time swimming in the ocean, which was fun and invigorating," he wrote. "We played baseball, threw horseshoes, and went sight-seeing. We were allowed to go into town on pass every 10 days."

The regiment spent 10 months on Maui before returning to Oahu for six months of ranger training and other exercises.

DEPLOYMENT TO GUADALCANAL

In January of 1944, the regiment headed for the island of Guadalcanal in the Solomon Island Chain of the South Pacific. Although under Allied control, the island still caused suffering for its 'guests'. Bill wrote in his memoir, "We landed on

Guadalcanal, a mosquito-infested, God-forsaken swamp area and malaria hole — it was miserable! We took training in the jungles and swamp lands and seemed to be wet most of the time, especially our shoes and feet."

DUTY ON NEW BRITAIN

United States landing craft and soldiers approach the beach at Arawe, New Britain, Dec. 1943.

In April, the regiment boarded a Landing Craft-Infantry (LCI) that transported them to the island of New Britain, about 900 miles away. Allied forces had first landed on New Britain in December of 1943. Another landing occurred in March of 1944, a month prior to the 185th Infantry Regiment's arrival.

"This was a sorry journey," he recalled in his memoir. "Everyone was seasick, and we stayed busy passing and emptying helmets over the side of the boat." Once off the vessel, "we had to walk several miles knee-deep in mud to get to our camp grounds underneath the coconut trees."

The Allies had already secured some of the key parts of the island by the time the 185 Regiment had arrived, but Japanese forces were still in the jungle and skirmishes still occurred. The regiment helped to keep open the important port at Cape Gloucester so that ships carrying supplies could freely enter and depart.

The regiment's stay on New Britain wasn't a pleasant experience. "At night we would always hear rats moving, coconuts falling on our tent, and land crabs as big as coconuts scratching under our bunks," he wrote.

The men passed the time taking classes and wondering where they would head next. New Britain proved to be pretty boring, except for experiencing a few minor earthquakes and rumblings.

JOURNEY TO LUZON, PHILIPPINES

By December of 1944, the regiment was on the move again. The 40th Division participated in a landing rehearsal at Lae, New Guinea. The men returned to Manus Island shortly before Christmas. "We occupied our time in dry dock,"

Bill recalled, "scraping the barnacles off the bottom of the ship. On Christmas Day, 1944, we enjoyed a holiday dinner of baloney and spam, which was a lot of 'baloney.'"

The regiment left Manus Island in early January of 1945 "in a convoy of approximately 1,000 ships of all sizes: aircraft carriers, battle ships, destroyers and many more," Bill wrote. "It was a sight to behold. How could we not win a war with this enormous show of force?"

The journey to the Philippines took the men through the Straits of Soriguo and along the western shore of Panay and Mindanao.

BATTLE ON LUZON, PHILIPPINES

Four years earlier, Japan had begun their invasion of the Pacific theater at the Philippine Islands. Now, in the late stages of World War II in the Pacific, General

Map of Philippines from 40th Division Book.

MacArthur had assigned the 8th Army (to which the 40th Division belonged) the task of liberating the Central Philippines.

Bill's ship landed at Luzon on January 9, 1945, according to his memoir. "After landing on Luzon on D-Day plus one, our ships were immediately firing on Japanese planes. One kamikaze plane landed on the top deck of one ship and exploded...I saw another go down in flames, but while walking up a road with Ray Hartman, a boy from Iowa, I suddenly found a plane spitting lead and aiming for little old me and Ray. I quickly dove into a pig pen (how nice to have one so close at hand) with Ray right behind and beside me. We both looked at each other, happy to be alive after our first encounter with real danger and death."

Bill on a Pacific island.

Bill continued, "Our company bivouacked several miles inland to regroup. The next morning, we were on our way (south) toward the Luzon Plain and Manila, with only slight opposition from rear guard troops."

Company F continued on toward the Zambales Mountains. Their initial objective was to recapture Clark Airfield where "charred planes and burned and black-looking corpses were strewn all around." Beyond the ghastly images, the men of F Company also had to be aware of the dangerous mines they couldn't easily see. As Bill recalled, "The Japanese buried many booby traps. There were mines all over. You never knew where they were. Mines of 100-550 pound aerial bombs ('Blockbusters') were buried fuse up ready to 'blow you to kingdom come.'"

Bill wrote that, "Towns in the vicinity were burned to the ground by the Japanese who were entrenched in cleverly designed caves and tunnels." It was Company F's job to flush out the hiding Japanese and capture or kill them. No easy task, as Bill remarked in his memoir, "Despite throwing everything at them (air and artillery bombardment, self-propelled guns, hand grenades, demolitions and flame throwers), some 3,000 Japanese had to be dislodged from their hunkered down positions. This was a taxing and dangerous

Baleta Pass, near Baugio, Luzon.

job, one of the most hair-raising experiences for a first or second scout, positions that put him on the point and in the spot of being the first one shot at and possibly killed. I was that 1st or 2nd scout at different times."

Not surprisingly, Company F had its share of casualties. Bill remembered, "During the Luzon campaign, our battalion and company lost many men and, of course, taking care of the wounded and getting them back to the medic stations was a harrowing and dangerous operation that fell to many of us. I helped carry three men. And one was a very heavy guy. After carrying his litter for what seemed like miles, the four of us had to go all the way back to our company's location and dig our foxholes for the night. The ground was rock solid."

When Company F finally did reach the Zambales Mountains they encountered the enemy in "a very horrifying incident" where they lost 85 of 160 men during a moonlit night attack by the Japanese. Bill recalled, "Our silhouetted figures were so obvious. The result was disastrous and fatal for some of the men. Small arms fire and mortar shells were landing all around us. Lying flat on the ground we prayed for the order to withdraw. Eventually, I and the others withdrew anyway."

The company tried again at daylight. "We went up that same mountain the next day and reclaimed it for a while, at least until we were run off with mortar and rifle fire. This withdrawal was hectic, as our quickest escape had a drop of about 20 feet, with the Japanese in pursuit. I remember my buddies and myself running like hell down the mountain. Once on level ground, we still had a 100-yard dash to negotiate along a line of trees, mostly in the open with bullets kicking at our heels. I thanked my God for getting us out of that hair-raising scrape."

In March, the 43rd Division relieved the 40th Division, which returned to Lingayen to regroup for their next offensive — the Panay Campaign.

PANAY CAMPAIGN

The Panay Campaign, fought on the Philippine Island of Panay, lasted from March 18-25, 1945. Bill wrote in his memoir, "The occupation of Panay and Negros Islands was a necessary prerequisite for the successful conclusion of the Philippines Campaign—so it was thought. Panay came first because of the fine harbor at Ililo and the protected shipping lanes of Guimaras Strait."

After disembarking from their Landing Ship, Tank (LST), Bill's platoon set foot on the island shortly after dawn and advanced 10 miles

Panay Island, Philippines, 1945.

on the first day, driving the Japanese guerrilla fighters deeper into the hills. With the help of medium-size tanks that blasted through a concrete wall, the men freed 500 civilians who had been held captive by the Japanese in a church.

The Japanese guerrillas who did survive were forced to forage for food. "Only patrol action was needed on Panay to investigate reports of Japanese foraging parties and to destroy those remnant groups attempting to descend into the lower plain for food," Bill recalled.

NEGROS CAMPAIGN

Their next objective was the island of Negros. Bill wrote, "The Negros Campaign ran from March 29 to June 15, 1945...Negros, the fourth largest of the Philippine islands, had been an important enemy air staging base during the Leyte operation.

Bill after Negros Campaign.

The island was also important for its sugar centrals, which the Japanese were using for the production of fuel alcohol."

For the next 72 days Bill and his comrades fought in a bitter struggle against the Japanese forces. Some of the fighting took place in the towns and some on the hills as the men of the 185th Regiment pushed out the enemy forces.

"We ate on the run," Bill remarked in his memoir. "...There were few hot meals...No wonder I dropped from 188 to 135 pounds in just four months."

"In the Army, hope gave us the added strength to persevere from day to day...We had to have faith that we would see our home and loved ones again..."

"Faith was a driving force for me, which I relied on a lot in combat. I had a rosary that someone gave me and which I hung around my neck, praying every night for a safe return home. I probably made promises to God during those trying times. I would like to think that I kept some of them."

Securing the 600-foot steel and concrete bridge over the Bago River was one of the most important objectives for the continued advance of the Allies. In the event of retreat, the Japanese had already wired the bridge for demolition. To secure the bridge, the Allies would have to make a surprise attack and overcome the Japanese bridge guards and electrical demolition control operators who were safely behind a pillbox on the north end of the bridge. The surprise attack mission fell to Bill's Company F of the 185 Regiment. A reinforced platoon landed at night to secure the bridge prior to the rest of the assault landing.

"How lucky can I get?" Bill remarked in his memoir. "…I was picked as one of 64 men of a reinforced platoon of Company F, 185th infantry, whose job it was to secure a five-span bridge over the Bago River."

"Moving inland, we observed nine Japanese driving carabao carts along the highway from the town toward the bridge. To avoid disclosing our presence by firing at the party, we raced silently for 2-1/2 miles parallel to the highway and reached the bridge first. I was lugging a bazooka, rifle and pack, with my 44-year old ammunition carrier behind me. Had the platoon opened fire before reaching the objective, the bridge guards would have been forewarned, the element of surprise lost, and the mission would have failed."

"Upon reaching the bank of the river, the platoon opened fire on the nine Japanese driving the carts, as well as the startled bridge guards, while the demolition squad cut the control wires. All the Japanese were killed in the brief fight. The bridge was secured at the cost of one American life. During this exchange, the first GI attempting to cross the bridge was killed and the second wounded. I was the third man to cross the bridge intact, zigzagging my way forward, which obviously paid off. What an experience in luck this all was. I could have been the one who was killed or seriously wounded. I was saved for better things in my life, maybe. Perhaps my prayers paid off."

"Twenty electrically controlled aerial bombs, ranging in size from ten 110-pounders to two 1,000 pounders, were found lashed to the bridge trusses or buried at the abutments."

"The main troop landing, which occurred three hours later, was unopposed. They found just a few of us guarding this big bridge until the rest of the battalion, about 100 men, arrived to reinforce us."

US Army 40th Infantry GIs and M4 Sherman tank move towards Bago River Bridge, Negros, 1945.

With the bridge secured, the landing battalions moved swiftly across the bridge and continued to the north, clearing out Japanese resistance.

"As we worked our way from town to town on Negros, it was a hairy and tense experience, never knowing when a bullet had your name on it or when you might step on a hidden mine in the road. There was danger everywhere waiting to happen. … There was no rest for us at night either, as we had to be on constant alert for bonsai attacks, which were really nerve-racking.

"Picture this — lying or crouching low in the foxhole, peering into the darkness hour after hour as your mind plays tricks on you, thinking you see the enemy, wondering if it is only your imagination, and also hoping that you have dug your foxhole deep enough to avoid having a grenade, bullet or bayonet find its mark, all the while wishing for daylight to arrive. You're feeling all alone, even though men were all around you feeling the same way."

"One night in particular I thought I heard some movement in front of my foxhole, so I held a grenade with the pin pulled and ready to throw. The anxiety was nearly overwhelming. I held that grenade so tight that my hand cramped up. When I was fairly sure that all was OK, I returned the pin to secure the grenade.

Your eyes would routinely play tricks on you as you strained to see things in the dark that you were imagining."

The danger wasn't limited to the enemy. There was also the threat of friendly fire. Bill recalled one occasion in his memoir, "We were vulnerable on the hilltops, too, more like mountaintops, really. I recall one incident at about three or four o'clock in the afternoon as we were starting to dig our foxholes and bivouac for the night when our own U.S. Air Force came overhead and bombed us with 100 pound bombs. One landed about 15 feet from me and really shook us all up…The bomb's impact lifted me a couple of feet out of my half-dug foxhole…I was stone deaf for a while…some guys were stone deaf for a week."

Danger also came from the jungle treetops by way of snipers. Bill recalled, "The heavy rain forests were spotted with snipers both on the ground and in the trees. You looked for them but they were hard to see. We were very vulnerable in the forests."

In spite of the constant danger, it was clear that the Japanese were losing ground and losing the battle. Bill remarked in his memoir, "Many times the Japanese intended to take a stand, but instead had to move under cover of darkness and keep moving because of the unexpected swiftness of our advance which went unhindered. He, the enemy, had to leave behind considerable supplies and equipment."

"From the beginning of the campaign in the Negros hills, regular drops of surrender leaflets had been made in all enemy-occupied areas. At the same time, Japanese prisoners volunteered to deliver appeals to still-fighting Japanese soldiers over a public address system, though the desired results were not immediate. But ongoing propaganda, coupled with the enemy's calamitous situation, eventually brought daily surrenders of groups averaging from five to ten men. They confirmed reports of supply shortages and loss of personnel, and acknowledged the hopelessness of not only their own situation, but that of the Japanese nation as well."

"After the Negros cam-paign, my division was re-

207

Inside cover of 40th Division History Book, Map of Division Movement.

lieved of its duty there and moved to Iloilo, Panay, the previously captured island. Many thanks to the good Lord, I was spared of harm on Negros. … I was eager to be relieved of the daily grind and tension endured in that place."

DISCHARGE

"While our company occupied the top of a hill on Panay, I went back to the battalion first aid station about a mile or two from the front lines, for treatment of jungle rot…my first time for first aid throughout my time in combat. When I returned to join the company I was told of some good and bad news by my buddy Ray Hartman. This time the rumor was true. All of the old men that had a lot of time overseas were being rotated back to the states. This meant me too, having 36 months of service in by that point."

"I said, 'you wouldn't kid me, would you, Ray?' He said, 'Honest to God, I wouldn't kid you about something as important as that.' But I was still skeptical, as there were always rumors floating around that were hard to believe, and we were often disappointed. According to this rumor, we were supposed to leave the next day."

"Well, the rumor was true and we left the company for the island of Leyte and stayed there three days waiting for a ship to take us to the states. I got on that ship with about 5,000 other G.I.s and never looked back. I had been in combat continuously for four and a half months, with the exception of three days' rest, and I was exhausted and tired of it all."

"The bad news, as I learned, was that the company we were leaving behind was moving forward to fight another day, and I felt sorry for them to have to endure more hardship."

"We were on that ship for 21 days to San Francisco, and the Golden Gate Bridge never looked so good." The date was April 5, 1945. And Bill Gabonay was finally back on U.S. soil.

Bill concluded his military service having earned ribbons and medals for meritorious service in the Asiatic Pacific Theatre, the liberation of the Philippines, and various other accomplishments, the biggest of which was the taking of the bridge on Negros Island, for which he received the bronze star.

Bill in front of house.

RETURNING HOME & FAMILY:

Bill and Marion's wedding in November 1947.

After Bill was discharged from the Army on June 17, 1945, he didn't look for a job for three months as he fought off the effects of the malaria he had contracted while in the Philippines. "About the same time every month it hit me hard for a day with chills and sweats," he recalled. "I became bedridden for 24 hours."

Bill married Marion Search of Bangor, Maine on November 29, 1947. The couple made their home in Indianapolis and later moved to suburban Beech Grove.

In the years ahead Bill and Marion were blessed with four sons: Paul, Will, Jim and Tom.

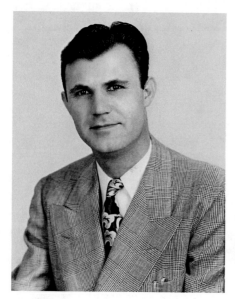

Bill when he worked for Eli Lily.

POST-SERVICE EMPLOYMENT

Bill worked at several different jobs during the first five years back from the war. In 1950, he accepted a job at Eli Lilly, a pharmaceutical company in Indianapolis, where he worked for 27 years. He worked in several different departments before being promoted to a machine operator position "taking charge of four machines that produced a million capsules in my 12-hour shift."

He was promoted again, this time to group leader. It was a position he held for 22 years until, following a couple of heart attacks, he retired in 1977 for medical reasons.

Bill and family.

RETIREMENT

In retirement, Bill and Marion moved to Greencastle, Indiana, where they lived out the rest of their lives enjoying the many benefits of small town, country living and playing host to their friends and family.

Bill Gabonay passed away at the age of 95 on October 2, 2012. A life-long Roman Catholic, he was buried in the Holy Cross Cemetery in Indianapolis. His wife, Marion died three years later in 2015.

Bill and Marion's 60th Anniversary.

Gabonay men at Bill's 80th birthday. Bill, center, sitting, with his sons and brother.

Story written by Bill's son, Paul Gabonay and edited by Ronald P. May. Much of Bill's material for his memoir came from, Infantry 40th Division, The Years of World War II, *copyright 1947 by the 40th Division, Army and Navy Publishing Company, Baton Rouge, Louisiana.*

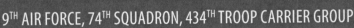

Adventures on a Troop Carrier
C-47 Pilot Flies into Japan Following the Atomic Bomb

Robert Kearns was born in Peoria, Illinois on September 22nd, 1922 to Edward and Mae Kearns. While he was still a child, his family moved to Indianapolis. Bob attended Cathedral High School, graduating from there in 1940.

Following high school, he enrolled at the University of Illinois and began a civil engineering degree while participating in the required Reserve Officer Training Corps on campus. During the summers he worked as a technical aid at his father's company, Edward J. Kearns Construction Engineers Company in Indianapolis.

Lt. Robert Kearns, Alliance Army Air Base, NE, April 1944.

Edward enlisted in July of 1943, joined the Army Engineers and served in Europe. He received a Bronze Star for meritorious service in leading his men across the Rhine River to Straussberg, Germany.

Bob enlisted with the Army Air Force in November of 1942, at the age of 20, and became an Aircraftman (AC). He served for about a year in that capacity.

Capt. Edward Kearns.

MILITARY TRAINING

His primary goal in joining the Army Air Force was to become a pilot. And, at the end of February in 1943, he began that journey as he received orders to begin

his pre-aviation cadet basic training at Army Air Forces Technical Command in Fresno, CA.

Following his basic cadet training he attended North Dakota State University for 10 weeks for his college training detachment and then reported to Santa Anna for 10 weeks of Preflight Pilot School. From there he went to Condor Field Air Academy at 29 Palms, CA for 10 weeks of Primary Pilot training. Next, he attended the 10 week Basic Pilot Training at Merced, CA, graduating from there in February 1944. He progressed to Advanced Pilot training at Ft. Sumner Army Air Force Pilot School in New Mexico for 10 weeks, graduating from there on Aug 4, 1944. Finally, he attended the 16-week course on Two Engine Replacement Training at George Field in Illinois

Following his training, Bob was assigned to fly the C-47 "Skytrain" transport planes for the Army Air Force. "I wanted to fly fighters," he said, "but I was too tall — I was a quarter inch over six feet. It sure did disappoint me." The cutoff for flying fighters was a very strict and literal six feet, and there were no exceptions — not even for a minute 1/4-inch difference.

C-47.

An Adaptation of the Douglas DC-3 civilian plane, the C-47 was built by the Douglas Aircraft Company and became a workhorse for the Army Air Forces. The aircraft was used to carry airborne troops to their drop zones as well as tow gliders. When not carrying personnel, the large plane was used to transport equipment. At 64 feet long and with a wingspan of 96 feet, the 'whale' of a plane could carry large loads. A crew of three flew the plane: Pilot, Co-Pilot and Navigator or Loadmaster.

Bob was assigned to the 74th Squadron of the 434th Troop Carrier Group in the 9th Air Force. The group would go on to provide airborne combat troops for operations in Normandy as well as Southern France, the Netherlands and finally Germany.

An unfortunate training accident, however, precluded Bob from taking part in those operations. His squadron, which was preparing for deployment to Europe, was in their final phase of training in late 1944. During his last flight training exercise on Thanksgiving evening, Bob's flight ended in disaster.

It was snowing and Bob's crew was in line for taking off along with the other planes of the squadron for a night formation. Just before take-off, Bob discovered that his dashboard lights were not working properly. At the last minute, just as he was beginning to lift off, he decided

Paratroopers in C-47.

to abort the take-off. His co-pilot, Hal Cohen, mistook Bob's hand signal for aborting the flight and the ensuing confusion with the throttle control resulted in the plane coming down, spinning out of control across the grass at the end of the runway, and jumping over a creek and into a cornfield. "I was so glad to see a corn field," Bob remembered.

The impact of the landing caused a fire in one of the engines and soon flames were threatening to engulf the cockpit. Hal Cohen started out of the cockpit ahead of Bob, but as he entered the cargo hold of the plane he fell down. Bob, who was following at a hurried pace right behind Hal, found himself suddenly standing on top of his co-pilot. As there was no other space for stepping off of him, Bob had to return to the cockpit (flames had already reached it) and wait for Hal to stand up and exit the plane. While in the cockpit, Bob's flight suit caught on fire and flames spread to his head and face. When it was his turn to exit the plane, he dove out and into the nearby creek to snuff out the flames, which saved his life.

Bob, who was the only crewmember badly injured, went to the infirmary with burns to his face and head. He spent the next five weeks in the hospital as the rest of his crew and the squadron left for duty in Europe.

DUTY IN THE PACIFIC

After recovering from his burns, Bob was sent to Guam and entered the Pacific Theater of the war, flying C-47s out of the Guam Air Depot at Harmon Field.

Harmon Field, Guam Air Depot.

Lieutenants Anger and Kearns with Hiroshima in background on one of the remaining buildings still standing, Oct. 24, 1945.

His flight missions took him to different islands in the chain of Pacific Islands near Japan, including Saipan and Iwo Jima. On one occasion he transported a General's jeep from Iwo Jima to Tokyo.

Toward the end of the war, Bob began flying troop missions between Guam and Japan. "I landed in Hiroshima one day after the bomb was dropped," he said. "We took an American medical team in." Bob would make two other trips to the devastated city to drop off medical teams in the days afterward. Although there were concerns about the exposure to radiation, the Allied Forces pushed forward in their mission to assist, stabilize, and occupy Japan.

Hiroshima, Oct. 1945.

Mark of man and cart on bridge, Hiroshima.

While in Hiroshima Bob took a photograph of a bridge that showed the outline of a man, a horse and a cart that were burned into the asphalt when the atomic bomb was dropped. He wrote on the back of the photograph:

"This bridge was a mile from the blast in Hiroshima. Evidently there was a man, a cart and a horse on the bridge at the time. The blast knocked them down and then the heat wave passed over them. Where they had fallen the asphalt was not melted, but all around them it was. If you look closely you can see the figures on the asphalt — horse, cart and man. Was hard to photograph, but quite plainly seen."

Sometimes, Bob would pick up troops from Tokyo and bring them back to Guam. Other times he would fly over Japan with some passenger troops who hadn't been assigned occupation duty and wanted a glimpse of the island from the skies.

The adventures weren't always from the cockpit of his plane. Bob recalled one adventure in Guam from the cab of an Army jeep. It was on Easter Sunday of 1945.

Aerial view of Tokyo.

"I took a jeep with three other guys into the jungle," he recalled. "We got stuck in the mud. While the other guys were trying to push us out, I looked up and saw a Japanese soldier in front of me. He was wearing a fresh U.S. uniform and had been hiding out in the jungle. When the other guys saw him, they all took off. We didn't have any weapons. I knew a little Japanese and I was able to

218

speak to him. Before long, he was helping us get the jeep unstuck." Bob and the other men with him took the Japanese soldier back to the air base for processing as a prisoner of war.

Bob made it back home to Indianapolis on Christmas Day of 1945 for a furlough before heading back to Guam to finish his final months of military service. He left the Pacific for good in late April of 1946 on a garbage scow ship from Saipan to Hawaii. Three months later, in July, he was discharged from military service.

By war's end, the Kearns family had a father (Edward) and two sons (Robert and his younger brother, James, who was a cadet at the time the war ended) serving in the Armed Forces.

Service Parade
✶ ✶ ✶ ✶ ✶ ✶ ✶ ✶ ✶ ✶ ✶ ✶ ✶ ✶ ✶ ✶

FATHER, TWO SONS IN SERVICE

CAPT. E. J. KEARNS   **CADET JAMES KEARNS**   **LT. ROBERT KEARNS**

Mr. and Mrs. Edward J. Kearns of 412 East Maywood avenue have three stars hanging in their window for the three men in their family who are now wearing khaki. First there is their son, Capt. Edward J. Kearns, who is in the engineers and has been overseas for several months. Then there are his two sons, Lt. Robert E. Kearns, first pilot in the troop carrier command, flying a C-47 transport ship. He is stationed at George field, Lawrenceville, Ill. Pvt. James Kearns in ASTP at the University of Illinois. The captain's wife and daughter are at present living at Indianapolis, Ind.

Article from *Peoria Journal.*

Dana Carolyn DeWitt

LIFE AFTER THE WAR

Following his discharge, Bob enrolled at Butler University. On March 15th, 1947 he married Dana Carolyn DeWitt, whom he had met in 6th grade.

Bob completed the bachelor's degree he had started prior to the war, graduating in 1948. He then got a job with Eli Lilly Pharmaceutical in Indianapolis, working in machine productions. Later he also earned a graduate degree from the University of Notre Dame.

Bob ended up back in Japan during the Korean War. He was activated in 1950 by the Air Force and sent to Tokyo, Japan where he spent the next 13 months. He flew politicians and media representatives from Tokyo into Seoul, Korea.

After returning from Korea, Bob remained on active duty with the Air Force and pursued a graduate degree in oral opinion at the University of Notre Dame. He was then hired by the university and taught Air Force ROTC for three years from 1951–1954.

Bob came back to Indianapolis following his discharge from the active Air Force and resumed his job at Eli Lily, working in pharmaceutical productions. He traveled the world including the countries of England, France, Japan and the island of Saipan.

Bob and Dana's weddding, 1947.

Bob at desk in foreground in office, 1952.

Robert Kearns, 1963.

Bob and Dana raised a family of five kids: Carolyn, Sharon, Michael, Chris, and Kelly.

Bob retired in 1983. For many years he enjoyed traveling and was most proud of his trip to Russia. He and Dana attended countless Elder Hostels in their retirement.

After sharing 63 years of marriage with Bob, Dana died in 2010.

Today Bob lives at Hoosier Village Retirement Center in Zionsville, Indiana. The 95-year old veteran of World War II and Korea listens to audio books and enjoys visits from his family.

Bob and children at Niagra Falls, 1964.

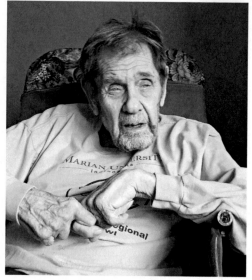

Bob in 2016.

Occupation Duty in Japan
Veteran Served in Japan and Returned Years Later

Ray McDonald has had two very different experiences with living briefly in Japan. The first was as a young Army Air Forces clerk assigned as part of the occupying forces at the close of World War II. The second was some 50 years later, as he and his wife came for short visits six years in a row to spend time with their grandchildren who were living there. Those visits are like bookends to his life of service as a soldier and later his life as a civilian.

Born July 6, 1927 in Gary, Indiana, he was the third of three children raised by his parents, Ray and Easter McDonald. (His mother was named 'Easter' because she had been born on Easter Sunday.)

He discovered an early interest in printing as he attended Horace Mann High School in Gary, Indiana, where he took a typing class and was introduced to printing. "A friend of mine invited me to a printing course," Ray recalled, "and that changed my life." He loved it enough to take four years of printing in high school.

His love for printing led him to apply for an after-school job at Burke Printing Company in Gary, where he did bindery work, delivered jobs, and distributed type.

When Ray wasn't working at Burke Printing Company, he was working for his own little printing enterprise. He and a friend, Carl Johnson, started a small printing business in the McDonald family's basement. "We bought a small printing press,

Ray in high school.

some type and got started," recalled Ray. "Our business was named 'Quality Print Shop.'"

Soon Ray and his friend were printing documents and flyers for church, for friends and for their school. The printed items ranged from dance programs, to tickets, or greeting cards. They also printed stationary and promotional material with service symbols to promote the war bond drives.

Typing and printing weren't the only skills Ray picked up in school. He also learned about military structure and discipline. ROTC was compulsory for young men growing up during World War II. "I loved it!" Ray exclaimed. "I became a Major and Adjutant, 2nd in command. I loved to march and loved close order drill."

Nearing his high school graduation in June of 1945, Ray and some buddies went to the recruiting office in downtown Gary to enlist in the service. They had set their sights on joining the Navy, but Ray's eyesight did not meet the Navy's requirements. Recalled Ray, "When I was asked to walk toward an eye chart and read a certain line I suddenly heard the recruiter say, 'Stop, that's far enough, you don't pass.' So, I could not join the Navy with some of my friends."

Ray wasn't disappointed. "I knew if I waited, I would be drafted," he said. "I wanted to go into the service." Although some older friends and brothers of friends had died while serving in combat, the sober reality of war didn't deter him from wanting to serve.

While waiting to be drafted, Ray continued working at Burke Printing Company. "I asked if I could stay until I was drafted," he said, "and they said, 'Sure.'

They were happy to have me stay on, as I had been working there the past three years and had enjoyed the work."

Ray didn't have to wait long for his opportunity to join the armed forces. He had signed up for the draft in July, and two months later, on October 15th, 1945, he left for Camp Atterbury in Indiana for processing into the U.S. Army.

His time in the Army was quite brief, however, as the Army Air Force was also looking for men and selected Ray to join them. Ray wasn't disappointed. "I was happy to go into the Air Corps," he said, "because I thought it would be more fun than going into the Army as a doughboy."

Ray was sent to Harlingen Army Air Base in Harlingen, Texas for his basic training. "One barracks mate from Kentucky was not used to showering every day," recalled Ray. "We had to pin him down in the shower and use a heavy bristled brush and laundry soap on him for him to get the message. He did."

When the Army Air Force discovered that Ray knew how to type, he was assigned to clerk typist school at SAC Field (Strategic Air Command) in San Antonio, Texas. "I really enjoyed it," he remembered.

Ray, sitting 1st row, 4th from right, with his training squadron, Dec. 1945

McDonald with gas mask, right.

While waiting for the school to start, he was made a drill instructor and was in charge of a barracks full of basic training personnel. "I marched them to and from classes during basic training," he said. "I was responsible for their well-being and had a room in their barracks." When he finished his clerk training, he worked at the headquarters office until he received orders to the Replacement Depot in Greensboro, NC.

In July of 1946, he left for his long anticipated deployment overseas. "We thought we were going to Europe," he said. After a few weeks in North Carolina, Ray and the others with him boarded a troop train and rode across country to Fort Lewis, Washington. They soon learned that they were on their way not to Europe but to Japan.

"It didn't make any difference to me that we were headed to Japan," remembered Ray. "You did what they wanted you to do. Besides, it was all a new experience."

For a 19-year-old native of Gary, Indiana, Japan seemed as far away as the moon. But the country and its people soon became significant in Ray McDonald's life.

Even while getting ready to deploy to Japan, Ray was still getting schooled in the art of language and grammar. "My mother was very good about writing to me frequently, and I wrote often also," he recalled. "The first paragraph or so of each of my mother's letters contained corrections of grammar, spelling and sentence structure of my previous letter. She could not avoid acting the part of a teacher, no matter what she was doing."

After a few weeks in Seattle, Washington the men finally boarded a Liberty Ship in August of 1946 and headed toward Yokohama, Japan. "I was with a friend and we had top bunks, which gave us more room and more air," Ray remembered. "It took a couple of weeks to get to Japan."

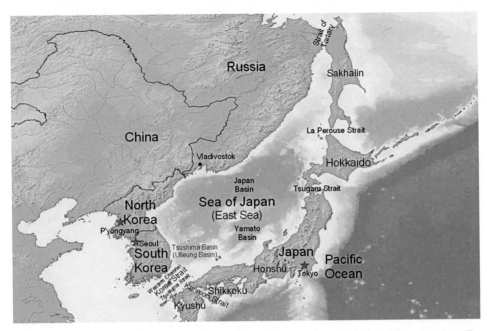

The men arrived in Japan and were transported to Johnson Army Air Base. "I received my orders to ship out to Chitose Army Air Base on Hokkaido Island for duty with the 49th Fighter Squadron, 5th Air Force," said Ray. During the war the squadron had flown P-38 planes. In the postwar era they were flying cargo and passenger planes along with supporting the training jumps for the 11th Airborne, which was stationed nearby.

The final leg of the journey to Chitose Army Base involved both a train and a ferry. "We boarded a train for the northernmost Japanese island, Hokkaido," said Ray. "I was distressed to see the Japanese people huddled in other railroad passenger cars while we had more than enough room for us. This was their country and we were spacious and had all the room we needed."

HQ building, Chitose Army Air Base.

He continued, "During the night, the train was placed on a ferryboat to go across Tsugaru Strait to Hokkaido Island. The train continued on to Chitose Army Air Base, near Sapporo, the capital city."

The base had been a Japanese naval air base during the war. According to Wickipedia:

> After Japan's surrender in 1945, ending World War II, the United States Armed Forces took over the base, being primarily under the control of the United States Army Air Forces, and later the United States Air Force Fifth Air Force. The base was used largely as a maintenance and logistics facility in the late 1940s prior to the Korean War, under the operational control of the 314th Air Division, Johnson Air Base.

Ray was stationed at Chitose Army Air Base from August 1946 to April 1947. "It was good duty," he recalled. "I worked in the headquarters building in the officers' classification, taking care of maintaining officer's records." He was at home in front of a typewriter, handling the documents that delineated an officer's record of duty.

Life was pretty good in Japan for the young man from Gary, Indiana. "The food was excellent," he recalled. "The hot baths were a treat. Some evenings, after dinner, we got in them and talked and relaxed."

Although winters could be rough there, those working at the base could mostly stay cozy. Recalled Ray, "Since we had heavy snow on Hokkaido Island, we had a building connected to the headquarters building from which all of the barracks and other buildings were also connected. Thus, we never had to go outside in snowy weather."

But, life in Japan wasn't quite like the comforts of home, as Ray learned. "We had a few mice running around the barracks and across our bunks on occasion," he said. "The headquarters bathrooms had running water but we had none for the barracks. We had a porcelain unit in the floor and we had to squat to relieve ourselves. A Japanese man would come along and scoop out the waste in buckets, called "honey buckets," and it would be used as fertilizer on their fields. We were not allowed to eat any of the local food."

During his tour of service in Japan, Ray was promoted in rank from Corporal to Sergeant.

Ray had mixed reactions in his interaction with the Japanese citizens inside and outside of the base gates. "One of the guys who cleaned our barracks had been a pilot in the Japanese Air Force," he recalled. "But there was no tension between us."

There was a little less interaction with civilians outside the base. "In town the people steered away from you," he said. "It bothered me."

Following his tour of service in Japan, Ray returned to the United States on a troop ship from Yokohama. It was not a pleasant voyage. "I was bunked in the bow of the ship in very close quarters," he recalled. "I got seasick and spent a miserable time for a few days in the latrine or head of the ship. I was glad to see San Francisco and the Golden Gate Bridge when we returned."

In April of 1947, Ray was officially discharged from military service. "After my discharge, I was glad I had done the service," he said. "I got overseas and got to experience some things I would never have experienced. I learned from the Army Air Forces the ability to get along with all kinds of people and adjust to the character and circumstances of people."

He also appreciated the responsibility and work experience he received in the service. "The Army and Air Force gives responsibility to people regardless of age," he said. "I had a good experience with that. I think I was a pretty good clerk and typist. It helped me on my professional career. I loved the Army experience. But

Ray and Fro.

Ray and Fro's wedding.

I didn't want to stay in. I wanted to go to college and get on with the rest of my life."

On his way home from Japan, Ray stopped to visit some distant relatives of his mother's in Dallas, Texas. "They owned a large printing company, Johnston Printing Company," he said. "They suggested I attend college and study advertising before deciding what I wanted to do."

The plan sounded like a good one to Ray. He returned home and worked in a steel mill for the summer and then applied to the University of Illinois, which had a new campus at Navy Pier in Chicago. When he later checked on the status of his application, he discovered they would not accept him because they weren't taking anyone from outside of Illinois. Ray scrambled and quickly enrolled at Indiana University Extension in East Chicago, IN for his freshman year, where he spent a year studying liberal arts.

A friend of his from the Army had attended Butler University in Indianapolis and had invited Ray down for a visit. Ray learned that Butler University had a great veteran's program. He applied for admission and started at Butler in the summer session of 1948. He majored in marketing/advertising and graduated with his bachelor's degree in 1950.

A degree was not the only thing that Ray earned at Butler. He also earned the heart of a woman he had met there and was engaged to marry.

Ray met Froso (Fro) Manolios in his college typography class in 1949 and began dating her. Fro was an Indianapolis native and was Greek. Since Ray wasn't of Greek descent, Fro's parents didn't care much for him. In fact, he never even met them until his wedding day. He and Fro were joined in marriage on February 10th, 1951. Ray's relationship with her parents quickly warmed after the wedding, and they got along quite well thereafter.

Together the husband and wife team raised three children: John, Bob and Sue. Today, the family consists of their children's spouses, seven grandchildren and five great-grandchildren.

Ray's college work had steered him toward a long and fulfilling career in commercial marketing and advertising. Recalled Ray, "My entry into advertising was in mechanical production, which was buying typesetting, engravings and

McDonald family photo.

the final plates or films for magazine and newspaper ads. From there I went to corporate advertising and marketing. In every responsibility I was involved in purchasing printing, and over the years probably purchased several million dollars of printing materials."

He worked for several different companies in the Chicago area until 1991. He and his wife then moved to Indianapolis, where he continued to work part-time as a sales manager before switching to the insurance business as a senior enroller. He also served as a K-12 substitute teacher in the Hamilton Southeastern public school system. He retired for good in 2003, after having actively worked for 42 years full-time and for 10 years part-time.

While family and work have been important to Ray, so has his relationship with God. Faith in God and regular worship attendance have always been a vital part of his life. Even while in the Army! "I always went to chapel on Sunday," he said. "None of my friends did." He continued that faith life even when he went overseas with the Army. "In Japan I went to chapel. I enjoyed it. It helped me a lot."

Both Ray and Fro have been active members in Presbyterian Churches throughout most of their marriage.

Today, while well into retirement, Ray still dabbles with the printed words that have shaped much of his life. He serves on the activities committee at Hoosier Village Retirement Center in Zionsville, Indiana where he and his wife live. He uses his personal computer to design and print many of the publicity sheets for upcoming events.

He has also written his unpublished personal memoir, *My Life…As I Remember It,* and updates it regularly as new events occur in his and his families' lives. Ray and Fro also stay active in their children and grandchildren's lives.

Even Japan worked its way back into Ray's life story in his later years. He and Fro traveled to Kobe, Japan near Osaka and spent a month there for six consecutive years, from 1995–2000, to care for their grandchildren as their son, Bob, and his wife came to the U.S. for corporate meetings with Procter & Gamble Company. "Everyone we came into contact with from Japan was wonderful," he exclaimed. "It was wonderful!"

They even made it to the city of Hiroshima. "We saw the one building partially standing and the museum there," he recalled. "It was tragic to look at the things that had happened there. Most of Hiroshima had been built back up by the time we were there. You wouldn't know anything had happened except for the museum and lone standing building."

Although Ray didn't personally get back to Sapporo, his son did. "When son, Bob, was in Japan with Procter & Gamble Company, he sometimes flew to Hokkaido Island on business," said Ray. "The international airport for Sapporo is located where Chitose Army Air Base used to be. It was interesting to think that he would be walking on the same location where I was stationed over 50 years before."

Japan remains a part of the man who once served there in the Army Air Force in the devastating and tragic aftermath of World War II. The country has changed. It is now an ally of the United States, and it has recovered from the ravages of war. Ray has changed also. The 19-year-old kid who first served in Japan has lived a full life. He has enjoyed a long career and raised a wonderful family.

Both Japan and Ray are enjoying the fruits of labor and the blessings of peace.

This story is based on the unpublished memoir of Ray McDonald, My Life as I Remember It, *and an interview by this book's author.*

Gunner on the High Seas

Veteran Maintains Guns on a Landing Craft Infantry (LCI)

"I always liked to work with my hands," said Donald Spees of Zionsville, Indiana. "It was easy for me." He used those hands to maintain and fire the guns from a Landing Craft Infantry Navy vessel during World War II.

Don was born on September 17th, 1926 in Indianapolis. He was one of five children born to Byron and Amelia (Weiland) Spees. His family moved from Indianapolis to Zionsville (a small town northwest of Indianapolis) when he was in the first grade.

Following the example of his older brother, Robert, Don enlisted in the Navy following his graduation from Zionsville High School in 1944. He spent nine months completing basic training and Gunnery school at Great

Seaman Donald Spees at Boot Camp, Great Lakes, 1944.

Lakes Naval Training Center in Chicago. He was then sent to Detroit, Michigan for his Advanced Gunnery School. He was trained to repair and maintain 50-caliber, 20mm and 40mm guns.

Following his training, Don was assigned to a Navy Landing Craft Infantry ship, LCI 429. The LCI, an amphibious ship that could pull up close to shore before sending off her troops, was 158 feet long and 23 feet wide. She could haul 250

LCI 351

LCI 429

Gunners Mate with LCI gun.

infantry troops who were stacked in bunks five high. The crew of the LCI carried four officers and 24 enlisted crew. Depending on her load, she could travel at speeds between 12-16 knots.

Unlike the larger ships in the Navy, LCIs were not given names. They were identified only by a hull number. Don's ship was #429. It had been built by the New Jersey Ship Building Corporation and was commissioned into the Navy on July 10, 1943. It was assigned for duty in the Asiatic-Pacific theatre of combat.

DUTY IN THE PACIFIC

Don joined the ship in early 1945. LCI 429 had already delivered invasion troops to Eastern New Guinea, Hollandia and the Philippines before Don came aboard at the Philippines.

After reporting to the ship, he was assigned to one of the 20mm guns onboard. LCI 429 had four of the 20mm guns and two of the 40mm guns. Used for antiaircraft defense, the double-barrel heavy machine guns fired 450 rounds per minute. Their range could reach up to 4,800 yards, but the weapon was most effective between 1,000-2,000 yards.

Four men were assigned to each 20mm gun. One man was the gunner who stood under the shoulder harness of the weapon and fired it. Another man served as a sight setter. The other two men were ammunition loaders for each barrel.

Gun Crew fires a 20mm canon.

"I was never in an area where they were shooting back at you," recalled Don of his time on the gun. While Don didn't recall ever firing one in combat, he did fire the weapon during the frequent training evolutions in the Pacific.

"There were 15 ships in my group," Don remembered. "Anytime we moved out, we stayed together." And whenever they moved out, it was for the purpose of dropping off troops at shore.

"We could drop our anchor 500 yards before the beach and run up to the shore," Don remarked on his ship's ability to bring their cargo of infantry close to shore. Once the ship had arrived near shore, the troops descended via two bow ramps on either side of the ship.

LCI 429 carried both Army infantry and Marines. "We all talked to one another," Don recalled of the interaction between his Navy crew and the cargo of fighting forces.

Don was in the Philippines when the war ended in August of 1945. "You never saw so many rockets go off!" he said of the many ships firing in Leyte Gulf at war's end. "Leyte Gulf was solid with ships. It was a big celebration!" The LCIs and many other Navy ships were in the gulf getting ready for the invasion of mainland Japan. "Although we *were* kind of disappointed we didn't get into the action," Don admitted.

OCCUPATION DUTY

LCI 429 stayed in the Philippines for a while after the war ended. She then was assigned to support the occupation of Japan and service to China from September 8th–December 16th, 1945. She went to Nan King in China

Allied Troops descend an LCI.

Don Spees with a woman at the USO in Shanghai, China, 1945.

and hauled Japanese troops back to their mother country, which was now an occupied area. "They were a pretty raggedy bunch," he said of their appearance.

Don recalled enjoying some liberty in Nan King. "I rented a car with a few buddies," he said. "It was real interesting to see how the people were living there."

During the post-war service on his LCI, Don also got to experience a typhoon. "We knew it was coming," he said of the typhoon. "They (Navy Brass) sent us into a channel leading to another body of water and kept us closer to the shore." The crew lowered the anchor and rode out the storm. "When you are 17, you are not smart enough to be scared," Don said. "If they sent me back today, I would be."

LCI 429 returned to the U.S. in January of 1946. For her service during World War II, she earned five Battle Stars. In addition to the Asiatic-Pacific Campaign Medal, the ship's crew also earned the Navy Occupation Service Medal and the China Service Medal.

After returning to the U.S., Don was discharged and given enough money to get back home. By the time of his discharge, Don had risen in rank to a 1st Class Gunners Mate.

LIFE AFTER THE WAR

After returning home from the war, Don attended Butler University on the G.I. Bill and graduated in 1950. He enrolled in Dental School at Indiana University in Bloomington. He stayed there for one year before transferring to the Indianapolis campus. He graduated with a Doctor in Dentistry degree in 1954 and, that same year, opened his dental practice in Zionsville, Indiana, where he worked for the next 45 years.

During his first five years in dental practice, Don taught part-time clinical classes at the Indiana University Dental School in Indianapolis. "You can't teach without learning a lot yourself," he said.

He recalled four black boys in his class. Two were struggling. He didn't think they were able to handle the academics, but the director of dental school said they needed black dentists in the black neighborhoods and for Don to make it work. Don gave them extra time and attention and got them through. "I felt good about that," he said.

He used his hands to care for the teeth of many people over his 45 years of service. "I was really happy with it," Don said as he thought back over his long career. "Good solid people! It was a good life." He retired from his practice in 1994.

Another part of his "good life" has been his wife and family. His wife, Jerrie, was in 8th grade when Don was in high school. He started dating her in 1946, after his return home from the war. They married in November of 1953.

Don and Jerrie in college.

Don Spees and his family.

Don hunting quail, 1994.

Jerrie became a teacher and later a guidance counselor. She served for 20 years in the Zionsville School system.

Together Don and Jerrie raised five sons: JB, Mike, Tim and Tom (twins) and Kevin. Those children have produced 12 grandchildren for Don and Jerrie.

Kevin followed in the footsteps of his father and became a dentist himself. He serves in the same Zionsville community as his father once did.

The extended Spees family enjoyed many fun times at a cabin on Lake Freeman, a reservoir near Monticello in Northwestern Indiana. The cabin was purchased by Don's father.

In his spare time, Don loved to hunt quail and fish. "I had bird dogs," he said with some pride. "I really enjoyed them." He liked raising the dogs as much as

hunting with them. "I didn't care how many birds I shot," he said, "I just enjoyed the dogs. I loved seeing the dogs perform. I was proud of them."

Don's wife, Jerrie died in February of 2016. She and Don enjoyed their 62 years of life together.

Today, at the age of 91, Don still uses his hands to enjoy life and people. He plays cards with the other residents of Hoosier Village Retirement Center in Zionsville, Indiana. And he often wins.

Don's hands have done a lot over his lifetime. He has maintained and fired large guns from his Navy ship. He has provided dental care for

**Don receiving recognition for his military service at Hoosier Village.
(Photo by Ann Marie Shambaugh, Current of Zionsville)**

thousands of mouths. He has loved a wife, raised a family, hunted, fished, prayed to God and played thousands of hands of cards.

"Hands down," that's a pretty good life by any comparison.

Experiment in the South Pacific
Veteran Experiences Racial Integration during WWII

E d White of Indianapolis was a long-time educator in the Pike Township and Decatur Township school districts. But long before he walked the halls of school buildings as a teacher or administrator, he spent almost three years walking some of the islands of the South Pacific during World War II. And that walk included an early experience with a racial integration experiment.

Born on May 26, 1922 in Petersburg, Indiana, Ed was the third of eleven children raised by his parents, Luther and Georgia White.

After graduating from Petersburg High School in 1940, Ed enrolled at Indiana Central College in Indianapolis and began a degree in physical education on a partial athletic scholarship. Having played basketball in high school, Ed was interested in coaching and knew that teaching physical education was the road that would help him get there. However, his pursuit of a degree was cut short in 1943 when he was drafted into the Army.

TRAINING

Following his induction and initial training at Fort Benjamin Harrison in Indianapolis, Ed reported to Camp Stoneman, CA (near San Francisco) for infantry training. "It was during a stage when the U.S. was speeding up the training due to fear of a Japanese invasion of Hawaii," Ed recalled of the fast-paced training cycle.

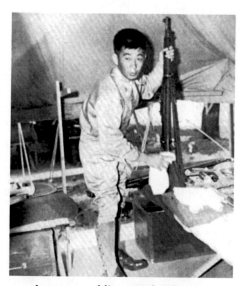

Japanese soldier, 298th Infantry.

Ed and Peanuts.

From California he shipped off to Hawaii, where he reported to the 298th Infantry Regiment at Schofield Barracks.

The regiment was made up largely of federalized National Guard service members from Hawaii, which was still a U.S. Territory at the time. It would not be approved for statehood until 1959.

Among the native Hawaiian Guardsmen in the 298th Regiment were over 700 soldiers of Japanese descent. They were mostly Nisei, second generation Japanese Americans, who a year earlier had been transferred into the all-Japanese 100th Battalion.

Ed, whose upbringing was in mostly white small town Indiana, was exposed to a unique integration between native Hawaiians, Japanese Nisei, and American forces; an experience that would serve him well later as an educator during the tumultuous days of racial desegregation in the public school system.

Ed served as a radio operator in the regiment. "I spent a lot of time transmitting with the key," he recalled of his time practicing with the radio handset.

The 298th Regiment spent a year in Oahu. They provided jungle warfare training to infantry divisions which were passing through and on their way to the Pacific theater of operations.

DEPLOYED TO THE SOUTH PACIFIC

In late 1944, it was the 298th Regiment's turn to deploy to the Pacific theater. Their first stop was the island of Espiritu Santo. Part of the New Hebrides archipelago in the South Pacific, Espiritu Santo is the largest island in the nation of Vanuatu.

"The Marines would make the initial landing and then our outfit would come in to clean it up," Ed

Men serving on Espiritu Santo in WWII.

explained of his regiment's role in the island hopping campaigns.

Cleaning up meant snuffing out the remaining pockets of Japanese resistance in the interior of the island, and setting up more permanent infrastructure for Allied occupation — things like building barracks and establishing communication between various company outposts.

Initially, that meant a lot of hiking. "It was pretty strenuous duty," said Ed. "I had to carry the radio along with my backpack and my weapon."

Communication was essential for setting up the infrastructure. "We handled all the internal communications between companies and battalions," Ed recalled. "All communication came through the regimental message center."

At times he pulled all-night duty on the switchboard in the message center. At other times, he was out on location at some of the outposts. He recalled spending time on the mountainous northern part of the island overlooking the harbor. He and other regimental members were lookouts who observed the flow of ship traffic into the

Radio operator.

245

Ed, left, and his buddies on Guadalcanal.

harbor, making sure no enemy ships came in.

After four months on Espiritu Santo, the 298th Regiment relocated to Guadalcanal for more of the same work.

After another four months, the regiment moved on to the islands of Tulagi and then American Samoa for repeat performances, before finally returning to Oahu for rest and replenishment.

While in Hawaii, Ed took a furlough to return to Indianapolis and visit his wife, Mary (Sinclair), whom he had married in 1942 prior to being drafted in the Army. He was still at home when the war suddenly came to an end with the surrender of Japan.

Ed spent the remaining months of his Army service at Fort Knox, Kentucky and was honorably discharged in 1946.

Soldiers on Guadalcanal.

LIFE AFTER WAR

Ed didn't waste any time starting a family with Mary. God blessed them with four children: Dennis, Steve, Dale and Anita.

He also didn't waste any time returning to college to continue his pursuit for an education degree. He completed his education at Butler University in 1949 and, that same year, began working at Pike High School of Indianapolis teaching English and serving as an assistant coach.

Ed completed his Master's Degree in School Administration at Butler University in 1953. He put his new degree to work serving from 1957–1965 as Principal at Pike High School.

In 1965, Ed became the Assistant Superintendent of Decatur Township Schools in Indianapolis. When several years later the Superintendent became ill, Ed assumed the top role and continued serving until 1983, when he retired.

He spent much of his time as superintendent in complying with the United States Justice Department's Desegregation ruling of 1971 against the Indianapolis Public School system — a ruling that eventually required one-way busing of African-American students from the inner city school districts out to the suburban and mostly white schools. "I spent more time in the Federal Courts than in the schools," Ed recalled.

He added, "In order to meet the racial integration requirement, the student population at Decatur Township Schools had to be 15% minority." Racial integration also meant having to hire a certain percentage of African-

Ed and Mary.

Ed White's graduation from Butler University.

Ed's retirement.

American teachers, who, because of the Federal Court ruling, were in high demand.

Ed not only oversaw the implementation of the integration in his school district, he also had to deal with the upset parents and students on both sides of the racial divide. "No one liked it," he recalled.

"But some good came out of it," Ed said as he thought back through the years of struggle. "One day at school I saw a little black boy and a little white boy holding hands and walking down the hall together."

To Ed White, that meant that desegregation had begun to produce its fruit of integration. "That gave me some personal satisfaction, knowing that we opened the door and got things going (toward racial integration.)"

Ed White retired from school administration in 1983. His career spanned eight years of teaching, eight years of serving as a principal and 18 years of leading Decatur Township schools as their Superintendent.

Ed and Mary's 50th anniversary.

In retirement Ed enjoyed golfing, reading and following the Colts. He moved to Hoosier Village Retirement Center in his latter years.

Ed's beloved wife, Mary died in 2010, after the couple had enjoyed 67 years together, 40 of which were spent in Decatur Township. The couple enjoyed watching their four children begin families of their own. Today that family has grown to include seven grandchildren and 12 great-grandchildren.

In the spring of 2016, Ed went to Washington, D.C. with Indy Honor Flight to see the World War II Memorial erected in his honor. It was an emotional and fulfilling day — one with a surprising and festive conclusion as the members of his family welcomed him and the other veterans home from their trip and home from a war they had fought so long ago.

Ed's zest for life and learning continued into his last years. "I've told the Lord that I am ready to go when he is ready to take me," said White. "But I'm in no hurry."

The Lord called Ed home on July 27th, 2016. He was 94 years old. He was buried in the Washington Park North Cemetery in Indianapolis.

Ed White and his family following his Honor Flight.

ON THE HOME FRONT

Duty Over Fear

Courageous Brit Delivers Milk During Air Raid Sirens Before Coming to America

Hilda Browning, Age 17, Women's Land Army.

During World War II, British citizens learned to deal with frequent air raid sirens as German bombers approached their airspace.

Most people sought out shelter when they heard the sirens. But not Hilda (Cawthorne) Browning! A member of the British Women's Land Army, she had the job of delivering precious milk to rural villagers. And air raid sirens didn't deter her.

Hilda Martha Cawthorne was born on January 14, 1927 in the little village of Treeton, near Sheffield, England. She was the last of 8 children born to Herbert & Hilda Mary Cawthorne. Her father died when she was only 8.

Hilda attended school through the 8th grade and then, at the age of 14, began working full-time. Her first job was at a canteen in the village of Treeton, fixing meals for the office staff at the local coal mine.

At the age of 16, she began working at a high school cafeteria in Rotherham. "I liked that better," she said. "I saw people my own age."

While Hilda enjoyed working at the cafeteria, what she really wanted to do was go into the Army. Her older brother, Herbert, was serving in the British Green Berets.

On February 25, 1944, her wish came true. Hilda enrolled in Britain's Women's Land Army. She was 17 years old.

WLA students learning how to milk cows, England, 1942.

The Women's Land Army (WLA) was Britain's answer to the critical need for additional labor force on farms. "We replaced the men on the farms," she explained. "They took all of our men for the war."

Hilda was assigned duty on a farm in Cherry Hinton, England, near Cambridge. It was about 100 miles from where she had grown up. She began working for a farmer. "When he found out I could add, he put me on a milk route with a little pony and a float (a cart)," she said. "I had to get the horse (named Betty) ready each morning. I loaded the cart, delivered the milk, (her route included 30 rural families), came back and washed the bottles. Then in the afternoon I had to help milk the cows. It was an experience," she said.

It was an experience that she liked. "I liked delivering because I got to meet different people," she said. "I especially enjoyed pay day. (Customers paid their milk bill once a week.) Some families invited me into their homes to have some tea and a piece of cake."

Hilda was also in danger of "meeting" other things while delivering milk — German bombers! Germany began bombing England in 1940 and continued to do so intermittently throughout the war. She recalled that hearing air raid sirens was just a way of life growing up in England during the war years. "You just got used to it," she said.

Near end of the war Hilda had the opportunity to meet some German prisoners of war. There was a British POW camp near Cambridge. One day some of the prisoners were brought out to visit the farm she worked on. Hilda remembered feeling anxious at first when she saw them. "But they were nice," she recalled. "Some even spoke English. They didn't want the war any more than we wanted it."

Hilda met her husband, John in 1944. He was from West Virginia and was serving as a military policeman in the U.S. Army. His duty was in France, but he spent some of his furlough in England. Spotting Hilda and her girlfriend one day coming back from the village library, he and his buddy asked if they could carry the girls' books. He was soon carrying young Hilda's heart.

In May of 1945, Hilda heard on the radio that Germany had surrendered. "It was a relief," she said.

A month later, on June 9th, 1945 she became one of the many war brides. John had come over to England from France on a weekend pass. He and Hilda were married by a Justice of the Peace in Cambridge and then escaped to Yorkshire for a one-day honeymoon. John returned to France the next day. It was almost a year before she saw him again.

John arranged for his young wife to join him in the U.S. following his discharge from the Army. She got released from her service in

WLA Girl leads a bull at a farm in Britain, 1942.

Hilda Browning, Age 19, WLA.

John and Hilda, 1945. (She was 18.

Hilda Browning at age 25.

the Women's Land Army (having faithfully served for 2 years), boarded a ship with many other war brides (many with babies), and headed to America for a long-awaited reunion with her husband.

The couple lived briefly with John's parents in West Virginia. A few years later they moved to Indianapolis where John found work in construction.

The Browning's were blessed with four children: John David (1947), Patricia (1950), Michael (1952), and Susan (1958). They enjoyed a 54-year marriage before John's death in 1999.

In between raising a family, Hilda attended classes once a week in preparation for her citizenship test. She became a naturalized U.S. citizen in the 1950s.

At the age of 58, she even went back to school to get her high school GED diploma.

Hilda returned to England in 1952, six years after coming to the U.S., to visit her sick mother. She went back to England to visit her family every two years after that.

While it has been at least 12 years since she last traveled back to England, a bit of England recently came to her. In June of 2015, 70 years after leaving her motherland, Hilda received a certificate and a medal via Royal Mail from British Prime Minister David Cameron for her service in the British Land Army.

"She's been a trailblazer," remarked Susie, Hilda's youngest daughter. "I feel like she is one of the bravest women I've ever known. She left her family, married a U.S. citizen, endured being apart from her husband for a year, and then came to the U.S. to begin a new life."

A classic case of duty over fear!

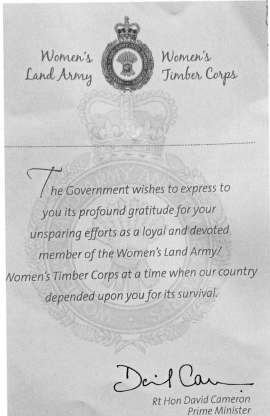

Statue to commemorate the Women's Land Army and Timber Corps at the National Memorial Arboretum, Alrewas.

Hilda's medal and WLA Certificate

The certificate states:
"The government wishes to express to you its profound gratitude for your un-sparing efforts as a loyal and devoted member of the Women's Land Army/ Women's Timber Corps at a time when our country depended upon you for its survival."

On a Farm at the Homefront

Veteran's Sister Reflects on Life Before, During and After War

Marilyn (Collings) Fowler grew up on a farm in western Indiana. Born in West Union (Parke County), Indiana on March 6th, 1923, she was the second youngest of 5 children in the family raised by her parents, Boyd and Fannie Collings.

In childhood, she spent much of her time with her younger brother, Duane, who is two years her junior and served in the Army Air Forces during World War II. Today, at the age of 95, she recalls much of the childhood she once shared with Duane.

"When he was a youngster in preschool his legs would swell and our dad had to carry him around," she recalled. "They took him to a doctor and finally got his legs healed."

Healed legs led to lots of outdoor activities. Even in the winter! "We lived on a farm next to a hill," she said. "In the winter we could slide down the hill. I was a house cat and didn't go out much.

Marilyn Fowler in high school, 1942.

But they (her siblings) finally talked me into it. They didn't tell me I was going to have to cross the road. I slid across and right into a barbed wire fence, which caught me in the forehead. He was worried about me," she recalled of Duane who was six or seven at the time.

Sibling concern gave way to sibling rivalry one day at the mailbox. Marilyn recalled, "I was nine and he was seven, I think. It was his turn to get the mail, but I got to the mailbox first. I thought to myself, 'He can't reach the box, so I will just give the mail to him.' Well, he hauled off and punched me in the stomach,

Collings Children (Marilyn lower left).

and I passed out. He thought he had killed me, but I was fine." She then added, "He was a good brother."

Marilyn was also a good sister, often deferring to her younger brother on what to play. "He always wanted to play some kind of ball games," she said. "I would play that with him and then insist he would have to play house with me. He would talk me out of it by saying we did that yesterday. As we got older we played a lot of baseball out on the road. There wasn't a lot of traffic then."

One of the occasions that a lone car did drive down the country road, Marilyn caught sight of a young man who changed her life. His name was Edward Roston Fowler. He had moved with his family from Illinois and lived two houses up the road from the Collings. "I saw his smile and that was it," she said of her fast fall into love. "Just watching him drive by was all it took."

Fast love progressed into fast marriage for the star struck couple. "I was still in high school when we got married," Marilyn said. "I ran away with him (to elope)." The couple married on August 15th, 1940. "We thought it was going to be kept a secret," she said. "But our marriage license was printed in the Indianapolis paper and everyone found out."

Ed and Marilyn.

"He was a hard worker," Marilyn said of Ed. "If anyone had trouble people would call him to help even if he wasn't feeling well. He was a workaholic."

Marilyn graduated from Mecca High School in 1942, six months after the Japanese attack on Pearl Harbor. Tragically, her mother was not around to see her graduate. "She had cancer and died my senior year, at

Christmas time," recalled Marilyn. "She suffered so with it! It was just heart breaking. We couldn't help her."

Following her graduation, Marilyn and Ed had an opportunity to move to a different farm. "After finishing high school my sister and her husband had job offers in Waveland, Indiana," she recalled. (Waveland is located south of Crawfordsville near Turkey Run State Park.) "They didn't want to move that far, so we asked if we could take the jobs. We were dirt poor at that time." They rented a home from the farm owners they worked for. Marilyn did some housekeeping and Ed worked on the farm.

Ed assisted on that farm for a while and then purchased a farm nearby. "It was a good community," remembered Marilyn. "An older couple across the road considered us as their children. The neighbors there were so kind and took us under their wings," recalled Marilyn. We stayed there for 65 years."

Marilyn and Ed's house.

ATTACK ON PEARL HARBOR

On December 7th, 1941 Japanese forces attacked the Navy base at Pearl Harbor, Hawaii. "It was very upsetting," Marilyn recalled after hearing the news of the bombing. "War is fought by the young people — families from our community had several sons that had to go. You hate to see anyone have to go to war."

Included among the men going off to war was Ed's brother, Allen and Marilyn's own little brother, Duane. "Duane was the only one who went off to war (of the siblings)," she said. "Dad offered to help him stay out of the service as a farm hand, but Duane wanted to go because his friends were going."

LIFE DURING WORLD WAR II

War ration book and coupons.

Pauline and Duane.

"Ed had a brother in the Navy and we were always anxious to get letters from him and Duane," said Marilyn. "I wrote them and tried to keep them up with the news."

Inside one of her letters she included a little bit of Indiana. "I sent a letter to Allen, who was in the Navy out on a ship," she said. "I included a little dirt in the letter and said, 'Be aware this is Indiana soil and you better come back to it.'" The soil was not just a creative reminder that he was missed back home; it was also a plea for him to stay safe. "He was overseas and when they went overseas you didn't know what might happen," she said.

Reflecting further on her anxiety she said, "We had so many friends beside our family that were in the war, and you just never knew if they were going to come back again or not. Sometimes, we worried because we didn't know how much danger they were in."

Marilyn recalled receiving letters from Duane every few weeks. "I heard more from him when he was in the states than when he was overseas," she recalled.

In addition to writing letters, Marilyn and Ed also tried to look in on Duane's wife,

Pauline, whom he had married during a short leave from training in 1944. "We tried to help take care of Duane's wife in Waveland (IN) while he was gone," she said. "She went out to Colorado and then she came back, and we tried to look after her."

In addition to the absence of many men who reported for military service, the war created other impacts for the people back home — food

Ed and Marilyn early in their marriage.

shortages! "There were a lot of things you couldn't buy," Marilyn said. "You had to get permission or tickets to get some things," she said referring to the war ration books.

Like many families, Marilyn and Ed grew as much food as they could. "We always had a garden," she said referring to the Victory or War Gardens the government had encouraged to reduce the demand on food at home so that more could be sent overseas to support the service men.

The war finally came to an end in August of 1945. "I can't remember where I was, but I know it was a really joyous time in town when the war ended," recalled Marilyn. "A lot of the kids in the town were gone. I was relieved that Duane and Allen survived and got home safely."

Allen and Duane came back home and got on with their lives. "Neither one of them liked to talk too much about their war years," Marilyn remembered. "I just hope we never, ever have a war like that one again."

Sadly, some years after his return from the war, Ed's brother, Allen died. "We don't know what happened to him," Marilyn said. "They found his body in the woods, and he was dead. Nobody knows anything about it."

LIFE AFTER THE WAR:

Not yet having children of their own, Marilyn and Ed began helping out with some of their neighbors' kids. "Our neighbor called and asked if we would keep their children (Dale and Joan Cheatham) while he took his wife to the hospital," she recalled. "We kept the children for a week. Their mother died, so we took care of those children until he could find someone else. We adored those children, and I still hear from them today. Dale still lives in the Waveland area, and Joan lives in Evansville. Dale's son is doing the farming now."

Marilyn and Ed's interest in children went beyond the Cheatham family. "We took care of most of the farm kids in the neighborhood when there was a need," said Marilyn.

Bob, Ed and Marilyn in 1972.

SON ROBERT

In 1952 Marilyn and Ed brought a son into their world. "We didn't have any children naturally, but we adopted one," explained Marilyn. Their son, Robert, had been born on January 1st, 1952. "We went to the hospital and got him," she recalled. "The doctor we had was taking care of the mother and he told us about it," she said. "When the baby was born we were told to come to a certain place in the hospital to pick up the baby."

Their son Bob brought much joy into Marilyn and Ed's lives. He graduated from Waveland High School and then attended Purdue University, pursuing an agriculture degree. Following his graduation, he worked for the farm division of the Eli Lily Company. He now lives in the Fishers, Indiana. "He's a good son," said his proud mother, Marilyn. "And he has a good wife. They are down here every week to do something for me. They bring me surprises."

Marilyn, left, and other teacher's aides in Waveland, 1971.

Seven years ago Bob's birth record was located, providing some information about his birth mother. "I gave him the information I had because I felt like anyone would want to know his family background," said Marilyn. "He has connected with his biological mother (who lives in Illinois) and discovered that he has two sisters."

INVESTING IN OTHER CHILDREN'S LIVES

Once Bob was grown, Marilyn began investing in the lives of other children. She began to volunteer her time at the local school. "I worked as a teacher's aide at the Waveland School," she said. "I had the 5th–6th grades (for three years). Prior to that, I worked with the Kindergarten children (for two years). I got to sit on the floor and talk to them."

DEATH OF HER HUSBAND, ED:

Life took an unexpected and difficult turn for Marilyn on August 28th, 1978 — the day that her husband, Ed, suddenly died. He was only 59 years of age. Marilyn's 38-year marriage to him was more brief than what she had hoped for but deeply appreciated nevertheless. Ed was buried at the Memory Gardens Cemetery in Rockville, Indiana.

LIFE AFTER ED'S PASSING

Marilyn continued to live in their home on the farm after Ed's passing. She enjoyed a connection to the land and its memories that had been a part of her for so long.

"I lived on a farm all my life, so I liked it," she said. "Sometimes I was a farmhand. I couldn't always do it right, but I could get down to the field. I had trouble making a ridge with the disc."

She also enjoyed feeding those who worked the land. "When it's the season for haymaking you had extra people to cook for," she recalled of those early years. "But those people were just like grandparents."

Marilyn also remembered the close fellowship enjoyed by nearby farmers in her years with Ed. "You didn't have much free time but we had a lot of farmers about the same age" she recalled. "So

Marilyn and her grandson.

265

Marilyn and her great-grandchild, Eleanor Kathleen.

we got together as four couples and played cards with each other. We had picnics and family reunions at Turkey Run State Park."

INVESTING IN CHILDREN/FAMILY

While others did the farming after Ed's passing, Marilyn continued to invest in the lives of children — neighbor children as well as children in her growing family. "I have two grandchildren from Bob: Jason and Chelsea."

"The greatest thing in life right now is my great-granddaughter, Eleanor Kathleen," said Marilyn. "She was a year-old last May."

SAD DAYS, TOO

Much of life has been great for Marilyn. But not all of it! There were sad days also. The deaths of her husband and mother were the most difficult. But even those had a way of turning out favorably in the end. Reflecting on her mother's death she said, "The saddest days were when my mother was going through cancer and my dad had to give her up when she died," she said. "He later married her sister, who had never married. She was taking care of her parents and they died. So both were alone and decided to get married. So my dad married two girls from the same family. It was fine with me because he was lonesome without mom. He couldn't have found a better wife than my mom's sister. She was a nice lady. She took good care of Grandma and Grandpa and helped Daddy farm."

MOST IMPORTANT LIFE LESSONS

When asked about life's most important lessons Marilyn replied, "Be careful what you say so you won't hurt somebody by saying the wrong thing. And try to show the love of the Lord. I'm glad to know that my family is all involved in churches and living the Christian life. I think Ed would be very proud of them. Maybe he's watching and knows."

MARILYN'S FAITH LIFE

Marilyn's Christian faith has always been an important part of her life. It remains so now, even though she can't get out and attend services. "I don't go to church anymore, but every Sunday I watch about five church services on television," she said. "I listen to Charles Stanley and David Jeremiah. I am one who has a hard time being in crowds. I'm the lone ranger I guess."

Marilyn and some of her family.

And she remains fervent in prayer. "I count my blessings every night. I sometimes think the Lord might get tired of hearing me. I pray for all my family and many friends every night."

DAILY LIFE

Today at the age of 95 she has slowed down quite a bit, but she still finds joy and meaning in some activities. "I still work puzzles and read the newspaper every day," she said. Most of the time she is content to sit and reflect on her life and on the blessings she has known — the best of which have been her family.

"I sit here and look at the pictures of my family and I just feel really glad about the type of life they have," she said. "They aren't rich, but they aren't poor. We have stayed together as a family. I still keep in touch with my nieces and nephews. My sister had four children, and my brother had one son, and Duane has two boys. My niece stayed with us growing up."

Family is what is most important to Marilyn. Family is why she came to Hoosier Village Retirement Community in Zionsville in 2014. She wanted to be closer to her son, Bob and her brother, Duane who also had moved there. When Duane later moved over to the Health Center, Marilyn made a point of walking over there at least once a week to visit him.

Brother and sister recently moved to a new retirement community in Westfield, Indiana. And Marilyn visits with him as often as she can. "He doesn't say much," she said of their visits.

Perhaps words aren't as important as physical presence for a brother and sister that have been a part of each other's lives for almost 100 years. The two started out together in life as they grew up on a farm in Parke County, Indiana. With 90+ years behind them, and their spouses and other family members gone, they are content to end their earthly journey in the same way it had begun — together.

Duty with the SPARS

New York City Native Shares Her Experience Serving with the Coast Guard

The following is a personal written reflection by Kay Gray of her decision to join the SPARS and her service experience.

It's December 8, 1941 on a Thursday morning. I'm seated at my typewriter at my very first job with Dun and Bradstreet in New York City. We're all busy typing when a message comes over the loudspeaker. All typewriters go quiet.

We're told that at 12:00 everyone should report to the top floor cafeteria for an important message on the radio.

Everyone is quietly sitting at the tables in anticipation of the important message. We had heard rumors of something terrible happening far way over the ocean in a place called Pearl Harbor. Most of us had never heard of that place, and since there was, of course, no TV or radio that would operate without electricity and an antenna; most of us had no more information than just that.

Then over the radio comes the distinguished voice of our President, Franklin Delano Roosevelt telling us about "a day that will live in infamy…" We are at war!!!

At war!! My father was in the artillery in the World War. (There was only one "World War" at that time.) War was a terrible thing. Why did the Japanese people want to have a war with us?

And so time went by, with more and more of my friends enlisting in the military service and leaving the area. I began to want very much to help out in some way – but I had to be 20 years old to enlist, and that meant quite a few months of waiting.

MAKE A DATE WITH UNCLE SAM

ENLIST WITH COAST GUARD

SPARS

APPLY NEAREST
COAST GUARD OFFICE

At last I was 20, and I had given a lot of thought to it. I decided to enlist in the Coast Guard SPARS ("Semper Paratus Always Ready," the Coast Guard Motto).

Biltmore Hotel. Palm Beach. Florida

SPARS in uniform.

And so, on a hot summer day, I got in line for the train to Palm Beach, Florida. It was a hot, sweaty, dirty ride of three days — of course no air conditioned cars; no air conditioning at all in those days, except for the movie theaters! Strangely enough, they were the first things to be air conditioned when nothing else was. I suspect that's because it was easier to cool one big open space than rooms or trains.

You've heard of "boot camp" and how tough it was. Ours was indeed tough. Oh, yes! We were bunked four to a room in a tourist hotel that had been taken over by the government for the SPARS' training. In Palm Beach, Florida, about two blocks from the Atlantic Ocean. Very rough duty, indeed!

We had some military training, and also the work that we would be doing when we took over the men's jobs, as they were called to active duty. That was our job, to free up the men. And in that way we served our country.

Oh, yes, the ocean. After two weeks of most intensive training, we were allowed some time off and could walk over to the beach. Being a girl from Long Island, New York and accustomed to the frigid Atlantic waves of Jones Beach, I was amazed at the warm water of the Florida waves. Just like waves in a bathtub! How strange.

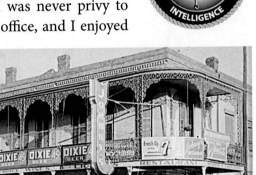

After boot camp I was stationed in New Orleans in the Intelligence Office, right downtown at the foot of Canal Street, the main avenue, overlooking the Mississippi River. There was some spy stuff going on, but actually the confidentiality extended to the office employees, and I was never privy to anything very exciting. It was a friendly office, and I enjoyed the secretarial work and exploring the town of New Orleans with all its French aspects. (I adored the French language!!)

After a year, I was transferred to Washington, D.C., where I spent about a year at the Coast Guard Headquarters, until the war finally was over and we all went home.

Johnnys Restaurant, New Orleans, 1940.

There were WACs (Army), WAVEs (Navy), SPARS (Coast Guard) and Marines. (I think they were just called "Women Marines.") We women did not serve overseas, but we freed up the servicemen to go over and do the hard work. That was our function. We were all very proud to be in the service of our country in time of war.

That time was very different from these days of the Iraq war. Everyone was very aware of it, and

Group of SPARS.

all were involved. Housewives went to work in the war factories, all dealt with food rationing, gas was rationed (my father gave up his car and we moved from the country into the city so he could easily get to work in New York.) There were War Bond drives; actors and actresses would publicly support the drives and would also travel around to entertain the troops. Many famous actors joined the services, and not only in the entertainment capacity. Glenn Miller, probably our most famous and beloved band leader, raised millions of dollars for the war effort and was abroad entertaining troops when he was killed in a plane which disappeared while flying from London to Paris.

It's a little different today.

That was my experience as a SPAR during World War II.

~ Kay Gray

Ennis and Kay wearing their uniforms today.

MORE INFORMATION ON THE COAST GUARD SPARS

The Coast Guard Women's Reserve was approved by congress in November of 1942. It was created to help free men to serve at sea and abroad in the war effort. Between 1942–46 approximately 10,000 women volunteered to serve in the newly formed women's reserve force.

Volunteers took an oath, received military training and wore uniforms. Their training and uniforms closely resembled that of the Navy WAVES. It was the insignia that identified them as women of the Coast Guard.

The name, SPARS, was coined by the newly appointed director of the Coast Guard Women's Reserve, Dorothy Stratton. It was the acronym for the Coast Guard Latin motto and its English translation: Semper Parratus, Always Ready.

Stratton had previously served as the Dean of Women at Purdue University in West Lafayette, Indiana before leaving to become a Navy WAVE officer.

There were both officer and enlisted positions in the SPARS. The enlisted training lasted for 6 weeks and included instruction in physical education, military organization, personnel, hygiene, and current events. Recruits underwent testing and classification training to determine their suitability for different positions or advanced training.

Once trained, the women filled shore-side positions around the nation, including Alaska and Hawaii. Most of the enlisted positions were in the fields of administrative assistance (Yeoman) or supply (Storekeeper), but there were also other specialized positions available.

The Coast Guard Women's Reserve (SPARS) was inactivated on July 25, 1947.

From the Farm to the Big Apple
Indiana Farm Girl Served with WAVES in New York City

BEGINNINGS

Fern (Caplinger) Metcalf grew up on a 100-acre farm in Switzerland County in Southeastern Indiana. Born on March 19, 1923 in Moorefield, Indiana she was one of five children born to her parents.

"We lived on a farm with no electricity or running water," she wrote in her personal life reflections. "My mother canned 400 or more jars of tomatoes each year as there were Mom, Dad, 5 children and Grandma and Grandpa living in our home."

Her Christian faith took root early in her life. "When I was 12, I accepted Christ as my Savior," she wrote. "This was during a two-week period of revival meetings. I was baptized the last Sunday of August in a creek."

Fern (Caplinger) Metcalf, SuperWave

Fern graduated from Vevay High School in Vevay, Indiana in 1941.

In 1941, Fern got a job at McCauley's Candyland candy store in Madison, Indiana. "I made a dollar a day," she wrote. "It was selling homemade candy and ice cream; and we also had sandwiches to sell. They made hard candy in the shape of little fish. It was very popular with mothers sending candy to their sons in the service."

In 1942 she enrolled at an all-girl Baptist Bible School in Chicago, Illinois. Following that year of education, she returned to her home in Indiana and resumed working at the candy store in Madison.

275

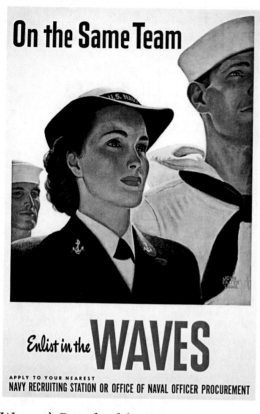

On the Same Team

Enlist in the WAVES

APPLY TO YOUR NEAREST
NAVY RECRUITING STATION OR OFFICE OF NAVAL OFFICER PROCUREMENT

Although her life was spent mostly on the farm, her mind was on travel. "As a small child I got the desire to travel," she wrote. "I had no way to accomplish this until I saw the poster wanting me to serve my country."

The poster was the one of Uncle Sam pointing outward toward the person viewing it. She saw it in the local post office in Madison, Indiana in May of 1943. She wrote, "I took some candy to mail for my boss and saw the sign of Uncle Sam pointing his finger at me. The sign said Uncle Sam needs you. I went in the Post Office, mailed the candy and then went over to the Navy recruiter and picked up an application for the Navy WAVES." (Women Accepted for Volunteer Emergency Service, which was the Women's Branch of the U.S. Navy Reserve)

Because she was only 20 years old at the time, she needed to get her parents' permission to join the WAVES. "I went home to Moorefield, Indiana that weekend and my Dad signed it for me," she wrote. Knowing well her spirit for adventure — much of what she had received from him — her father did not try to talk her out of joining.

After taking her entrance exam she waited for her official orders. They finally came in July, directing her to report to New York City. "I took the bus to Cincinnati, and caught the train to New York," she recalled. "I had never taken a train before."

BASIC TRAINING

Basic training for WAVE recruits was held at Hunter College in the Bronx, New York. Fern wrote of her experiences there. "I got off the train at Grand Central Station. A Wave in uniform met us. There were about ten of us. The WAVE took us to Boot Camp located at Hunter College in the Bronx. This had been an all-girls college that the Navy leased for their training of us WAVES."

"We were taken to the dorms and shown our beds and then to the mess hall to eat. The first day we ate our lunch when we arrived. We were fitted for our uniforms, and then sent to a classroom where we received our Blue Jacket Manual and assignment for the next day's lesson. We were then assigned our barracks. These had been the student rooms. Ours was a two room apartment. Our room had two

Boot Camp at Hunter College.

double bunk beds. There were twelve of us in this room. There were twelve in the other room to share two bathrooms, two ironing boards, and two irons. We then ate dinner and had the rest of the day off to get acquainted with our roommates."

"We were awakened by the officer of the day and lined up to shower and dress and be downstairs and in the yard for roll-call. We answered with a loud 'HERE' when our name was called. We formed our column and marched to mess hall for breakfast. We then marched to the parade ground and a Marine taught us to march. The Marine was tall and good-looking. I made a mistake and he took me out of formation and showed me the step. I, on purpose, 'goofed' again. The third time he whispered in my ear, 'you do this again and your "butt" will be on the next train back to Indiana'. I became the best marcher in the group."

"As we marched we sang our WAVE song: *'Waves of the Navy; We are marching out to sea; And we won't be home again until there is VICTORY'.*"

Like every branch of military service, the WAVES had their own uniforms which Fern remembered consisting of "a purse, shoes, our suits and a wool overcoat." Although it was the summer when Fern began her training, she and the other WAVE recruits were issued only winter wool uniforms, which she recalled were quite hot. She wasn't issued her summer uniforms until the following year in May of 1944.

Uniforms were not the only change to Fern's former appearance. "I had not cut my hair for ten years," she wrote. "I wore my hair page-boy style. They made me get it cut. I went to the beauty shop on campus. She hooked me up to this machine that had these curlers on straps that came down from the machine. She cut my hair then placed this monster curler on my hair and it curled my hair to a neat, tight fuzz. I cried, but this did not change anything."

The Navy also had a new language she had to learn. "We had classes out of the Blue Jacket manual," she recalled. "This taught us the Navy language, such as 'head' for the restroom, 'ladder' instead of stairs, etc. We were also shown pictures of enemy planes that we were to identify."

Practically every aspect of Fern's life was dictated by the Navy. "Boot camp was getting up when the officer said, going to bed with lights out, eating when and how long the powers that be that ruled our every move ordered."

Following their dinner each evening the WAVE recruits had some free time back in their rooms before the required time for lights out. "Most of us studied for the lesson for the next day, did wash by hand, ironed, etc.," recalled Fern.

While there was much that the Navy required of Fern, she recalled feeling extremely privileged to serve. And this included a deep gratitude for others who had served and died. "I remember walking across campus one evening and two sailors were lowering the flag and another sailor was playing Taps. I saluted, of course, but I was so emotionally moved the tears ran down my cheeks as I stood there."

Eleanor Roosevelt and WAVES at Hunter College.

The WAVES, created by Congress in July of 1942, had a special celebration on their 2nd anniversary in July of 1944. And a special guest came to Hunter College to help the new recruits celebrate. Fern wrote: "Eleanor Roosevelt visited us to celebrate our second anniversary. I was selected as a Shore Patrol, so I was at the gate where she and the admiral entered. She and the admiral came to the mess hall. I was at the end table. We all stood at attention when they entered. The admiral said "at ease." So I put my hand on the table. Mrs. Roosevelt came over and patted my hand and told us how proud she was of each of us serving our country."

Fern missed participating in her graduation from basic training. She explained, "One night I got sick and they put me in the hospital; so I did not get to graduate with my unit. I made up the classes and received my Hospital Apprentice Second Class rating. I got through boot camp without many scars."

"I was then assigned to the Hospital Corps School. I made good grades, so I graduated with a rating of Pharmacist Mate third class. I received $78 a month."

NAVY DUTY

Following her training, Fern remained in New York. "I came to New York from my home that was a hundred-acre farm near Moorefield that had a population of 74 at this time. New York was sure a culture shock for this country girl. The New Yorkers talked so fast. They would say to me 'if you are going to say something, say it'. I had to slow my Indiana twang."

Fern served as a WAVE in 4 different locations throughout New York. "I was assigned to duty at Brooklyn Naval Hospital" she wrote of her first assignment. "I was promoted to Pharmacists' Mate 3rd Class at the beginning of my service. My barracks was in an apartment building that the Navy had purchased for our housing. I enjoyed this service. I took the temperature and pulse of thirty patients on the ward that I was assigned to. I gave baths, back rubs,

In Brooklyn, Jan. 1944.

served their meals as there was only the one nurse and me on the day shift. I also gave shots and medicine. It was a very full day."

"We had a patient that had syphilis. The Nurse warned me to be sure and sterilize the thermometers well, as we used them over and over in those days. I had a cup with clean ones and another container to put the used ones in. I finished the thirty patients and put the used thermometers in the autoclave."

Fern described a mishap that took place one day with the autoclave. "The autoclave is an oven heated by steam. The thermometers only read up to 106 degrees and the autoclave was much higher causing the thermometers to explode. There was glass and mercury all over the oven. We cleaned this up with shop rags. We played with the mercury as we cleaned it up. Now (if it happened today) they would seal off the whole ward, I am sure."

Fern at home on the farm while on leave Nov. 1943.

Staten Island Feb. 1944 next to a captured German tank with a sign that reads: Join to help capture more.

"While in Brooklyn I went on weekends with the Chaplain to the Marine unit where we sang and the Chaplain gave a short encouraging speech there. There were four girls that went with him. I saw many badly injured there."

"The Navy then transferred me to Procurement as a Doctor and Dental assistant. I had to stand by the dentist and chart the cavities of the new recruits' teeth. These were girls joining the WAVES. I also tested their eyes and hearing and urine for sugar. This was at 44 Wall St and 33 Pine in New York City."

"I was then transferred to Rochester, New York to do the same at the Navy center there. We had both men and women in Rochester. This was smaller, and I got to know the other workers there more than in New York City. I was stationed at the YWCA in Rochester."

"There were just we four that worked in Procurement in Rochester with Dr. O'Kane. He was in the Navy (I forgot his rank), but still a 'down home type of doctor.' One Friday I forgot my black tie. At work, we wore a blue tie. He took off his black tie and gave it to me to wear to Erie, Pennsylvania so I would not be out of uniform. He made a sign over the lab where I tested urine for sugar. 'Ye Olde Urine Shoppe by Cappy.'"

"In Rochester we interchanged our duties of checking urine, blood, and teeth, and assisted Dr. O'Kane. It being a small work unit, we all became good friends. I was called 'Cap' or 'Cappy,' as my last name was Caplinger. Jack Holmes lived by a cemetery. He would steal fresh flowers from new graves and take then to his girlfriend as if he had bought them. He also brought flowers to work."

"I was transferred back to New York City for a short time. And I was next sent to Samson Naval Hospital in upper New York. This was far from anywhere. No one liked being at Samson, especially after New York City. I went back to tending to patients there. The wards were bigger but there were more people to help by this time as more girls had joined."

FERN'S INJURY & MEDICAL DISCHARGE

A back injury at Sampson Naval Hospital in August of 1944 proved to be the end of the road for Fern's service in the WAVEs. She explained, "I was injured and was shipped back home with a medical discharge. I hurt my back and have had three surgeries on it after leaving the Navy."

As she looked back over her exciting and pack-filled year of Navy duty with the WAVES she wrote, "I enjoyed the Navy experience, and it did a great deal in maturing me in a hurry. We tended to the injured, after all, and we saw so many badly injured men."

"I was treated so well in the Navy. We women ate on one side of the mess hall and the men on the other. They tried so hard to keep us ladies, they treated us with velvet gloves, as the saying used to be. I am still proud to be an American.

"I did receive valuable training that I used when I got out of the service as a nurses-aid at Grant Hospital in Columbus, as an x-ray tech in Cleveland, and also as a dental assistant to Dr. Seiple in Columbus. I would have to say I got what was advertised."

And, concerning her time in New York City she wrote, "I liked New York City, as there was so much to see and do. I went to Radio City Music Hall and with each movie shown there was a live act, between the double feature. I saw Gypsy Rose Lee strip. She had more clothes on when she finished than some have walking down the street these days. She was so graceful; it was almost like ballet movements. I saw the Ink Spots, The Mills Brothers, and many others that I do not recall at this time. We service people got in the movies just by paying the tax. I went to the Statue of Liberty several times. I also enjoyed the many museums located in New York City."

MEETING AND MARRYING BILL

Fern in Winter Uniform, Dec. 25, 1943.

The Navy not only provided Fern with a great opportunity for serving her country, it also provided her with the opportunity for meeting the man whom she would marry. Fern met Willard (Bill) Stucky while she was serving in Brooklyn. He was in the Army and stationed in Brooklyn at the time. It was a fast fall into love followed by a fast wedding. "We met in July and married December 17, 1943," Fern wrote.

Less than a week after getting married, Fern endured one of her worst bouts of homesickness. "Have you ever been so homesick that you cried until your chest hurt," she wrote? "This was my Christmas in 1943, my first Christmas away from my family. Bill received a furlough, so he went home with my blessings. Then I was alone. Bing Crosby was singing "White Christmas" from every corner of my world, which was New York City then. However, it passed, and I lived to see many more Christmases without going back to Moorefield, Indiana."

In 1944 Bill was transferred by the Army to attend Pre-Medical School in Pittsburgh, Pennsylvania. Fern recalled, "I would go each weekend to Erie, Pennsylvania (half-way for each of us to travel). We had to show our marriage license to get a hotel room, as we were in uniform."

LIFE AFTER THE NAVY

Following her discharge from the Navy Fern attended college in Pittsburgh for a time. She and Bill then moved to Cleveland where she got a job working for the city of Cleveland. The couple then moved to Denver where Fern resumed college at the University of Denver. Fern and Bill's marriage ended in divorce after a few years.

Fern transferred to Ohio State University and continued her education. While in Columbus, Ohio she met Bob Metcalf, whom she later married. The couple settled in Troy, Ohio and raised two children: Clark and Rebecca. Bob died in 1989.

Fern remained in Troy after Bob's death and kept active as a Sunday School Teacher and volunteer at Troy Christian Church.

HONORED FOR HER SERVICE

In these latter years Fern has been honored for her service as a WAVE. In 1994, she was recognized for her 50-year anniversary as a disabled veteran. She was selected as the Grand Marshall for the Memorial Day Parade in Troy, Ohio.

Fern Waving to the crowd as Grand Marshall of the parade.

On April 21, 2007, Fern went on an Honor Flight to Washington D.C. While visiting the World War II Memorial, she was approached by a female Navy Sailor. "She asked if I was in WWII and I answered, 'Yes, I was in the Navy,'" Fern wrote. "She grabbed me and put her arm around me and had a friend take our picture. She said, 'I have to send this to my mom and tell her, 'see there were other women that joined the Navy before me.' She then took me to the Indiana pillar and took my picture there."

Fern at the Indiana Pillar of the World War II Memorial.

Fern and her group was also honored by famous World War II veteran and Senator, Bob Dole. She wrote, "There were chairs set up at one place, and Senator Bob Dole was there to meet us."

Even the founder of the Honor Flight Network, Dr. Earl Morse from Springfield, Ohio, honored Fern with some of his time. "We took the bus to the Vietnam, Korean, and Lincoln Memorials. I, by this time, had walked my quota. I got into a wheelchair and Mr. Morse (yes, the founder of the organization) took me around. He had been there often, so he filled me in on all the details. It was great!"

Today, Fern is 95 years old and lives in a retirement home in Troy, Ohio.

Fern with Navy Sailor at World War II Memorial.

Fern holding her service photo.

A Rosie the Riveter
Woman helped build P-47 fighter planes in Evansville

Sixteen million men left the United States for combat during World War II. Others had to take their place in the factories, many of which had been converted to making weapons, munitions, vehicles and aircraft to help support the war effort. And in many cases the "others" were women.

Referred to by the popular image and name, "Rosie the Riveter," more than two million women became laborers in factories throughout the United States in the mid 1940s. Betty Robling of Mooresville, Indiana was one of them.

Born April 7th, 1924 in Bridgeport, Illinois (17 miles west of Vincennes), Betty graduated from Bridgeport High School in 1943. Having learned of a job opening with Republic Airlines in Evansville, she moved there that same year and became a riveter, helping to build P-47 fighter aircraft.

Betty Robling, 1945, Evansville, Indiana.

The P-47, known as the Thunderbolt, was one of the largest and heaviest single-engine fighter aircraft in the Army Air Forces' arsenal. It was used extensively both in the European and the Pacific theaters of war.

Republic Airlines had begun building the fighters at its Farmingdale plant on Long Island, New York. When demand for the plane exceeded the production capabilities of that plant, a new plant was built in Evansville, Indiana. The new plant produced 110 of the planes.

P-47 Thunderbolt.

Betty recalled, "I weighed only 95 pounds and sat at a table with a vice where I placed rivets into small sheets of metal used for different parts of the plane." Her job consisted of both placing the rivets into the pre-drilled holes and bucking the end of the rivet so that it would collapse down on the inside of the piece of metal, locking it into place. "It was a fine job," she said. "And it was good money; about $42 a week."

Ironically, Betty's future husband, whom she had not yet met, was also working on planes at the same time as Betty. Hubert Robling from Petersburg, Indiana was serving as an aircraft mechanic with the 8th Air Force in Europe.

It wasn't until January of 1947 that the couple met for the first time, when Hubert's best friend brought him down to Evansville for a visit. Love blossomed

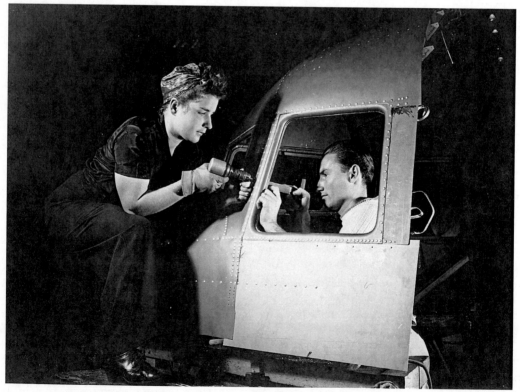

A Woman riveter at the Long Beach, Calif., plant of Douglas Aircraft Company.

quickly, and seven months later, on August 23rd, the couple became husband and wife. "The best thing that ever happened to me was when I met Hubert," Betty said!

The young couple settled in Mooresville, Indiana. Hubert had already begun working for Allison Transmission and had found an apartment in the Mooresville community.

In 1950 the couple built a home together. "I helped put the roof on and the siding," said Betty. "And we laid our own hardwood floors." The Robling's lived in the home for the next 40 years, and raised three boys: Jim, Danny and Tom.

After Hubert died in 1990, Betty sold the home to her oldest son, Jim, and moved into a nearby apartment. She has kept busy with involvement at the Free Methodist Church of Mooresville, where she has been a member for the past 57 years.

Betty and Hubert.

Her congregation, along with two others churches in the community, organized "Churches in Mission" 27 years ago to provide food, clothing and financial resources to people in need. "Kathleen Mills and I were the first people to walk into the doors and volunteer," Betty said. "It's just a wonderful place!"

She has filled every position in her years of service at Churches in Mission, but the work she has enjoyed most is restoring donated dolls, which are then made available as Christmas gifts for children. "It's my favorite job," she said. "Last year I restored 202 dolls. And I've probably done 100 already this year. I'm called the 'doll lady.'"

Betty and Hubert, 1978.

Betty and one of her dolls.

An avid doll collector for 40 years, Betty cleans the donated dolls and then repairs or replaces their articles of clothing. It's a far cry from her earlier life of bucking rivets on fighter aircraft.

Today, at the age of 94, she maintains a full and active life. She enjoys her four grandchildren and three great-great grandchildren. And each day is another opportunity for her to make a difference in the lives of others.

P-47D Wicked Rabbit, Tennessee Aviation Museum.

Acknowledgments

First, I thank the veterans of this volume who allowed me the privilege of hearing and sharing their stories. It has been an honor and blessing to know them and, in many cases, some of their family.

I thank the administration of Hoosier Village Retirement Center for allowing me to interview the veterans of that community as part of my overall ministry as campus chaplain. I commend them for seeing the value of this project not only for the individual veterans but for the whole community who will now be able to know and celebrate the service of these men and women.

I also thank BHI Foundation for underwriting the publishing cost of this book. BHI is the corporation that owns and manages Hoosier Village and three other retirement communities in Indiana. It has demonstrated a clear commitment to honoring veterans not only by providing funds for this book but also by recently having the BHI Foundation underwrite the cost for building a veterans' garden at Hoosier Village. The garden consists of a block wall with medallions of each of the five branches of military. Each veteran is honored with a brick consisting of his

BETTY L. RENNER WOMENS' ARMY CORPS 1941-45		W. THOMAS SCHEMMEL ARMY 1962-64	FRANCIS DARRELL THOMAS MARINES 1946-47	
ROBERT W. RENNER AIR FORCE 1941-45	FRANCIS SCHIFFHAUER ARMY 1942-45	HOUSTON SWENSON ARMY 1954-56	SCOTT THOMPSON ARMY 1943-45	
FRANCIS REUTER ARMY 1945-47		CARL SCHLAGETER ARMY 1963-65	JERRY TOMLINSON AIR FORCE 1944-45	
WILLIS A. ROOSE NAVY 1943-46	STEVE SWIGONSKI AIR FORCE 1948-72	MARY (JANE) SWIGONSKI AIR FORCE 1949-52	

or her name, branch and years of service. Built at the very center of the campus behind the large flagpoles, it is a lovely garden/memorial that serves as a reminder to all who drive or walk past it to remember those who have served. I am blessed to see that memorial every day.

My continued thanks also go out to the *Martinsville Reporter Times* Newspaper and editor, Stephen Crane for graciously granting me permission to use in my book four of my previously submitted veteran stories which they published as articles in their newspaper. These include the stories of Hilda Browning, Gene Groves, John Redmond and Betty Robling. I am pleased that my 6-year partnership with them as a freelance writer continues today. I don't know of any other daily newspaper that so regularly features the military service stories of veterans and prints them on the front page. As they say in the Navy, "Bravo-Zulu" — job well done in honoring the veterans of Morgan County, Indiana.

I wish to also thank editor Kathy Linton of the *Hendricks County Flyer* for printing the story on veteran Rodney Sieck and allowing my use of that article for his chapter in my book.

Robin Surface of Fideli Publishing, also the publisher of my first volume, has done another fine job in designing the layout and cover for this second volume. I thank her for a job well done.

I also want to express my gratitude to Dominick Oto, a fellow veteran, published author and lover of World War II history. He went with me on my Europe trip to visit World War II sights. He has been a great encourager for my writing as well as a great inspiration as he has shared his own writing journey with me.

My thanks also go to my good friend, Christina Johnson (a veteran herself) who encouraged my pursuit of a 2nd book and offered her assistance whenever possible. Her friendship and support have been a great blessing to me.

Finally, I thank you, the readers, for taking the time to read this book. As you do, you take part in a noble task of remembering and passing on the legacies of those veterans who have served us. Let us also keep in our thoughts and prayers those who are serving us today in the Armed Forces.

MORE ABOUT THE PARTNERSHIP WITH BHI SENIOR LIVING AND THE BHI FOUNDATION

I am grateful for the partnership with BHI Senior Living and the BHI Foundation in supporting my work of preserving resident veteran stories. I am especially grateful to the BHI Foundation for covering the publishing costs of this book.

BHI Senior Living Inc. is a faith-based, non-profit organization which operates 4 Continuing Care Retirement Communities (CCRCs) in Central Indiana: Columbus, Fort Wayne, Frankfort and Indianapolis. Its mission is to enhance the quality of life for older adults within a secure environment which supports their needs, values, interests, and independence while encouraging personal and spiritual development.

BHI communities offer spacious, maintenance-free apartment homes and cottage homes; a wide variety of on-campus amenities and services; a pet-friendly environment; a full-time chaplain; and an on-site continuum of senior healthcare services — from assisted living and memory care, to skilled nursing and rehabilitation services. Each community welcomes people of all faiths, beliefs and traditions.

The BHI Foundation is an arm of BHI Senior Living designed to help fulfill each community's goal of ensuring that every resident who lives at one of the Continuing Care Retirement Communities is empowered to live life to the fullest. It's a lifestyle filled with opportunities to enhance wellness; enjoy exceptional services, amenities, and activities; and live in a community filled with good neighbors and caring staff. BHI Foundation Inc. is a 509(a) (3) supporting organization.

The BHI Foundation sponsors many programs to enhance the lives of residents including:

- **Wellness Program** — The BHI Foundation contributes to the funding for Wellness programs in each community. This support allows each community to offer fitness programs, staffing, equipment, and more so residents receive the benefit of comprehensive mind/body/spirit care.

- **Benevolent Care: The Good Neighbor Fund** provides financial assistance to residents whose financial resources have been depleted. This ensures that residents who join a BHI community may remain there for the duration of their years.

- **Employee Support Programs** — These include scholarship tuition assistance for BHI professionals wishing to advance their training and further their education to better serve the residents' needs. Additionally, the BHI Loan Repayment Assistance Program assists healthcare professionals in paying off the student loans they may have acquired while training.

- **Christian Service Award** — These grants support incoming residents who have been dedicated to a lifetime of Christian service.

- **Special Gifts and Projects** — The BHI Foundation supports individual projects specific to each BHI community's needs. These projects improve and enhance residents' quality of life. Several of these projects have focused on honoring resident veterans, including the building of a beautiful Veterans Garden at Hoosier Village and the funding of Honor Flight Guardian Sponsorship which pays the way for volunteers who accompany community veterans on an Honor Flight trip to Washington D.C.

FOR ADDITIONAL INFORMATION ON THE BHI COMMUNITIES, VISIT:

www.bhiseniorliving.org

FOR ADDITIONAL INFORMATION ON THE BHI FOUNDATION, VISIT:

bhiseniorliving.org/foundation

ABOUT THE AUTHOR

A native of Erie, Pennsylvania, Ron May has served as a Chaplain, Pastor and Freelance Writer. Following graduation from college and seminary he spent 25 years in full-time church ministry as a Lutheran Pastor. For 22 years of those years, he was also serving as a Navy Reserve Chaplain. More recently he served as a Hospice Chaplain.

In 2012, following his retirement from the Navy, he began work as a freelance writer, submitting the stories of military veterans and senior citizens for publication in local newspapers. He published his first book: *Our Service Our Stories* in the fall of 2015. It tells the service stories of 36 World War 2 veterans from Central Indiana. His current book is the 2nd volume in what he hopes will eventually be a 4 volume set of World War II veteran stories.

In 2016, Ron received the Distinguished Citizen's Award presented by the Indiana Daughters of the American Revolution for his work in preserving Indiana veteran stories.

In 2018, Ron wrote and performed his first dramatization on World War II correspondent, Ernie Pyle. He continues to perform this drama for local groups and organizations to preserve the legacy of the man who became the best known and loved correspondent.

Ron currently serves as Chaplain at Hoosier Village Retirement Center in Zionsville, Indiana and resides in Carmel. When he is not writing or serving as Chaplain, Ron can be found on a bicycle exploring Central Indiana, on a path hiking local trails, or on the gridiron officiating high school football games each fall.

To correspond with Ron, have him interview a veteran ,or arrange to have him as a guest speaker, you can contact him by email at **ron@ronaldpmay.com** or by phone at 317-435-7636.

www.ronaldpmay.com

Follow him on Facebook @ OurServiceOurStories